NORTHERN NEW YORK

AND THE

ADIRONDACK WILDERNESS.

SAMUEL de CHAMPLAIN

From the Painting by Th Hamel after the Moncornet Portrait

HISTORICAL SKETCHES

OF

NORTHERN NEW YORK

AND THE

ADIRONDACK WILDERNESS:

INCLUDING

TRADITIONS OF THE INDIANS, EARLY EXPLORERS,
PIONEER SETTLERS, HERMIT HUNTERS, &c.

BY

NATHANIEL BARTLETT SYLVESTER,

OF THE TROY BAR.

Ye who love the haunts of Nature,
Love the sunshine of the meadow,
Love the shadow of the forest,
Love the wind among the branches,
And the rain-shower and the snow-storm,
And the rushing of great rivers,
Through their palisades of pine trees,
*   *   *   *   *
Listen to these wild traditions.
    —*Song of Hi-a-wat-ha.*

TROY, N. Y.:
WILLIAM H. YOUNG.
1877.

Reprinted by
HARBOR HILL BOOKS
Harrison, New York
1973

Sylvester, Nathaniel Bartlett, 1825-1894.
Historical sketches of northern New York and the Adirondack wilderness.

1. Adirondack Mountains. 2. New York (State)—History. 3. New York (State)—Description and travel. 4. Iroquois Indians. I. Title.

F127.A2S9   1973   917.47'53'044   73-5937

ISBN 0-916346-00-5

Entered according to Act of Congress in the year 1877, by

NATHANIEL BARTLETT SYLVESTER,

In the Office of the Librarian of Congress at Washington.

EDWARD GREEN,
PRINTER, TROY.

Printed in U.S.A.

TO THE MEMORY

OF

𝔐𝔶 𝔒𝔫𝔩𝔶 𝔅𝔯𝔬𝔱𝔥𝔢𝔯𝔰,

AN ELDER AND A YOUNGER,

WHO, IN THEIR EARLY MANHOOD,

BOTH DIED THE SAME YEAR,

THIS VOLUME

IS

AFFECTIONATELY DEDICATED.

PREFACE.

A few years ago I published in the Troy *Times*, at the solicitation of its editor, an article entitled "John Brown's Tract, or the Great Wilderness of Northern New York." Since then, my attention, in leisure hours, has been drawn irresistibly to the subject, and that meagre and cursory article has grown into the book now presented to the reading public.

But if the newspaper article was unsatisfactory, I fear the book will be deemed scarcely less so when the wealth of historic incident and legendary lore which clusters about the territory of which it treats is considered, upon which, in this volume, I have, as it were, but opened the door.

In the olden time, Northern New York was disputed ground. It was claimed by the Iroquois of Central New York and by the Algonquins of Canada; by the French colonists of the St. Lawrence, and by the Dutch and English settlers of the Hudson. It was surrounded by the war-trails of the Indian, and by the war-paths of the armies of colonial times. Hence from its first discovery and exploration by Samuel de Champlain in the summer of 1609 to the close of the war of 1812 with Great Britain, it was the theater of continuous strife between rival powers contending for its mastery. Of the history of this long period much has been written, but more of it still lies buried in our colonial archives. In the following pages I have attempted hardly more than to awaken the attention of the historical student to this most interesting field of research.

To several friends who have kindly assisted me in this task in the use of books of reference and otherwise, and who have aided me with many valuable and practical suggestions my thanks are due. Among them I desire to mention Messrs. John M. Francis, Benjamin H. Hall, James Forsyth, Alexander G. Johnson, Jerome B. Parmenter, William H. Young, Edward Green, and Cha's C. Giles, of Troy; Messrs. Joel Munsell and Henry A. Holmes, State Librarian, of Albany; Messrs. P. Porter Wiggins, A. S. Pease, D. F. Ritchie, E. J. Huling, and J. P. Butler, of Saratoga Springs; Mr. Charles D. Adams, of Utica; the late Nelson J. Beach, of Watson; Dr. Franklin B. Hough, and Mr. W. Hudson Stephens, of Lowville; and Mr. John E. Pound, of Lockport.

TROY, N. Y., 9th April, 1877.

CONTENTS.

———•———

VI.   CONTENTS.

CHAPTER XIX.—SISTERSFIELD.

CHAPTER XX.—JOHN BROWN'S TRACT.

CHAPTER XXI.—THE HUNTER FOSTER AND THE INDIAN DRID.

CHAPTER XXII.—SMITH'S LAKE.

CHAPTER XXIII.—NUMBER FOUR.

CHAPTER XXIV.—JAMES O'KANE.

CHAPTER XXV.—JAMES T. WATSON.

CHAPTER XXVI.—LAKE BONAPARTE.

CHAPTER XXVII.—THE LEGEND OF THE DIAMOND ROCK.

CHAPTER XXVIII.—THE TWO WATER WHEELS.

VIII. CONTENTS.

CHAPTER XXIX.—THE STORY OF TOM GARNET'S DREAM.

CHAPTER XXX.—THE ST. LAWRENCE OF THE OLDEN TIME.

CHAPTER XXXI.—THE COUNTY OF CHARLOTTE.

CHAPTER XXXII.—OSWEGO AND THE WESTERN WAR-PATH.

CHAPTER XXXIII.—SARATOGA AND THE NORTHERN WAR-PATH.

NORTHERN NEW YORK

AND ITS

GREAT WILDERNESS

―・●・―

CHAPTER I.

NORTHERN NEW YORK,

Land of the forest and the rock;
Of dark blue lake and mighty river;
Of mountains rear'd aloft to mock
The storm's career, the lightning's shock—
My own green land forever.
　　　　　　　—*Whittier.*

I.

ITS ATTRACTIVENESS.

Northern New York, although it has within it, and along its borders, ten populous cities,* and villages without number, is still mostly covered by its primeval forests. Of a truth, it may be said to be a vast wilderness, surrounded by a narrow fringe of settlements.

And although in great part a gloomy solitude which is seldom trodden by the foot of man, yet it is completely surrounded by the world's great routes of travel, over which the business and the pleasure of half the continent yearly pass under the very shadows of its aboriginal woods.

Northern New York not only has a Great Wilderness within its borders, but it has also within it a Lesser Wilder-

* Albany, Troy, Cohoes, Schenectady, Utica, Rome, Syracuse, Oswego, Watertown, Ogdensburgh.

2

ness.* The Lesser Wilderness would itself be a famous one, were it not lost sight of in the overshadowing grandeur of the Greater.

Northern New York abounds in grand, beautiful and picturesque scenery, unsurpassed anywhere. It teems with undeveloped mineral wealth and forest products. It has been for centuries the theatre of stirring events—the pathway of contending armies—the battle-ground of nations. It is therefore rich in historic incident and legendary lore. In a word, it is one of the most attractive and interesting parts of our country.

II.

ITS ANCIENT NAMES.

As long ago as the year 1570, Abraham Van Ortelius was the distinguished geographer of Philip II. of Spain. In that year Ortelius published his "Universal Geography." It was a work of such rare merit that it won for him the title of "The Ptolemy of his Age." In this work was a map of New France.

As then known to Europeans, New France comprised almost all that had been discovered of North America.

In this map New France was divided into nine provinces. What is now known as Labrador was called *Terra Corterealis*. The district which lies between Labrador and the Saguenay River was named *Saguenai*. The country along the St. Lawrence between the Saguenay and the Ottawa

* The Lesser Wilderness lies at the head waters of the Mohawk river, on the highlands that rise northerly of Oneida Lake, and between the eastern shore of Lake Ontario and the upper valley of the Black river.

River was called *Canada*.* The region above the Ottawa, and in the angle between it and the St. Lawrence, was called *Chilaga* (Hochelaga). The territory south of the St. Lawrence which now embraces Maine and Nova Scotia was named *Norumbega*. The country which lies to the south of the St. Lawrence and east of the river Richelieu was called *Moscosa*. The region lying south and west of Moscosa, embracing what is now Northern New York, was called *Avacal*. The territory out of which Virginia and the great middle states have since been formed was named *Apalachen*, while the whole great region from which the Gulf states were formed was called *Florida*, "the land of flowers."

By this it seems that the earliest name applied by Europeans to the region now known as Northern New York was *Avacal*.

On later maps the country lying on both sides of Lake Champlain is called *Ir-o-coi-sia*, "the hereditary country of the Iroquois."

This last name, it seems, was also given to this region at a very early day, as it appears on a map of the New Netherlands of the year 1616, lately found in the royal archives at The Hague.

III.

IT IS AN ISLAND.

The region which is covered by the Great Wilderness of Northern New York is a vast elevated plateau that rises into lofty mountain peaks in the interior, but which slopes

* Canada is an Indian name signifying a mass of huts. See Chateaubriand's Travels.

gradually down on every side into deep depressions or valleys.

In these deep valleys run the natural water-courses which almost entirely surround Northern New York, making of it an island, as will appear upon an examination of its boundaries.

On the north of it flows the great river St. Lawrence. To the east of it is the Hudson River, running southerly into the Atlantic ocean, and the waters of Lake Champlain and its tributaries flowing northerly through the river Richelieu into the St. Lawrence. On the south of it the Mohawk River runs easterly into the Hudson; while the waters of the Oneida Lake run westerly through the Oswego River into Lake Ontario. On the west is Lake Ontario, from which runs the St. Lawrence, completing the encircling chain of almost a thousand miles of living waters.

The Indian could paddle his canoe around it finding but two short carrying places. One was from the Hudson at Fort Edward to the Wood Creek that runs into Lake Champlain; another was from the Mohawk at Fort Stanwix to the other Wood Creek that runs into the Oneida Lake. These obstacles were long since overcome by artificial means, and Northern New York is now entirely surrounded by navigable waters.

IV.

THE HIGHWAYS OF NATIONS.

The remarkable depressions or valleys which surround Northern New York, and through which run its natural and artificial watercourses, have always been great routes of travel.

Through them first ran the old Indian trails.* After the white man came, for more than two hundred years they formed the pathways of armies. When the long wars were ended, these routes were thronged with hardy pioneers on their way to the great West; and now the products of the West, the commerce of the world, come back through these thoroughfares.

And after sixty years of smiling peace other armies travel through them, armies of summer tourists, in search of health or pleasure on their way to Saratoga, the Adirondacks, Lake George, the Thousand Islands, the gloomy Saguenay, Sharon, Richfield, Trenton Falls, Clifton, Avon, Massena, Niagara, the great lakes, and the prairies beyond. In a word, to the thousand attractions which lie in and around Northern New York.

* The Indian trails were well-worn paths of a foot or more in width, and sometimes a foot in depth. See Morgan's League of the Iroquois.

CHAPTER II.

HO-DE-NO-SAU-NEE-GA.

" Or shall we cross yon mountains blue,
   Whose streams my kindred nation quaff'd ?
And by my side, in battle true,
   A thousand warriors drew the shaft ?
Ah ! there in desolation cold,
   The desert serpent dwells alone,
   Where grass o'ergrows each mould'ring bone,
   And stones themselves to ruin grown
Like me, are death-like old.
   Then seek we not their camp,—for there—
   The silence dwells of my despair !"
         —Campbell's Gertrude of Wyoming.

I.

THE HO-DE-NO-SAU-NEE.

At the time of its first exploration by Europeans in the early years of the seventeenth century, Northern New York formed a part of the territory and hunting grounds of the great Indian league or confederacy, called by the English the "Five Nations," by the French the "Iroquois," and by themselves the "*Ho-de-no-sau-nee*," or the "People of the Long House."

Their country, called by them *Ho-de-no-sau-nee-ga*,* and extending from the Hudson to Lake Erie, from the St. Lawrence to the valleys of the Delaware, the Susquehanna and the Alleghany, embraced the whole of Central, of Northern, and large parts of Southern and Western New York.

It was divided between the several nations by well defined boundary lines running north and south, which they called "lines of property."

* See Morgan's League of the Iroquois.

The territory of Northern New York belonged principally to the Mohawks and the Oneidas, the Onondagas owning a narrow strip along the eastern shore of Lake Ontario.

The line of property between the Mohawks and the Oneidas began on the St. Lawrence river, at the present town of Waddington, and running south, nearly coincident with the line between Lewis and Herkimer counties, struck the Mohawk river at Utica.

The country lying to the east of this line of property, embracing what is now the greater part of the Wilderness, formed a part of *Ga-ne-a-ga-o-no-ga*—the land of the Mohawks. The territory lying westerly of this line, including the fertile valley of the Black River, and the highlands of the Lesser Wilderness, which lies between the upper valley of the Black River and Lake Ontario, belonged to *O-na-yote-ka-o-no-ga*, the country of the Oneidas.

It was the custom of the Indians, whenever the hunting grounds of a nation bordered on a lake, to include the whole of it if possible, so the line of property between the Oneidas and Onondagas bent westerly around the Oneida Lake, giving the whole of that to the Oneidas, and deflected easterly again around Lake Ontario in favor of the Onondagas.

These three nations claimed the whole of the territory of Northern New York. But the northern part of the Great Wilderness was also claimed by the Adirondacks, a Canadian nation of Algonquin lineage, and, being disputed territory, was the "dark and bloody ground" of the old Indian traditions, as it afterward became in the French and English colonial history.

II.

TWO FAMILIES OF NATIONS.

The Indians who inhabited the Atlantic slope and the basin of the great lakes were divided into two great families´of nations. These two great families were known as the Iroquois and the Algonquin families.* They differed radically both in language and in lineage, as well as in many of their manners and customs.

The principal nations of the Iroquois family were grouped around the lower lakes. The Five Nations of Central New York—the Iroquois proper—were the leading people of this family. To the south of the Five Nations, on the banks of the Susquehanna, were the Andastes, and to the westward, along the southern shore of Lake Erie, were the Eries. To the north of Lake Erie lay the Neutral Nation and the Tobacco Nation, while the Hurons dwelt along the eastern shore of the lake that still bears their name. There was also a branch of the Iroquois family in the Carolinas— the Tuscaroras—who united with the Five Nations in 1715, after which the confederacy was known as the Six Nations.†

Surrounding these few kindred bands of the Iroquois were the much more numerous tribes of the great Algonquin family.

To the people of Algonquin speech and lineage belonged the Horicons, the Mohicans and other tribes of River Indians who dwelt along the Hudson, and the Pequots,

---

* Parkman's Pioneers of France in the New World.
† See Colden's Five Nations.

Wampanoags, Narragansetts, and all the other New England tribes.*

Northward of the Iroquois were the Nipissings, *La Petite Nation*, and *La Nation de l'Isle*, and the other tribes of the Ottawa. Along the valley of the St. Lawrence were the Algonquins proper—called Adirondacks by the Iroquois, the Abenaquis, the Montagnais, and other roving bands around and beyond the Saguenay.

Thus were the Indian nations situated with respect to each other when Samuel de Champlain, in the early summer of 1609, entered the territory of Northern New York from the north, and Henry Hudson, in the beginning of the coming autumn, approached it from the south.

III.

THE "PEOPLE OF THE LONG HOUSE."

Among all the Indians of the New World, there were none so politic and intelligent, none so fierce and brave, none with so many germs of heroic virtues mingled with their savage vices, as the true Iroquois—the people of the Five Nations. They were a terror to all the surrounding tribes, whether of their own or of Algonquin speech. In 1650 they overran the country of the Hurons; in 1651 they destroyed the Neutral Nation; in 1652 they exterminated the Eries; in 1672 they conquered the Andastes and reduced them to the most abject submission. They followed the

---

* After the defeat of King Philip of Pocanokett in 1675-6, a part of the Wampanoags and Narragansetts fled from their ancient hunting grounds, and settled at Schaghticoke, on the Hudson, and were afterward known as the Schaghticoke Indians. See paper by John Fitch in His. Mag. for June, 1870.

3

war-path, and their war-cry was heard westward to the
Mississippi, and southward to the great gulf. The New
England nations, as well as the River tribes along the Hudson, whose warriors trembled at the name of Mohawk, all
paid them tribute. The poor Montagnais on the far-off
Saguenay would start from their midnight sleep, and run
terror-stricken from their wigwams into the forest when
dreaming of the dreadful Iroquois. They were truly the
conquerors of the New World, and were justly styled "The
Romans of the West." "My pen," wrote the Jesuit Father
Ragueneau in 1650, in his *Relations des Hurons*, "My pen
has no ink black enough to describe the fury of the Iroquois."

They dwelt in palisaded villages upon the fertile banks
of the lakes and streams that watered their country. Their
villages were surrounded with rudely cultivated fields, in
which they raised an abundance of corn, beans, squashes
and tobacco. Their houses were built within the protecting
circle of palisades, and, like all the tribes of the Iroquois
family, were made long and narrow. They were not more
than twelve or fifteen feet in width, but often exceeded a
hundred and fifty feet in length. They were made of two
parallel rows of poles stuck upright in the ground sufficient-
ly wide apart at the bottom to form the floor, and bent
together at the top to form the roof, the whole being nicely
covered with strips of peeled bark. At each end of the
wigwam was a strip of bark, or a bear skin, hung loosely for
a door. Within, they built their fires at intervals along the
center of the floor, the smoke passing out through openings
in the top, which served as well to let in the light. In every

house were many fires and many families, every family having its own fire within the space allotted to it.

From this custom of having many fires and many families strung through a long and narrow house comes the signification of their name for the league, "The People of the Long House." They likened their confederacy of five nations, stretched along a narrow valley for more than two hundred miles through Central New York, to one of their long wigwams. The Mohawks guarded the eastern door of this long house, while the Senecas kept watch at the western door. Between these doors of their country dwelt the Oneidas, Onondagas and Cayugas, each nation around its own fire, while the great central council fire was always kept brightly burning in the country of the Onondagas. Thus they were in fact as well as in name the people of the long house.

Below are given in the order of their rank therein, the Indian names of the several nations of the league.*

Mohawks—*Ga-ne-a-ga-o-no.* "People Possessors of the Flint."

Onondagas—*O-nun-do-ga-o-no.* "People on the Hills."

Senecas—*Nun-da-wa-o-no.* "Great Hill People."

Oneidas—*O-na-yote-ka-o-no.* "Granite People."

Cayugas—*Gwe-u-gweh-o-no.* "People at the Mucky Land."

Tuscaroras—*Dus-ga-o-weh-o-no.* "Shirt Wearing People."

* See Morgan's League of the Iroquois.

IV.

THEIR GOVERNMENT.

It may of a truth be said that this wild Indian league of the old savage wilderness, if it did not suggest, in many respects it formed the model after which was fashioned our more perfect union of many states in one republic.

The government of this "League of the Iroquois" was vested in a general council composed of fifty hereditary sachems, but the order of succession was always in the female and never in the male line. That is to say, when a sachem died his successor was chosen from his mother's descendants, and never from his own children. The new sachem must be either the brother of the old one or a son of his sister—so in all cases the status of the children followed the mother and never the father. Each nation was divided into eight clans or tribes, which bore the following names :

| Wolf, | Bear, | Beaver, | Turtle, |
| Deer, | Snipe, | Heron, | Hawk. |

The spirit of the animal or bird after which the clan was named, called its *To-tem*, was the guardian spirit of the clan, and every member used its figure in his signature as his device.

It was the rule among them that no two of the same clan could intermarry. If the husband belonged to the clan of the Wolf, the wife must belong to the clan of the Bear, the Deer, and so on, while the children belonged to the clan of the mother, and never to the father's clan. In this manner their relationship always interlocked, and the people of the whole league were forever joined in the closest ties of consanguinity.

The name of each sachemship was permanent. It was the name of the office, and descended with it to each successor. When a sachem died the people of the league selected the most competent brave from among those of his family who by right inherited the title, and the one so chosen, was raised in solemn council to the high honor, and dropping his own received the name of the sachemship. There were two sachemships, however, that after the death of the first sachems of the name, forever remained vacant. These sachemships were *Da-ga-no-we-da* of the Onondagas and *Ha-yo-went-ha* (*Hi-a-wat-ha*) of the Mohawks. *Da-ga-no-we-da* was the founder of the league. His head was represented as covered with tangled serpents, and *Hi-a-wat-ha* (meaning "he who combs") straightened them out, and assisted in forming the league. In honor of their great services their sachemships were afterward held vacant.

There was another class of chiefs of inferior rank to the sachems, among whom were the war chiefs whose title was not hereditary, but who were chosen on account of their bravery and personal prowess, their achievements on the war-path, or their eloquence in council. Among this latter class were found the most renowned warriors and orators of the league, such as King Hendrick and Red Jacket, but they could never rise to the rank of sachem.

The whole body of sachems formed the council league. Their authority was entirely civil, and confined to the affairs of peace. But after all, the power of the sachems and chiefs was advisory rather than mandatory. Every savage to a great extent followed the dictates of his own wild will, controlled only by the customs of his people and a public sentiment that ran through their whole system of affairs, which was as inflexible as iron.

V.

THEIR FESTIVALS AND RELIGIOUS BELIEF.

The Indian was a believer in spirits. Every object in nature was spiritualized by him, while over all things in dim and shadowy majesty, ruled the one Great Spirit, the supreme object of his fear and adoration, whom he called *Ha-wen-ne-ya*. There was likewise an Evil Spirit, born at the same time with the Great Spirit, which he called *Ha-ne-go-ate-ga*—"The Evil-Minded." There was also *He-no*, "The Thunderer," and *Ga-oh*, the "Spirit of the Winds." Every mountain, lake, stream, tree, shrub, flower, stone and fountain had its own spirit.

Among his objects of worship were the Three Sister Spirits—the Spirit of Corn, the Spirit of Beans, and the Spirit of Squashes.* This triad was called *De-oha-ko*, meaning "Our Life," "Our Supporters." Upon the festal days sacred to the Three Sisters they were represented by three beautiful maidens, each one gaily dressed in the leaves of the plant whose spirit she represented.

The *Ho-de-no-sau-nee* observed five great feasts every year. There was the New Year's Festival, or the "Sacrifice of the White Dog," which was celebrated with great pomp for seven days early in February. Then as soon as the snow began to melt, and the sap to flow from the maple trees, and the sugar boiling began in earnest, came the Maple feast. The next great festival was the *A-yent-wa-ta* or

---

* See Morgan's League of the Iroquois.

Planting festival, which came on as soon as the leaves on the butter-nut trees were as big as squirrels' ears, indicating the time for planting corn. The third feast was *Ha-nan-da-yo*, the Feast of Strawberries, which came in the moon of roses. The fourth was *Ah-dake-wa-o*, the Feast of the Green Corn Moon, and the last was the Harvest Festival, observed at the gathering of the crops in autumn.

Dwelling forever among the wildest scenes of nature, himself nature's own wildest child, believing in an unseen world of spirits, in perpetual play around him on every hand, his soul was filled with unutterable awe. The flight or cry of a bird, the humming of a bee, the crawling of an insect, the turning of a leaf, the whisper of a breeze, were to him mystic signals of good or evil import, by which he was guided in the most important affairs of life.

The mysterious realm about him he did not attempt to unravel, but bowed submissively before it with what crude ideas he had of religion and worship. To his mind everything, whether animate or inanimate, in the whole domain of nature, is immortal. In the happy hunting grounds of the dead, the shades of hunters will follow the shades of animals with the shades of bows and arrows, among the shades of trees and rocks, in the shades of immortal forests, or glide in the shades of bark canoes over shadowy lakes and streams, and carry them around the shades of dashing waterfalls.*

In dreams he placed the most implicit confidence. They were to him revelations from the spirit world, guiding him to the places where his game lurked and to the haunts of his enemies. He invoked their aid upon all occasions.

* See Charlevoix's Voyage to North America.

They taught him how to cure the sick and revealed to him his guardian spirit, as well as all the secrets of his good or evil destiny.

VI.

THEIR SOCIAL LIFE.

The Iroquois were extremely social in their daily intercourse. When not engaged in their almost continual public feasting and dancing, they spent the most of their time in their neighbors' wigwams, playing games of chance, of which they were extremely fond, or in chatting, joking and rudely bantering each other. On such occasions their witticisms and jokes were often more sharp than delicate, as they were "echoed by the shrill laugh of young squaws untaught to blush."*

In times of distress and danger they were always prompt to aid each other. Were a family without shelter, the men of the village at once built them a wigwam. When a young squaw was married, the older ones, each gathering a load of sticks in the forest, carried her wood enough for a year. In their intercourse with each other, as well as with strangers, their code of courtesy was exact and rigid to the last degree.

But the Indian is still the untamed child of nature. "He will not," says Parkman, "learn the arts of civilization, and he and his forest must perish together. The stern unchanging features of his mind excite our admiration from their very immutability; and we look with deep interest on the fate of this irreclaimable son of the wilder-

* Francis Parkman.

ness, the child who will not be weaned from the breast of his rugged mother.   *   *   The imprisoned lion in the showman's cage differs not more widely from the lord of the desert than the beggarly frequenter of frontier garrisons and dramshops differs from the proud denizens of the woods.   It is in his native wilds alone that the Indian must be seen and studied."*

*Parkman's Conspiracy of Pontiac, vol. I, p. 44.   Consult also Schoolcraft's Works, Clark's History of Onondaga, Heckewelder's History of Indian Nations, The Iroquois, by Miss Anna C. Johnson, Documentary History of New York, Cusick's History of the Five Nations, Charlevoix's Letters to the Duchess de Lesdiguières, and Jesuit Relations of 1656-57, and 1659-60.

4

CHAPTER III.

EARLY EXPLORERS.

Westward the course of empire takes its way ;
The four first acts already past,
A fifth shall close the drama with the day ;
Time's noblest offspring is the last.
—Bishop Berkeley.

I.

JACQUES CARTIER.

The great River St. Lawrence, which serves to drain the larger part of the waters of Northern New York into the ocean, was discovered and first explored by Jacques Cartier, an eminent mariner of St. Malo.

St. Malo is a quaint medieval seaport town of the ancient province of Brittany, on the northern coast of France. The city is built on a huge rock that seems to rise like a wall out of the sea, it being separated from the mainland by a salt marsh, which is covered by the waters at high tide. St. Malo has long being celebrated as the nursery of a race of daring and hardy navigators, and among the most famous of them all is Jacques Cartier. He was born at St. Malo in the year 1494, and passed his boyhood there in watching the waves come in from the awful unknown Atlantic, whose mysteries had then but just been solved by Columbus, and of which he was destined to become one of the most eminent explorers.

In the year 1535, Cartier was sent on a voyage to the New World by Francis I, King of France, at the instigation of Philippe de Chabot, his Grand Admiral, in quest of gold and empire. The little fleet with which Cartier sailed

consisted of three ships only, ranging from forty to one
hundred and twenty tons burden. This fleet was under the
command of Cartier, who was styled the "Captain and
Pilot of the King." In his ship's company were several of
the young nobility of France, among whom were Claudias
de Ponte Briand, cup-bearer to the Lord Dauphin, Charles
de Pomeraces, John Powlet and other gentlemen.

Before venturing upon their long and perilous voyages to
the dreary, cheerless solitudes of an almost unknown and
unexplored ocean, the daring but devout navigators of
those days were accustomed to attend upon the solemn
offices of religion as if they were departing to

> " The undiscovered country, from whose bourne
> No traveler returns."

So, just before setting sail, this company of adventurers all
went, on Whitsunday, in solemn procession to the Cathedral
Church of St. Malo, where each was absolved and received
the sacrament. Then, all entering the choir of the church,
they presented themselves in a body to the Lord Bishop of
St. Malo, and received his blessing.

They embarked on the 19th of May, and, after a stormy
passage, arrived off the coast of Newfoundland on the 7th
of July. On the 10th day of August in that year, which
day was the festival of Saint Lawrence, they discovered and
entered the broad bay which forms the mouth of the great
river, and named it in honor of the saint.

Proceeding on their voyage up the wild stream, they
passed the dark gorge of the *Saguenai*, and arrived at the
island of Orleans, that lies a short distance below the city
of Quebec. On account of the abundance of wild grapes
found upon this island, which hung in clusters from all the

trees along its shores, Cartier named it the Isle of Bacchus.
Continuing his voyage, Cartier soon reached the narrows
in the river opposite the rocky cliffs of Quebec. This
stronghold was then occupied by a little cluster of Indian
wigwams, and was called by the savages *Sta-da-co-ne*. Its
chief, whose name was *Don-na-co-na*, met Cartier and his
strange band at the landing, made a speech to them, and
gave them some bread and some wine pressed from the wild
grapes that grew so abundantly along the shores of the
river and upon all its islands.

These Indians told Cartier that many days' journey up
the river, there was another Indian town that gave its name
to the river and to the country around it. Taking on
board some Indian guides, Cartier proceeded up the river
in quest of this wonderful city of the great forest state.
Upon arriving at some dangerous rapids in the now narrow-
ing river, Cartier left his ships, and launching his small
boats, went up the stream with but two white companions
and his Indian guides. In a few days they led him to the
spot where now stands the beautiful city of Montreal.

On the island of Montreal Cartier found an old palisaded
Indian town, containing many wigwams, built long and
narrow after the fashion of the Iroquois. In this village
were more than a thousand savage inhabitants of Iroquois lineage. It was the famous Indian *Ho-che-la-ga*,
the capital of the great forest state that lay along the St.
Lawrence above the Ottawa. Like *Sta-da-co-ne* at Quebec,
it was one of the centers of Indian population on the great
river.

Cartier landed at *Ho-che-la-ga* on the second day of October, amid the crimson and golden hues of the lovely Cana-

dian autumn. So glorious, so wild, so fair, so savage
a scene these wondering mariners of the Old World had
never seen before.

When Cartier and his two bearded white men, clad in glittering armor and gorgeous attire, landed at the Indian village
Ho-che-la-ga, on the wild island of Montreal, the half-nude
savages crowded around them in speechless wonder, regard-
ing them more as demi-gods than men. They even brought
their chief, whose name was *Ag-ou-han-na*, who "was full
of palsy" says an old narrative, "and his members shrunk
together," and who was clad in rich furs and wore upon his
head a wreath or crown of red feathers, and laid him upon
a mat before the captain that he might give the useless
limbs a healing touch—such was their simple faith in the
power of the strange pale faces. "Then did *Ag-ou-han-na*,"
continues the old chronicler, "take the wreath or crown he
had about his head, and gave it unto our captain. That
done, they brought before him divers diseased men, some
blind, some cripple, some lame and impotent, and some so
old that the hair of their eye-lids came down and covered
their cheeks, and laid them all along before our captain, to
the end that they might of him be touched, for it seemed
unto them that God was descended and come down to heal
them."*

Then the Indians led Cartier to the top of the mountain
at whose foot their village nestled. Planting a large cross
of cedar wood upon the summit of the mountain, Cartier
solemnly took possession of the great forest state of *Ho-che-
la-ga* in the name of the French king, and named the

* Pinkerton's Voyages, vol. xii, p. 653.

mountain on which he stood Mount Royal, from whence comes the modern Montreal.

On the 5th of October, Cartier left *Ho-che-la-ga*, and regaining his ships, passed a long and gloomy winter in that part of the river called Lake St. Peters.

In the spring Cartier returned to France. In 1541 he made another voyage to *Ho-che-la-ga*. After his return to his native city of St. Malo from his last voyage to the New World his name passes out of history. It is supposed that he lived in retirement and died at a good old age.

When Champlain, upon his first voyage in 1603, sixty-eight years after Cartier's visit, landed upon the still wild and savage island of Montreal, scarcely a vestige of *Ho-che-la-ga*, the ancient Indian metropolis on the great river, remained to be seen. All its savage glory had departed forever. Its Iroquois race of house-builders had been driven to their new hunting-grounds in the rich valleys of Central New York. Champlain found the site of the village occupied only by a few families of a roving tribe of Algonquin lineage, who lived in some temporary huts built of the decaying remnants of the ancient village. Such was the fate of the old forest state *Ho-che-la-ga*, and its metropolis at Montreal. But its people found a more congenial home among their sister Iroquois tribes of the Five Nations, with whom doubtless they united in the great confederacy.

II.

SAMUEL DE CHAMPLAIN.

Samuel de Champlain, the discoverer of the beautiful lake of Northern New York that bears his name, was the founder of New France, and its first Governor General. No name in Canadian annals is more illustrious than his. He was born in Brouage Saintonge, about the year 1570, of a noble family. In his youth he served in the French navy, was pensioned and attached to the person of Henry IV of France.

In 1603, M. de Chastes, Governor of Dieppe, obtained permission from the king to found a settlement in North America. De Chastes appointed Champlain as his substitute, and Henry gave him the title of General Lieutenant of Canada. On the 15th of March Champlain set sail for America in a ship commanded by Pont-Gravé, an enterprising mariner of St. Malo.

They sailed up the St. Lawrence to the Sault St. Louis, being as far as Jacques Cartier had proceeded with his ships in 1535, and after carefully examining its banks, returned to France.

Upon his return, Champlain published his first work, entitled *Des Sauvages.* In the meantime De Chastes had died, and his concessions had been transferred to Sieur de Monts. De Monts was made Vice-Admiral and Lieutenant General of his majesty in that part of Acadia called *Norumbega*, with full powers to make war and peace, and to trade in peltries from lat. 40 to 46 N., in exclusion of all others. Armed with these plenary powers, De Monts and Champlain sailed for Acadia, and attempted a settlement at Port Royal, but returned to France in 1607.

Champlain's third voyage to America was undertaken at the solicitation of De Monts in the year 1608. In this year he founded his colony of Quebec, in the heart of the old, wild, savage wilderness, upon the site of the old Indian hamlet *Sta-da-cone*, found by Jacques Cartier seventy years before, under the sway of the royal chief *Don-na-co-na*.

In the beginning of the summer of the next year, (1609) months before Henry Hudson sailed up the North River, and eleven years before the Pilgrims landed at Plymouth, Champlain discovered and explored the lake which still bears his name, and planted on its shores the Cross and the Lilies of France.

At Quebec, during his hunting excursions with the Indians, while sitting around their wild camp fires, they had told him marvelous stories of a great inland sea filled with wonderful islands, lying far to the southward of the St. Lawrence, in the land of the terrible Iroquois. His curiosity was excited, and as soon as the melting snows of the next spring would permit, he set out upon a voyage for its discovery.

He was accompanied by two companions only besides his savage allies, who numbered sixty warriors, with twenty-four canoes. They were Hurons, Algonquins and Montagnais. The Montagnais were a roving tribe of the Algonquin family who inhabited the country of the Saguenay, called by the French the paupers of the wilderness.

After a toilsome passage up the rapids of the Richelieu, Champlain entered the lake—the far-famed "wilderness sea of the Iroquois." It was studded with islands that were clothed in the rich verdure of the early summer; its tranquil waters spreading southward beyond the horizon. From the thickly wooded shores on either side rose ranges of mountains, the highest peaks still white with patches of snow. Over all was flung the soft blue haze, sometimes called mountain smoke, that seemed to temper the sunlight and shade off the landscape into spectral-like forms of shadowy beauty. Who does not envy the stern old forest ranger his first view of the lake that was destined to bear his name to the latest posterity?

Champlain and his allies proceeded cautiously up the lake, traveling only by night and resting on the shore by day, for they were in the land of the much dreaded Iroquois, the hereditary enemies of the Algonquin nations.

On the morning of the 29th of July, after paddling, as usual, all night, they retired to the western shore of the lake to take their daily rest. The savages were soon stretched along the ground in their slumbers, and Champlain, after a short walk in the woods, laid himself down to sleep upon his bed of fragrant hemlock boughs. He dreamed that he saw a band of Iroquois warriors drowning in the lake. Upon attempting to save them, his Algonquin friends told him that "they were good for nothing, and had better be left to die like dogs." Upon awakening, the Indians, as usual, beset him for his dreams. This was the first dream he had remembered since setting out upon the voyage, and it was considered by his superstitious allies as an auspicious vision. Its relation filled them with joy, and at early nightfall they re-embarked flushed with the hope of an easy victory. Their anticipations were soon to be realized. About ten o'clock in the evening, near what is now Crown Point, they saw dark moving objects upon the lake before them. It was a flotilla of Iroquois canoes. In a moment more each party of savages saw the other, and their hideous war cries, mingling, pealed along the lonely shores.

The Iroquois landed at once, and barricaded themselves

5

upon the shore with fallen trees and brush-wood. The Algonquins lashed their canoes together with long poles within a bow-shot of the Iroquois barricade, and danced in them all night their hideous war dances. It was mutually agreed between the hostile bands that the battle should not come off till the morning. At the dawn of day the Algonquins landed, and the Iroquois marched, in single file, from their barricade to meet them, full two hundred strong. They were the boldest, fiercest warriors of the New World, and their tall, lithe forms and noble bearing elicited the warmest admiration of Champlain and his white companions. The chiefs were made conspicuous by their tall plumes. Champlain, who, in the meantime, had been concealed, now advanced to the front, with arquebuse in hand, clad in the metallic armor of the times. The Iroquois warriors, seeing for the first time such a warlike apparition in their path, halted, and stood gazing upon Champlain in mute astonishment. Champlain levelled his arquebuse and fired. One Iroquois chief fell dead, and another rolled lifeless into the bushes at his feet. Then there rose an exulting yell from the Algonquin allies, and clouds of feathery arrows whizzed through the air. But the bold Iroquois, panic-stricken at the strange appearance of a white man clad in glittering armor, and sending forth from his weapons fire, smoke, thunderings and leaden hail, soon broke and fled in uncontrollable terror toward their homes on the Mohawk, leaving everything behind them.

The Iroquois afterward became the friends and allies of the English, and this first forest encounter was the forerunner of a long and bloody warfare between the French and the English, and their respective Indian allies, of

which the soil of Northern New York often formed the
battle ground.

Four years afterward Champlain made a long journey up
the Ottawa River to the country of the Hurons. On his
return he discovered Lake Ontario, the name meaning in
the Indian tongue, the "Beautiful Lake." He fought
another battle with the Iroquois to the south of the lake in
Western New York. He explored its shores along the
western border of Northern New York, in the vicinity of
what was afterward known to the French as La Famine.
On his return he passed down the St. Lawrence to his
colony at Quebec, thus becoming the first explorer of the
Lake of the Thousand Isles.

In 1620 Champlain was made Governor-General of
Canada, and died at Quebec in 1635. In 1620 his wife accompanied him to Quebec. Madame de Champlain,* as
she was married to him when she was only twelve years
of age, was still very young. The Indians, struck with her
frail and gentle beauty, paid homage to her as a goddess.
"Champlain," says Parkman, "was enamored of the New
World, whose rugged charms had seized his fancy and his
heart, and as explorers of the Arctic seas have pined in
their repose for polar ice and snow, so did he, with restless
longing, revert to the fog-wrapped coast, the piney odors of
forests, the noise of waters, the sharp, piercing sun-light,
so dear to his remembrance. Fain would he unveil the
mystery of that boundless wilderness, and plant the Catholic

---

* Madam de Champlain was Hélène Bouté, daughter of Nicholas
Bouté, Secretary of the royal household at Paris. She remained four
years in America, returned to France, founded a convent of Ursulines at
Meaux, entered it as Sister Helen of St. Augustine, and died there in
1654.

faith and the power of France amid its ancient barbar-
ism."*

III.

HENRY HUDSON.

At the beginning of the seventeenth century, the little
Republic of Holland had already become one of the first
commercial and maritime powers of the world. In those
days hardy navigators and bold explorers were flocking
from every nation in Europe to sail under the Dutch stand-
ard in search of fame and fortune.

Among the most noted of these was Henry Hudson, a
mariner of England, who was the discoverer and first explorer of the river that now bears his name. Henry Hudson was born about the middle of the sixteenth century,
but of his early life little is known. His first voyage was
in 1607, in the employ of a company of London merchants,
to the east coast of Greenland, in the search for a northwest passage to India.

On the 6th of April, 1609, he began a voyage in the service of the Dutch East India Company, to the northern
coast of Asia. For some reason or other he turned his
ships toward North America, and on the twelfth day of
September in that year, discovered and entered the mouth
of the beautiful river now called by his name that serves to
drain the waters of the mountain belt of the Great Wilderness of Northern New York.

It is believed that Hudson explored the stream as far up

* See Parkman's Pioneers of France, Palmer's History of Lake Champlain, Champlain's Voyages de la Nouv. France, and Documentary
History of New York.

as the old Indian hunting ground called *Nach-te-nak*, which lies around and upon the islands that cluster among the "sprouts"* or mouths of the Mohawk.

In his voyage up the stream he had numerous adventures and two or three battles with the Indians, who were jealous of the strange intruders. The staunch little ship in which he sailed up the river was named the Half-Moon. He named the stream the River of the Mountains, which is a literal translation of the Algonquin name of it, *Ca-ho-ta-te-a*. It was reserved for his countrymen, who took the province from the Dutch in 1664, first to call it in honor of its immortal discoverer.

Hudson, a year or two afterward discovered the great northern bay, which was also named in his honor. His ship's crew then mutinied; he was sent adrift with eight men in a small boat upon the wild northern ocean, and was never heard of more.

From these explorations and discoveries by navigators sailing in the interests of rival powers, there sprang up conflicting claims to the territory of Northern New York. Out of these claims arose a long series of bloody conflicts between the French and the English and their respective Indian allies, of which the soil of Northern New York formed the battle ground, until the brave Montcalm yielded to the chivalrous Wolfe, one hundred and fifty years afterward, on the plains of Abraham.

Since these discoveries and explorations, two centuries

---

* The Mohawk, just before it flows into the Hudson, separates into four spreading branches, which the early Dutch settlers significantly called *Spruytes*, which is from the Danish *Spruiten* or Saxon *Spryttan*, from which comes our English word *Sprouts*.—Vide Annals of Albany, vol. 2, page 226.

and a half have passed away, and how manifold and vast
are now the human interests that lie stretched along the
lakes and rivers which are still linked with the names of
those three kindred spirits of the olden time, "romance-
loving explorers," each immortalized by his discoveries—
Jacques Cartier, Henry Hudson, and Samuel de Champlain.

CHAPTER IV.

THE GREAT WILDERNESS.

Where the red deer leaps and the panther creeps,
And the eagles scream over cliff and stream ;
Where the lilies bow their heads of snow,
And the hemlocks tall throw a shade o'er all.
—*Judson.*

I.

COUCH-SACH-RA-GE.

The gloomy solitudes of a great wilderness still cover the larger part of the territory of Northern New York.

On Governor Pownal's map of the northern British colonies of 1776, across the region that comprises the wilderness, is written the following inscription :

THIS VAST
TRACT OF LAND,
WHICH IS THE ANTIENT
COUCHSACHRAGE, ONE OF THE FOUR
BEAVER HUNTING COUNTRIES
OF THE SIX NATIONS,
IS NOT YET
SURVEYED.

So this great wilderness was the old Indian hunting ground, *Couch-sach-ra-ge* of the Iroquois, which, like the ocean and the desert, refuses to be subdued by man.

But a more euphonious Indian name for the great wilderness, or rather for the mountainous or eastern part of it, has long usurped the place of its ancient but more significant title *Couch-sach-ra-ge*. This name is Adirondack. The Montagnais, those wild rovers of the country of the Saguenay, who subsisted entirely by the chase, were often during the long Canadian winters, when their game grew scarce, driven by hunger to live for many weeks together upon the buds and bark, and sometimes even upon the wood of forest trees. This led their hereditary enemies, the more favored Mohawks, to call them, in mockery of their condition, *Ad-i-ron-daks* or *tree-eaters.** This Iroquois name of an Algonquin tribe, thus born in derision, was first given, it is said, by Prof. Emmons to the principal mountain chain of the wilderness, but it is now by common consent applied to the whole mountainous region of it.

In the year 1798, John Brown of Providence, Rhode Island, bought a tract of two hundred and ten thousand acres, lying in the western part of the wilderness, and made upon it a fruitless attempt at settlement. The name John Brown's Tract, so often applied to the whole region, comes from this purchase.

Can we not have some more appropriate name than either for the great wilderness, and is there one more full of wild significance than the old Indian *Couch-sach-ra-ge?*

II.

ITS GENERAL ASPECTS AND ITS IMPORTANT USES.

A line beginning at Saratoga Springs, and running westerly across the country to Trenton Falls, near Utica, on the Mohawk; thence northerly to Potsdam, near Ogdensburgh, on the St. Lawrence; thence easterly to Dannemora, near Plattsburgh, on Lake Champlain, and thence southerly to the place of beginning, will nearly coincide with the boundaries of the wilderness.

---

* On trouve aussi *Adirondaks* c'est-à-dire *mangeurs d'arbres*. Ce nom leur a été donné par les Iroquois pour se moquer de leur jeûne à la chasse. Il a été transformé plus tard en celui d' *Algonquins.—Jesuit Relations.*

A few small settlements confined to the fertile valleys of the streams, lie within these boundaries, while in many places the ancient woods stretch down beyond them to the very shores of the surrounding lakes and rivers, and cast their shadows over the great routes of travel.

The wilderness comprises greater or lesser parts of eleven counties of the state, and is quite the size of the whole state of New Jersey, or the state of Vermont or New Hampshire. To compare it with European countries, it is three-fourths as large as the kingdom of Holland or Belgium, or the republic of Switzerland, whose Alpine character it so much resembles.

The Great Wilderness of Northern New York is an upland region of a mean height of almost two thousand feet above the level of the sea. It is traversed by five distinct ranges of mountains, with well-defined intervening valleys. It contains within its borders more than a thousand lakes, and from its heights run numberless rivers and streams in every direction. Over it all is spread a primeval forest, "covering the land as the grass covers a garden lawn, sweeping over hill and hollow in endless undulation, burying mountains in verdure, and mantling brooks and rivers from the light of day." In this forest there is only here and there a feeble settlement to break the monotony of its almost interminable sweep.

This region has always been and will always be under the dominion of Nature. Its altitude renders its climate cold and forbidding, while its rugged surface and light soil render it in a great measure unfit for cultivation. While the tide of emigration has rushed around it for almost a century, and filled the West with people for thousands of miles

6

beyond it, this region, although lying along the borders of some of the oldest settlements in the New World, may still be said to be

> *   *   " A waste land where no one comes,
> Or has come since the making of the world."

But it is not without its important uses in the economies of the civilization that surrounds it, and which has tried in vain to subdue it.   It is a vast reservoir of pure living waters.   The state and city of New York, and the cities and villages that throng the borders of Northern New York, are all indebted to the superabundant waters of this wilderness reservoir for their canals and water courses, which are the perennial sources of their growth and prosperity.   And doubtless in the not distant future the cities of the Mohawk and the Hudson even down to the sea will need these waters for their daily use, and will extend their aqueducts into the wilderness, to draw them from the living springs among the mountains.

III.

THE ADIRONDAK PARK.

In this wilderness lies a natural park or pleasure ground, the grandest in the world.   Nowhere else do five thousand square miles of such grand old woods lie all unbroken so near the most busy haunts of men.

The city of New York has lately rescued a part of her territory from the tyranny of pavements—from the rule of brick and mortar, and placed it under the milder dominion of shaded walks and flower-covered lawns, and Central Park is the city's pride and crowning glory.

Nature herself has here formed a park that only needs preserving to be to the state all that Central Park is to the city. Let the state preserve that which Nature has so kindly bestowed with a lavish hand, as a breathing place for the sick and weary of her swarming population, and the *Ad-i-ron-dak* Park of *Couch-sach-ra-ge* will be her pride and glory.

IV.

GRAND DIVISIONS OF THE WILDERNESS.

The Wilderness of Northern New York may properly be divided into three natural grand divisions or belts, which extend across it diagonally from north-east to south-west. These natural divisions may be called the Mountain Belt, the Lake Belt, and the Level Belt. Each of these great belts comprises about one-third part of the Wilderness, and each is strongly marked by the distinguishing characteristics which suggest its name.

The Mountain Belt, whose greatest width is about forty miles, extends across the south-eastern part of the wilderness, from the southern half of Lake Champlain and Lake George to the middle valley of the Mohawk River. It is a wild, weird region, crowded to fullness with mountains and mountain masses of hypersthene and other of the upper Laurentian system of rocks. These stupendous mountain masses are surmounted with towering rocky peaks almost numberless and nameless. A bright lake or a fair mountain meadow sleeps in every valley between them, and a wild torrent dashes and foams through every gorge. This Mountain Belt of the wilderness is the Switzerland of the New World.

The Lake Belt is about thirty miles wide, and stretches centrally through the wilderness from the northern half of Lake Champlain one hundred and fifty miles to the head waters of the Black River in the northern part of Oneida county. This belt is a rugged region, by no means free from mountain masses and lofty peaks, but mainly consists of a depression in the rocky groundwork of the wilderness, forming a sort of valley, which runs parallel with the ranges of the Mountain Belt. It is dotted all over with a thousand lakes, each in its own wild way a gem of beauty, and it is navigable, with the exception of a few short carrying places, by canoes from one end to the other. The Lake Belt of the Wilderness is a belt spangled with jewels.

The Level Belt comprises the remaining north-western part of the wilderness, which slopes gradually off from the Lake Belt to the great plains that border the St. Lawrence. This belt is not altogether level, as its name indicates, but is only comparatively so when contrasted with the more rugged Lake and Mountain Belts. Its whole surface is covered with low, rolling, forest crowned hills, and studded with immense bare boulders, all composed of the granite and gneiss of the lower Laurentian system of rocks. Around these hills and huge bare rocks, countless streams wind through interminable woods. Like the other great belts, this is also filled with lakes and mountain meadows, some of which are of great size and beauty. The Level Belt of the Wilderness is a complete forest Arcadia—a hunter's paradise.

CHAPTER V.

MOUNTAINS OF THE WILDERNESS.

Why to yon mountain turns the musing eye,
Whose sun-bright summit mingles with the sky?
Why do those cliffs of shadowy tint appear,
More sweet than all the landscape smiling near?
—*Campbell's Pleasures of Hope.*

I.

THE LAURENTIDES.

The underlying rocky strata of the highlands of the Wilderness belong to the Laurentian system of Canada.

The great Canadian Laurentian mountain chain extends from the coast of Labrador along the northern shore of the St. Lawrence river to a point near the city of Quebec. From this point it recedes from the river inland for some thirty miles or more, until it crosses the Ottawa river above Montreal.

After crossing the Ottawa, the chain again bends southerly toward the St. Lawrence, and a spur of it crosses the great river at the Thousand Islands into Northern New York.

After thus, by its rugged broken character, forming the Thousand Islands in crossing the St. Lawrence, this great spur of the Laurentides spreads easterly to Lake Champlain and the Upper Hudson, southerly to the valley of the Mohawk, and westerly to the Black river, forming the whole rocky groundwork of the great upland region of the Wilderness.

II.

THE OLDEST SYSTEM OF ROCKS.

The Laurentian system of rocks constitutes the oldest known strata of the earth's crust.

These rocks were doubtless the first dry land that appeared above the primeval ocean, which, before they rose above its surface, enveloped the whole earth with one wide limitless waste of waters. Out of the dreary steaming depths of this boundless ocean, there came, in the course of the creation, these Laurentian rocks peering into the misty sunshine of the new world, ages upon ages before the softer rocks of the Apalachian chain of what is now the Atlantic slope were deposited in their ocean beds. Then doubtless there were ages of slow upheaval into the wear and tear of the fierce war of the elements of the still heated but slowly cooling surface of the young world. Then followed ages of slow depression, until the small Laurentian continent was again submerged, and the waves of the boundless sea again beat over the low sinking rounded rocks.

As the surface of the new earth gradually cooled and contracted, once more the Laurentian continent rose above the waters. This time it lifted into the sunshine the broken and corrugated mountain masses of the Upper Laurentian rocks that now constitute the ranges of the Mountain Belt of the Wilderness.

Then the crumbling pulverized materials of the old worn-out rocks began to settle in the warm muddy bed of the ocean that washed the shores of this slowly-rising Laurentian continent, and the sandstones, limestones, slates and shales of the less ancient geologic systems were formed.

After this came the upheaval of these newly deposited strata into the great Apalachian chain ; the ocean receded to its present coast line, and the continent became vastly enlarged, leaving the old Laurentian region far inland.

In the days of the Laurentian continent the region of the Wilderness was a *peninsula*, joined to the mainland by a narrow isthmus at the Thousand Islands. But this peninsula, although left by the final great upheaval far inland, was left by it surrounded by the remarkable depressions or valleys through which the water-courses now run that make it an island—the Island of Northern New York.

III.

MOUNTAIN CHAINS.

There are no less than five separate mountain chains or ranges which run through the whole length of the Mountain Belt of the Wilderness. These ranges are about eight miles apart, and run parallel with each other. They are not always quite distinct, but sometimes their lateral spurs interlock, and sometimes single mountains are so vast that they occupy the whole space between the ranges and choke up the valleys. They are not regularly serrated, but consist of groups of peaks, joined together by immense ridges, which rise continually higher and higher toward the north until they culminate in the highest peaks of the Adirondack range.

The Mountain Belt of the Wilderness presents on every hand an Alpine landscape, with its towering mountain peaks, deep yawning abysses, rough granite blocks, sweeping torrents, fresh fountains, and green meadows.

IV.

THE LUZERNE RANGE.

The most easterly of these five mountain ranges in the Mountain Belt is the Palmertown or Luzerne range. It begins at Ticonderoga, on Lake Champlain, runs down on both sides of Lake George, forming the beautiful highlands that surround that lake, and stretching southward across the upper Hudson, which breaks through it just above Glens Falls, terminates in the rocky forest-covered hills that bound the village of Saratoga Springs on the north.

Mount Defiance, of historic fame, stands guard over the ruins of old Fort Carrillon at Ticonderoga, rising seven hundred and fifty feet above the lake. The Indian name of this place was *Che-on-de-ro-ga*—"Sounding Waters." The French translated this to Carrillon, a chime. It was suggested by the chiming sound of the falls on the outlet of Lake George, near by.

French mountain, of this range, more than two thousand five hundred feet above tide water, overlooks with frowning brow the old battle-ground at the head of Lake George, rich in historic memories.

A spur of this range to the westward forms the Luzerne Mountains, whose highest peak is *Se-non-ge-non*—the great up-turned pot—now called Mt. Kettle Bottom.

V.

THE KAYADROSSERA RANGE.

The next range is the *Kay-ad-ros-se-ra*. They extend from near Crown Point, which is the old Indian *Tek-ya-dough-ni-gar-i-gee*—"Two Points,"—on Lake Champlain, down through Warren into Saratoga county, and running along a little to the westward of Saratoga Springs, in plain sight of the village, terminate in the highlands of Galway and Charlton. They derive their name from the old Indian hunting ground of which they form so conspicuous a feature. Lake *Scarron* (corrupted into Schroon) lies in the valley to the west of this range. The Hudson winds along for many miles in a deep gorge between its mountain masses. The Sacondaga breaks through from the west, and enters the Hudson in this gorge. Mount Pharaoh, whose Indian name is *On-de-wa*, is its highest peak, being four thousand feet above the sea.

VI.

THE SCARRON RANGE.

The third chain of mountains in the Great Wilderness is the Scarron (Schroon) Range. This range begins in the promontory of Split Rock on Lake Champlain, in Essex county, and running through Warren into the south-east corner of Hamilton, ends in the rounded drift hills that rise from the valley of the Mohawk in the eastern part of Fulton county.

Scarron (Schroon) Lake lies at the foot of this range, and Scarron (Schroon) River winds through its deep valleys. From this lake and river the range derives its name.

This name was given to this lake and river by the early French settlers at Crown Point, on Lake Champlain, in honor of Madame Scarron, the widow of the celebrated French dramatist and novelist, Paul Scarron, who was styled in his day " the emperor of the burlesque."

7

The maiden name of Madame Scarron, who afterward became the famous Madame de Maintenon, was Françoise d'Aubigné. Her grandfather was the celebrated Agrippa d'Aubigné, the soldier, prose writer and poet, the friend of Henry IV of France. Her father, Constant d'Aubigné, the Baron of Surimeau, was a profligate and libertine, and was thrown into prison at Niort for killing his wife and her lover, whom he had taken in adultery. While in prison he married Jeanne de Cardilhac, the daughter of the governor of the prison. Before his release, several children were born to him, among whom was Françoise, our heroine. After his release, her father went to Martinique with his little family, where he soon after died in the most abject poverty. Shortly after her father's death, Françoise returned to France with her mother, and after much suffering and many trials, found an asylum in an almost menial position in the house of her godmother, the Countess de Neuillant. She was in fact a mere drudge in the service of the Countess, minding poultry in the farmyard, in peasant's garb and wooden shoes.

In the same street with Françoise lived the poet Scarron, who was a paralytic and a cripple. Becoming interested in the sad story of the young girl, he offered to furnish the money to complete her education in a convent. Calling to thank her benefactor, the young, beautiful and intelligent girl captivated him at once, and he offered her his hand in marriage. She was seventeen, and he more than twice her age, but she accepted his offer. She brought the poor cripple the wealth of her youth, grace and beauty, and he conferred upon her in return an immortal name. The house of Scarron soon became the resort of the most gifted intel-

lects of Paris. Among its frequent guests were the great
Racine and the brilliant Madame de Sévigné.

But a more brilliant chapter opened in the life of the
poor prison-born Françoise. Her poet husband died, and
the still beautiful and fascinating woman this time captivated royalty itself by her wondrous charms. By some
means she became the secret governess of the natural children of Louis XIV, by Madame de Montespan, and soon became the rival of the latter in the affections of the volup-
tuous king. At length the queen, Maria Theresa of Austria,
died, and Louis, unable to make her his mistress, secretly
married the fascinating widow Scarron. The ceremony was
performed at midnight, in June, 1684, in the palace of Ver-
sailles, the Archbishop of Paris and Father la Chaise offici-
ating, only two or three others being present besides the king
and his bride. Thus Madame Scarron became the Queen
of France in fact but not in name. The king settled a large
estate upon her, named Maintenon, and made her Marquise
de Maintenon. As Madame de Maintenon, for nearly thirty
years she exercised a remarkable influence over the desti-
nies of France and of Europe.

Like Blanche of Castile, Agnes Sorel, Madame de Pom-
padour and Marie Antoinette, Madame de Maintenon is one
of the high historical characters of France. But unlike
theirs, there is an air of mystery about her career that renders it all the more fascinating. By some she was regarded
as a person full of crafty intrigue, who, with a subtlety
scarcely human, bewitched an aged monarch by her fascinating charms into humiliating subjection to her will. By
others she was regarded as a divinely appointed messenger,

with almost miraculous powers, to win a lascivious king from his immoral ways.

But the mountain chain, the lake, and the river, bear her more humble name—the name of her poor, poet husband, Scarron. Doubtless some former frequenter of the brilliant *salon* of the poor poet cripple, in sunny France, who had often been charmed by the exquisite grace and tact of his young and beautiful wife, had, in his lonely wanderings in the northern wilds of the New World, while indulging in the pleasing memories of the past, in the enthusiasm of his admiration for her, named the beautiful lake and stream in her honor. How full of meaning, then, is the name Scarron for this lake and river, and mountain chain, as it is written in all the old maps.

VII.

THE BOQUET RANGE.

The fourth chain is the Boquet range, named from the river that waters its base in Essex county. It begins in the high bluffs that border on Perou Bay, on Lake Champlain, and extends through the center of Essex, past the northwest corner of Warren into Hamilton, and through the south-east corner of Hamilton into the west end of Fulton county, and ends in the rocky bluffs that border East Canada Creek above where it enters the Mohawk. The highest mountain in this range is Dix Peak, in North Hudson, Essex county, which rises 4,916 feet above the sea level.

VIII.

THE ADIRONDAK RANGE.

The fifth range of mountains in the Mountain Belt of the Great Wilderness, is the Adirondak chain proper. This name, the origin of which is given in Chapter IV, was originally applied by Prof. Emmons, while making his geological survey of this region, to the remarkable group of high peaks of which Mount Marcy, the highest peak in the chain, forms the towering central figure. This fifth and last great range extends from Point Trembleau, near Port Kent, on Lake Champlain, in nearly a straight line through Essex, Hamilton and Herkimer counties, and ends on the Mohawk river in the rocky barrier through which that river has worn its channel at Little Falls. This chain is more than a hundred miles in length, and is the backbone of the Highlands of the Wilderness. It divides the waters that flow northerly into the St. Lawrence from those that run southerly into the Hudson.

Mount Marcy, the old Indian *Ta-ha-was*—" He splits the sky,"—was found by Verplanck Colvin to be 5,402 feet above the level of the sea. It is the highest land east of the Mississippi, save the White Mountains of New Hampshire, and the Black Mountains of North Carolina. Mount McIntyre, of this range, the Indian *He-no-ga*—" The Home of the ,Thunderer," is 5,201 feet, Mount Haystack is 5,006 feet, and Mount Skylight 5,000 feet above tide water. Upon the south side of Mount Marcy is a little pond or pool, called by the old guides Summit Water, and named by Verplanck Colvin " Tear of the Clouds." It is 4,326 feet above tide. A mile or two south of it is its twin pool, named

Moss Lake, which is 4,312 feet above tide. These sister lakelets are the highest pond sources of the Hudson. Moss Lake is margined and embanked with luxuriant *sphagnous* mosses, and is more of a mountain meadow than a lake. Hence its name. In it Colvin found numbers of beautiful minute white bivalve shells, but three-sixteenths of an inch in diameter.

Near the summit of these high mountains are found many rare arctic plants. Among them are the mountain golden-rod, the *Arenaria groenlandica*, (Greenland sand root), and the *Potentilla tridentata*, (white cinquefoil).

IX.

MOUNTAINS OF THE LAKE BELT.

The Mountain Belt terminates as well as culminates in the Adirondack range. Westerly and northerly of it in the Lake Belt the mountains are more scattered and broken, and are arranged in vast groups or clusters around some high peak that overlooks the wilderness of lakes.

One such group lies around Mount Seward, which is ten miles south of the Saranac lakes. Mount Seward, whose Indian name is *Ou-kor-la*—the "Great Eye"—is 4,332 feet above tide.

Another group lies around Mount Whiteface, whose Indian name is *Wa-ho-par-ten-ie*, and at whose base sleeps Lake Placid. Whiteface is 4,956 feet above tide. Upon its bare, storm-beaten summit some enthusiastic lover of the grand in nature has cut with reverent chisel, deep and clear into its everlasting rock, these words:

THANKS BE TO GOD FOR THE MOUNTAINS.

A third group surrounds Blue Mountain, in the Raquette Lake region. Blue Mountain is 3,824 feet above tide. Its old Indian name is *To-war-loon-da*—" Hill of Storms."

Still another group is gathered around Mount Lyon, which rises to the height of about 4,000 feet between the Chateaugay and Chazy lakes. This group consists of the spurs and broken ranges that cover the northerly half of Clinton county with their wild grandeur.

The chains and groups above named constitute the mountains of the Great Wilderness which were called by the early French explorers the "Mountains of St. Marthe."

X.

THE VIEW FROM THE MOUNTAIN TOPS.

From the summit of any of the high mountains of the Great Wilderness, the scene presented to the eye of the beholder is one of the most striking and sublime in the whole domain of nature. It is at once awfully grand and wildly beautiful beyond the power of language to describe. On every side peak after peak towers up into the clear, cold atmosphere above the clouds, their outlines growing softer and more shadowy in the distance, until the earth and sky commingle in the vast encircling horizon. In all the nearer valleys, full in view, sleep numberless mountain meadows and quiet lakes and lakelets, "pools of liquid crystal turned emerald in the reflected green of impending woods." Wonderful also are the hues and tints and shades of color which these mountains assume with the varying seasons of the year and with the daily changes of the weather, as the sky becomes bright and clear or dark and overcast. Now we see them clothed in the crimson and golden tints of the evening—now in the cold, leaden grey of the morning; now silvery mists creep up their shaggy sides and linger languidly in their valleys—then purple shadows flit across them and play upon their summits. Sometimes the air is so pure and clear after a storm breaks away, that all the mountains stand out with outlines so sharply defined, and their giant forms seemingly appear so near, that we fancy human voices might be heard from the farthest of them. Then again they are all mantled with the matchless soft blue haze, often called mountain smoke, which is that dim, impalpable but lovely illusion and sem-blance of a color, that indescribable appearance of the fleeting, the vanishing and the spiritual, seen nowhere else in nature's realm but among the mountains, that makes the bristling crags and towering peaks, and solid mountain masses seem for all the world like softly sleeping clouds, hanging low down in a far-off shadowy sky, or floating over the sleeping bosom of some distant mountain lake. Thus the scene forever changes, every day in the year, and every hour in the day presenting some new feature in the mountain landscape.

But more striking and more wonderful than all else is the corrugated, wave-like, billowy appearance of the whole mountain region, that so forcibly reminds one of the wide, rolling sea. It seems as though the ocean, in one of its wildest, maddest storms, had suddenly

"Stood still with all its rounded billows fixed
And motionless forever."

XI.

ALTITUDE OF MOUNTAIN PEAKS.

Below is a table showing the height of some of the principal mountains of the Wilderness, mostly as measured by Verplanck Colvin in his Adirondack survey:

Name.	Height in feet above tide.
Mount Marcy,	5,402
Mount McIntyre,	5,201
Mount Haystack,	5,006
Mount Skylight,	5,000
Mount Grey Peak,	4,984
Mount White Face,	4,955
Mount Clinton,	4,937
Mount South McIntyre,	4,937
Mount Dix,	4,916
Mount Little Haystack,	4,854
Mount Colden,	4,753
Mount Gothic,	4,744
Mount Redfield,	4,688
Mount Nipple Top,	4,684
Mount Santanoni,	4,644
Saddle Mountain,	4,536
Giant of the Valley,	4,530
Mount Seward,	4,384
Macomb's Mountain,	4,371
Ragged Mountain,	4,163
Mount Colvin,	4,142
Mount Lyon,	4,000
Mount Pharoah,	4,000
Mount Seymour,	3,928
Mount Bald Face,	3,903
Mount Devil's Ear,	3,903
Snowy Mountain,	3,903
Mount Wall Face,	3,893
Blue Mountain,	3,824
North River Mountain,	3,758
Mount Hurricane,	3,763
Mount Hoffman,	3,727
Bartlett Mountain,	3,715

8

CHAPTER VI.

MOUNTAIN PASSES.

I climbed the dark brow of the mighty Hellvellyn,
 Lakes and mountains beneath me gleamed misty and wide ;
All was still, save by fits when the eagle was yelling,
 And starting around me the echoes replied.
On the right Striden-edge round the Red-tarn was bending,
And Catchedicam its left verge was defending,
One huge nameless rock in the front was ascending,
 When I marked the sad spot where the wanderer had died.
—*Sir Walter Scott.*

I.

THE INDIAN PASS.

Among the stern and rugged features of the grim Wilderness, none are more awfully grand and imposing than the mountain passes over the highest ranges, and the dreadful gorges that so often furrow the mountain sides.

The most celebrated of these mountain passes is the Indian Pass over the Adirondack range in the town of North Elba, in Essex county. This pass was called by the Indians *Otne-yar-heh*—"Stonish Giants," *Ga-nos-gwah*—"Giants clothed with stone," *Da-yoh-je-ga-go*—"The place where the storm clouds meet in battle with the great serpent," and *He-no-do-aw-da*—"The Path of the Thunderer." Through this pass ran the old Indian trail which led from the head waters of the rivers that flow into Lake Champlain to the head waters of the forest branches of the Hudson, and through it now runs the trail of the tourist and modern hunter. The old Indian Pass is an appalling chasm of more than a mile in length, and more than a thousand feet in depth, cut through the solid rock between Mounts McIntyre and Wall Face. The bottom of this awful gorge is a

narrow ravine strewn with huge fragments of rock that
some Titanic force has hurled from the towering mountain
walls on either side.

On its westerly or Wall Face side, a perpendicular precipice or wall of rocks towers up to the giddy height of
thirteen hundred feet ; while on its easterly side is a steep
acclivity which rises at an angle of forty-five degrees, more
than fifteen hundred feet towards the lofty summit of Mount
McIntyre.   Near the center of this wondrous chasm,
high upon the shaggy side of Mount McIntyre, two little
springs issue from the rocks so near to each other that their
waters almost mingle.   From each spring flows a tiny
stream.   These streams at first interlock, but soon separating, run down the mountain side into the bottom of the
chasm, which is here 2,937 feet above tide.   After reaching
the bottom, one runs southerly into the head waters of the
Hudson, and the other northerly into the waters that flow
into the St. Lawrence.

Only a little while at mid-day does the sunshine chase
away the gloomy shadows of the perpetual twilight of this
awful chasm, and the snow and ice linger all summer in its
deep fissures.

The towering precipice on the side of Mount Wall Face
is the most striking feature of the old Indian Pass.   It
seems as if Mount McIntyre, suddenly, in some great con-
vulsion of nature, or by slow degrees, had sunk more than
a thousand feet below its former level, leaving this grand
perpendicular wall of solid rock on the side of Wall Face
to mark the extent of the great depression.   The scene
presented by this stupendous yawning chasm and awful
precipice is sublimely grand beyond description.   "In

viewing this great precipice," says Prof. Emmons, "no feeling of disappointment is felt in consequence of the expectation having exceeded the reality." "What a sight," says Alfred B. Street, "horrible, and yet sublimely beautiful—no, not beautiful, scarce an element of beauty there—all grandeur and terror."

II.

OTHER MOUNTAIN PASSES.

Between Mounts Dix and Nipple Top, another gloomy gorge extends across the Boquet range, called the Hunter's Pass. It is second in wild grandeur only to the famous Indian Pass. The height of the center of the Hunter's Pass is 3,247 feet above tide. In this pass also, two rivers take their rise whose waters seek the sea in contrary directions—the Boquet running northerly to Lake Champlain, and the Schroon southerly into the Hudson.

In the gorge next west of Nipple Top is the Elk Pass. This pass leads from the head of an easterly branch of the Schroon to a branch of the Au Sable, and opens upon the head of Keene Valley. Its summit is 3,302 feet above the level of the sea.

Between Russagonia or Sawtooth Mountain and Mount Colvin is the Au Sable Pass. It leads from the Lower Au Sable Lake to the head waters of the Boreas River, a branch of the Hudson. It is a water-gap, forming a natural gateway through the mountains.

The Opalescent-head Pass and the Avalanche Lake Pass are elevated mountain passes whose centers are more than four thousand feet above tide.

Then there is the *Ou-lus-ka* Pass, "the place of shadows," between Mount Seward and Ragged Mountain.

The Caraboo Pass runs around the peak of Mount Mc-Intyre, connecting the head of the Opalescent River with the head waters of the Au Sable.

The Great Elba Pass extends as a broad valley along the west side of Mount White Face, and the Ampersand Valley Pass lies between Ragged Mountain and Mount Seymour.

Then there is the Panther Gorge on Mount Marcy, whose very name makes one shudder, and the Gorge of the Dial —gloomy mountain gorges that impress the beholder with feelings of unutterable awe and terror.*

The reader's attention has so far been called to the more rugged features of the Mountain Belt of the Great Wilderness. In the following chapters I shall attempt to sketch some of its softer and more gentle aspects—its lakes and streams and mountain meadows.

* See Report of the Topographical Survey of the Adirondack Wilderness of New York for the year 1873, by Verplanck Colvin ; Natural History of New York, Part IV ; The Indian Pass, by Alfred B. Street, notes to poems of Charles Fenno Hoffman, and Hough's Gazetteer of New York of 1872.

CHAPTER VII.

MOUNTAIN MEADOWS.

The spring has passed this way.   Look ! where she trod
The daring crocus sprang up through the sod,
To greet her coming with glad heedlessness,
Scarce waiting to put on its leafy dress,
But bright and bold in its brave nakedness.
And further on—mark !—on this gentle rise
She must have passed, for frail anemones
Are trembling to the wind couched low among
These fresh green grasses that so lush have sprung
O'er the hid runnel, that with tinkling tongue
Babbles its secret troubles.   Here she stopped
A longer while, and on this grassy sweep,
While pensively she lingered, see ! she dropped
This knot of love-sick violets from her breast,
Which as she threw them down she must have kissed,
For still the fragrance of her breath they keep.
                      —*W. W. S., in Blackwood's Magazine.*

The Wilderness is mostly characterized by the rugged grandeur of its mountain scenery, yet it is not wholly without its softer aspects and more gentle features.   Among these none are more wildly beautiful than its Mountain Meadows.

In all the valleys between the mountain ranges, and scattered thickly about all through the lake and level belts of the Wilderness, are numberless mountain meadows, sleeping in their quiet beauty, veiled in the dreamy haze, the lovely mountain smoke of the short Adirondack summers.

In these wild mountain meadows Nature, in her playful moments, seems to have dressed the fairy scene in sharp contrast with the frowning grandeur of the mountain gorges.

Some of these wild meadows are broad expanses of waving grass—miniature prairies—often of miles in extent. Through the most of them a brooklet winds with sluggish

current, filled with speckled trout,—its banks covered with
the bloom of the crocus, the anemone, violets, grass pinks,
wild roses and azaleas.

Others are wide marshes or peat bogs, carpeted with
deep many colored *sphagnous* mosses, and covered with
clumps of low, bushy shrubs, among which the modest
Kalmia blooms beside the blue gentian and the flaming car-
dinal flower, and the curious side-saddle flower or pitcher
plant alternates with the rare yellow iris.

Among the largest and most famous of these mountain
meadows is the *Sacondaga Vlaie* in the northern part of
Fulton county, near which Sir William Johnston built his
hunting lodges, called the Fish House and the cottage on
the Summer House Point, (built in 1772,) at which he spent
several months in the summer. This vlaie is five or six
miles in length, and in many places more than a mile in
width. Through it runs the *Ken-ny-et-to* creek; and the
Mayfield creek runs into the Sacondaga at the Fish House.

Another of these natural meadows or miniature prairies
of equal size, also called the *Vlaie*, lies along the west bank
of the Black River, in Lewis county, between Lowville and
Castorland.

Many of these wild meadows cover extensive beds of
peat. It seems that a large share of the vegetable matter
of the soil of the wilderness has been washed into these
peaty beds. A beautiful feature of these beds is the rich
carpet of *sphagnous* mosses with which they are covered.
These mosses, late in the summer, sometimes drop their
delicate shades of green, and rival the autumn leaves in
the soft beauty of their hues and tints. These carpets of
the wilderness are then more beautiful than the fairest pro-

ducts of the Persian looms. At Number Four, near Fenton's, is one of these charming mountain meadows carpeted with brilliant mosses.

Around all these wild mountain meadows of the Great Wilderness, and along the borders of the brooks that wander through them, is always to be seen a wavy line of alders and shining willows. Along this line the shad bush hangs out in earliest spring its flag of truce, and the trailing arbutus peeps with bright eyes as it creeps forth beside the lingering snow-banks. Later in the season, the clematis—virgin's bower—twines, with its clusters of purple blossoms, and the sweet azaleas and wild roses mingle their fragrance with the violets and lilies that bloom among the grasses. Often in the sumptuous summer these meadows are all ablaze with the scarlet and purple flowers of the early autumn of warmer regions.

In many of these natural meadows of the wilderness may still be seen the remains of old beaver dams, and sometimes the decaying stumps of old trees once gnawed by beavers' teeth. These wild meadows were the beaver's favorite home when the old wilderness was the Indian *Couch-sach-ra-ge,* or "Beaver Hunting Country," and are now called by the hunters "beaver meadows." It is supposed that the beaver long since ceased to exist within the boundaries of the wilderness. The last one was seen in the vicinity of Bog Lake, by Charles Fenton, more than twenty years ago. Yet it is said that there are unexplored regions which lie at some distance from the frequented forest trails where a few colonies yet linger in their ancient home, unmolested by man.

Around all the wild meadows may be seen many a quiet

nook, where the deer comes in to crop his morning meal from off the juicy grasses, and the black bear to gather his supper of sweet wild berries. And here and there among them, " dells smile, fit haunts for fairies, where the thrasher pipes, the scampering squirrel barks, and the gliding rabbit jerks its long ears at every sound, and the ancient path of the whirlwind is seen, with the wrenched trees long since melted into the grass of a vista like an old settler-road, so that the eye looks in vain for the faint wheel track."

Such are some of the smiling and softer aspects of the grim old wilderness.

9

CHAPTER VIII.

THE DISCOVERY OF LAKE GEORGE.

> " The very echoes round this shore
>   Have caught a strange and gibbering tone
> For they have told the war whoop o'er,
>   Till the wild chorus is their own."
>   —*Goodrich.*

I.

THE GEM OF THE OLD WILDERNESS.

In the olden time, when the whole North Continent was a vast howling wilderness from the frozen ocean to the flowery gulf land, many bright, fair lakes lay sleeping in its awful solitudes, their waters flashing in the sunshine, like gleaming mirrors, and lighting up the somber desolation like jewels in an iron crown ; but the fairest and the brightest of them all was Lake George.

It was the gem of the old wilderness. Of the thousand lakes that adorn the surface of Northern New York, there is none among them all to-day so fair, none among them all so like " A diadem of beauty," as Lake George—its deepest waters as bright and as pure as the dew drops that linger on its lilies.

Its authentic history runs back for two hundred and forty years. Its forest traditions extend into the dim, mythical, mysterious and unknown romance of the New World. But its waters have not always been as pure as they are to-day, and we would all grow weary of its story, for it is a story of blood. In the following pages, therefore, I shall attempt to sketch a few only of the most noted incidents connected with its discovery by white men.

II.

ISAAC JOGUES.

The first white men who saw Lake George were the Jesuit Father Isaac Jogues, and his companions René Goupil and Guillame Couture. They were taken over its waters as prisoners—tortured, maimed and bleeding,—by the Mohawks, in the month of August, 1642.

Isaac Jogues, the discoverer of Lake George, was born at Orleans, in France, on the 10th of January, 1607, and received there the rudiments of his education. In October, 1624, he entered the Jesuit Society at Rouen, and removed to the College of La Fletche in 1627. He completed his divinity studies at Clermont College, Paris, and was ordained priest in February, 1636. In the spring of that year he embarked as a missionary for Canada, arriving at Quebec early in July.

At the time of his first visit to Lake George, Jogues was but thirty-five years of age. "His oval face and the delicate mould of his features," says Parkman, "indicated a modest, thoughtful, and refined nature. He was constitutionally timid, with a sensitive conscience and great religious susceptibilities. He was a finished scholar, and might have gained a literary reputation; but he had chosen another career, and one for which he seemed but ill-fitted." His companions were young laymen who, from religious motives, had attached themselves without pay to the service of the Jesuit missions.

III.

WAR IN THE WILDERNESS.

Thirty-three years before Jogues' first visit to Lake George, Samuel de Champlain, while on his voyage of discovery, had attacked the Iroquois on the shores of the lake that bears his name, and they had fled in terror from his murderous fire-arms to their homes on the Mohawk. Since then they had ceased to make war upon their hereditary enemies, the Canadian Algonquins, or the French colonists. But the Iroquois had by no means forgotten their humiliating defeat. In the meantime they had themselves been supplied with fire-arms by the Dutch traders at Fort Orange, on the Hudson, in exchange for beaver skins and wampum, and now their hour of sweet revenge had come.

The war with the Eries, the Hurons, and the other western tribes, had been undertaken by the Senecas, the Cayugas and Onondagas. It was left to the Mohawks and the Oneidas to attempt the extermination of the Canadian Algonquins and their French allies. They came near accomplishing their bloody purpose. But for the timely arrival of a few troops from France, the banks of the St. Lawrence would soon have become as desolate as the country of the lost Eries or that of the Hurons. The savages hung the war-kettle upon the fire and danced the war-dance in all the Mohawk castles. In bands of tens and hundreds they took the war-path, and passing through Lakes George and Champlain, and down the River Richelieu, went prowling about the French settlements at Montreal, Three Rivers and Quebec, and the Indian villages on the Ottawa. The Iroquois were everywhere. From the Huron country to

the Saguenay they infested the forests like so many ravening wolves.   They hung about the French forts, killing
stragglers and luring armed parties into fatal ambuscades.
They followed like hounds upon the trail of travellers,
and hunted through the forests, and lay in wait along the
banks of streams to attack the passing canoes.   It was one
of these hostile bands of Mohawks that attacked and captured Isaac Jogues and his companions.

IV.

CAPTURE OF JOGUES.

Father Jogues had come down the savage Ottawa River
a thousand miles, in his bark canoes, the spring before,
from his far-off Huron Mission to Quebec, for much needed
supplies.   He was now on his return voyage to the Huron
country.   In the dewy freshness of the early morning of
the second day of August, with his party of four Frenchmen and thirty-six Hurons, in twelve heavily laden
canoes, Father Jogues reached the westerly end of the
expansion of the St. Lawrence called Lake St. Peters.   It is
there filled with islands that lie opposite the mouth of the
River Richelieu.   It was not long before they heard the
terrible war-whoop upon the Canadian shore.   In a moment
more Jogues and his white companions and a part of his
Hurons, were captives in the hands of the yelling, exulting
Mohawks, and the remainder of the Hurons killed or dis-
persed.

Goupil was seized at once.   Jogues might have escaped,
but seeing Goupil and his Huron neophytes in the hands
of their savage captors, he had no heart to desert them,

and gave himself up. Couture at first eluded his pursuers, but, like Jogues, relented, and returned to his companions. Five Iroquois ran to meet Couture as he approached, one of whom snapped his gun at his breast. It missed fire, but Couture in turn fired his own gun at the savage, and laid him dead at his feet. The others sprang upon him like panthers, stripped him naked, tore out his fingernails with their teeth, gnawed his fingers like hungry dogs, and thrust a sword through one of his hands. Jogues, touched by the sufferings of his friend, broke from his guards, and threw his arms around Couture's neck. The savages dragged him away, and knocked him senseless. When he revived they gnawed his fingers with their teeth, and tore out his nails as they had done those of Couture. Turning fiercely upon Goupil they treated him in the same way.

With their captives they then crossed to the mouth of the Richelieu, and encamped where the town of Sorel now stands.*

The savages returned, by the way which they came, to the Mohawk with their suffering captives.

On the eighth day, upon an island near the south end of Lake Champlain, they arrived at the camp of two hundred Iroquois, who were on their way to the St. Lawrence. At the sight of the captives, these fierce warriors, armed with clubs and thorny sticks, quickly ranged themselves in two long lines, between which the captives were each in turn made to run the gauntlet up a rocky hill-side. On their way they were beaten with such frenzy that Jogues fell senseless, half dead, and covered with blood. After passing this or-

* Parkman's Jesuits in North America, p. 217.

deal again, the captives were mangled as before, and this time tortured with fire. At night, when they tried to rest, the young warriors tore open their wounds, and pulled out their hair and beards.

V.

THE DISCOVERY OF LAKE GEORGE.

In the morning they resumed their journey, and soon reached a rocky promontory, near which rose a forest covered mountain, beyond which the lake narrowed into a river. It was more than a hundred years before that promontory became the famous Ticonderoga of later times.

Between the promontory and the mountain a stream issued from the woods and fell into the lake. They landed at the mouth of the stream, and taking their canoes upon their shoulders, followed it up around the noisy waters of the falls. It was the Indian *Che-non-de-ro-ga*, " *the chiming waters.*" They soon reached the shores of a beautiful lake that there lay sleeping in the depths of the limitless forest, all undiscovered and unseen by white men until then. It was the fairest gem of the old wilderness, now called *Lake George*. But then it bore only its old Indian name *Caniaderi-oit*, " the tail of the lake."

Champlain, thirty-three years before, had come no further than its outlet. He heard the " chiming waters" of the falls, and was told that a great lake lay beyond them. But he turned back without seeing it, and so our bruised and bleeding prisoners, Isaac Jogues, and his companions Goupil and Couture, were the first of white men to gaze upon its waters.

"Like a fair Naiad of the Wilderness," says Parkman, "it slumbered between the guardian mountains that breathe between crag and forest the stern poetry of war."*

Again they launched their frail canoes, and amid the dreamy splendors of an August day glided on their noiseless course across the charming waters. On they passed, under the dusky mountain shadows, now over some wide expanse, now through the narrow channels and among the woody islands, redolent with balsamy odors. At last they reached the landing place, at the head of the lake, afterward the site of Fort William Henry, now Caldwell, famous as a summer resort.

Here they left their boats and took the old Indian trail that led from Lake George, across Indian *Kay-ad-ros-se-ra*, a distance of forty miles, to the lower castles on the Mohawk. It was the same trail afterward followed by the Marquis de Tracy, in October, 1666, on his way to the Mohawk castles, with his army and train of French noblemen, to avenge the death of the youthful Chazy.

This Indian trail, so often the war-path, led from the south end of Lake George on a southerly course to the great bend of the Hudson, about ten miles westerly of Glens Falls. From the bend it led southerly through the towns of Wilton and Greenfield, along in plain sight of, and but four or five miles distant from, Saratoga Springs, and through Galway to the lower castles on the Mohawk, four or five miles westerly of what is now Amsterdam, on the New York Central Railroad.

* Jesuits in North America, p. 219.

VI.

THE CAPTIVITY OF JOGUES.

After their arrival at the Mohawk towns, Father Jogues and his companions were again subjected to the most inhuman tortures, with the horrid details of which I will not weary the reader. Among the Mohawks Jogues remained for nearly a year, a captive slave, performing the most menial duties. Soon after his arrival, more Huron prisoners were brought in, and put to death with cruel tortures. In the midst of his own sufferings, Jogues lost no opportunity to convert them to Christianity, sometimes even baptizing them with a few rain-drops which he found clinging to the husks of an ear of corn that was thrown to him for food.

Couture had won their admiration by his bravery, and after inflicting upon him the most savage torture, they adopted him into one of their families in the place of a dead relation. But in October they murdered poor Goupil, and after dragging his body through the village, threw it into a deep ravine. Jogues sought it and gave it partial burial. He sought it again and it was gone. Had the torrent washed it away, or had it been taken off by the savages? He searched the forest and the waters in vain. "Then crouched by the pitiless stream he mingled his tears with its waters, and in a voice broken with groans, chanted the service for the dead."* In the spring, while the snows were melting, some children told him where the body of poor Goupil was lying further down the stream. The Indians, and not the torrent had taken it away. He found the bones scattered around, stripped by the foxes and birds.

* Jesuits in North America, p. 225.

10

He tenderly gathered them, and hid them in a hollow tree, in the hope that he might some day be able to lay them in consecrated ground.

Late in the autumn after his arrival he was ordered to go to some distant forest with a party of braves on their annual deer hunt. All the game they took they first offered to their god *Ar-rok-oui*, and then ate it in his honor. Jogues came near starving in the midst of plenty, for he would not taste the food offered to what he believed to be a demon.

In a lonely spot in the forest he cut the bark in the form of a cross from the trunk of a large tree. Then half clad in shaggy furs, in the chill wintry air, he knelt before it upon the frozen ground in prayer. He was a living martyr to the faith before whose emblem he bowed in adoration— a faith in which was now his only hope and consolation.

VII.

THE ESCAPE.

At length in the month of July, 1643, Father Jogues went with a fishing party to a place on the Hudson about twenty miles below Fort Orange. Some of the Iroquois soon returned, bringing Jogues with them. On their way they stopped at Fort Orange, and he made his escape.

Fort Orange was then a small octagonal palisaded fort, situated on the flats near what is now the steamboat landing in Albany, and was surrounded by twenty or thirty plain wooden houses. Albany was then a small fur trading station at the lower end of the great carrying place between the Mohawk and the Hudson which avoided the Cohoes Falls.

Jogues was secreted by the Dutch, and the savages made diligent search for him. Fearing his discovery and recapture by them, the kind-hearted Dutch paid a large ransom for the captive, and gave him a free passage to his home in France. He arrived in Brittany on Christmas day, and was received by his friends, who had heard of his captivity, as one risen from the dead. He was treated everywhere with mingled curiosity and reverence, and was summoned to Paris. The ladies of the court thronged around to do him homage. When he was presented to the queen, Anne of Austria, she kissed his mutilated hands—the hands of the poor slave of the Mohawk squaws.

In the spring of 1644, Jogues returned to Canada, soon to become a martyr to his faith in the valley of the Mohawk.

VIII.

THE LAKE OF THE BLESSED SACRAMENT.

For still another year the Iroquois war raged with unabated violence. Early in the spring of 1645, a famous Algonquin chief named *Piskaret*, with a band of braves, went out upon the war-path toward the country of the Mohawks. Upon an island in Lake Champlain they met a war-party of thirteen Iroquois. They killed eleven of the number, made prisoners of the other two, and returned in triumph to the St. Lawrence.

At Sillery, a small settlement on the St. Lawrence, near Quebec, Piskaret, in a speech, delivered his captives to Montmagny, the Governor General, who replied with compliments and gifts.

The wondering captives, when they fairly comprehended that they were saved from cruel torture and death, were surprised and delighted beyond measure. Then one of the captive Mohawks, of great size and of matchless symmetry of form, who was evidently a war chief, arose and said to the Governor Montmagny :

"Onnontio, I am saved from the fire. My body is delivered from death. Onnontio, you have given me my life. I thank you for it. I will never forget it. All my country will be grateful to you. The earth will be bright, the river calm and smooth ; there will be peace and friendship between us. The shadow is before my eyes no longer. The spirits of my ancestors slain by the Algonquins have disappeared. Onnontio, you are good ; we are bad. But our anger is gone. I have no heart but for peace and rejoicing."

As he said this he began to dance, holding his hands upraised as if apostrophizing the sun. Suddenly he snatched a hatchet, brandished it for a moment like a mad man, then flung it into the fire saying as he did so :

"Thus I throw down my anger ; thus I cast away the weapons of blood. Farewell war. Now, Onnontio, I am your friend forever."

Onnontio means in the Indian tongue "Great Mountain." It is a literal translation of Montmagny's name. It was ever after the Iroquois name for the governors of Canada, as Corlear was for the Governors of New York. Corlear was the Indian name for Arendt van Curler, first superintendent of the "colonie of Rensselaerswick," who was a great favorite of the Mohawks.

The captive Iroquois were well treated by the French

and one of them sent home to their country on the Mohawk, under a promise of making negotiations for peace
with his people, and the other kept as a hostage. The efforts of the captive chief who returned to the Mohawks
were successful. In a short time he reappeared at Three
Rivers with ambassadors of peace from the Mohawk cantons. To the great joy of the French he brought with him
Couture, who had become a savage in dress and appearance.
After a great deal of feasting, speech-making and belt-giv-
ing, peace was concluded, and order and quiet once more
reigned for a brief period in the wilderness.

But ambassadors from the French and Algonquins must
be sent from Canada to the Mohawk towns, with gifts and
presents to ratify the treaty. No one among the French
was so well suited for this office as Isaac Jogues. His, too,
was a double errand, for he had already been ordered by
his superior to found a new mission among the Mohawks.
It was named prophetically, in advance, "The Mission of
the Martyrs." At the first thought of returning to the
Mohawks, Jogues recoiled with horror. But it was only a
momentary pang. The path of duty seemed clear to him,
and, thankful that he was found worthy to suffer for the
saving of souls, he prepared to depart.

On the 16th of May, 1646, Father Jogues set out from
Three Rivers with Sieur Bourdon, engineer to the Governor,
two Algonquin ambassadors, and four Mohawks as guides.
On his way he passed over the well remembered scenes of his
former sufferings upon the River Richelieu and Lake Cham-
plain. He reached the foot of Lake George on the eve of
Corpus Christi, which is the feast of the Blessed Body of
Jesus. He named the lake, in honor of the day, "The

Lake of the Blessed Sacrament." For more than a hundred years afterward this lake bore no other name. When
he visited the lake before, as a poor, suffering, bleeding
prisoner, it was clad in the dreamy splendors of the early
autumn. Now its banks were robed in the wild exuberance
of leafy June.

When Sir William Johnson began his military operations
at the head of the lake in the summer of 1755, he changed
its name to Lake George in honor of England's Hanoverian
king. "Better," says an eminent historian, "had it been
called Lake Jogues in honor of its gentle discoverer."

From Lake St. Sacrament, Jogues proceeded on his way
to the Mohawk country, and having accomplished his political mission, returned to Canada.

Thus ended the first French and Indian war, which I
shall call the war of 1642.

IX.

THE MISSION OF THE MARTYRS.

But the work of Father Jogues was only half done.
Again, in month of September he set out for the Mohawk
country. On his way he again passed over the shining
waters of Lake St. Sacrament. Now it had doffed its summer dress, aud donned again the gold and crimson glories
of the autumn forests. This time he went in his true character, a minister of the gospel. But he had a strong presentiment that his life was near its end. He wrote to a
friend "I shall go and shall not return." His forebodings
were verified. While there in July he had left a small box
containing a few necessary articles in anticipation of an

early return. The superstitious savages were confident that famine, pestilence, or some evil spirit or other was shut up in the box, which would in time come forth and devastate their country. To confirm their suspicions, that very summer there was much sickness in their castles, and when the harvest came in the autumn they found that the caterpillars had eaten their corn. The Christian missionary was held responsible for all this, and was therefore doomed to die.

He arrived at their village of *Cach-na-wa-ga*, on the bank of the Mohawk, on the 17th of October, and was saluted with blows. On the evening of the 18th, he was invited to sup in the wigwam of a chief. He accepted the invitation, and on entering the hut he was struck on the head with a tomahawk by a savage who was concealed within the door. They cut off his head, and in the morning displayed it upon one of the palisades that surrounded the village. His body they threw into the Mohawk.

Thus died Father Isaac Jogues, the discoverer of Lake George, at his *Mission of the Martyrs, St. Mary of the Mohawks*, in the fortieth year of his age.* He was but an humble, self-sacrificing missionary of the Cross, yet his was

> " One of the few, the immortal names,
> That were not born to die."

---

* For a full account of the martyrdom of Father Jogues, see Parkman's Jesuits in North America, to which work I am indebted for many of the incidents above related. Also see Abridged Relations of Father Bressany, published in Montreal in 1852, which contains a portrait of Father Jogues.

CHAPTER IX.

LAKES OF THE WILDERNESS.

A mirror, where the veteran rocks,
May glass their seams and scars ;
A nether sky where breezes break
The sunshine into stars.
—*Houghton.*

I.

Among the softer and more gentle aspects of the Wilderness, are its numberless lakes, which, like its mountain meadows, are scattered all over its surface, sleeping in quiet beauty in all its valleys.

A boundless stretch of forest is grand, but when its somber shades are broken by the silver waters of a lake, its grandeur at once softens into the beautiful.

In the Old World, the associations of centuries of human experience cluster around each lake and river, and they are linked to the past by a thousand pleasing or painful memories. But here in this primeval wilderness, many of them are as new and fresh creations, so far as civilized man is concerned, as they were when left by the receding waters of the Primeval Ocean. No human blood or tears have ever been mingled with their waters. The wild fowl builds her nest near them, and there hatches her young brood ; the grey wolf comes tripping down the banks to drink ; the timid deer steps in to crop his juicy food ; the eagle rears her young on some steep jutting crag, or towering top-blasted tree ; the sleek otter slides in for his daily store of fish, and the panther's scream echoes around their lonely shores to-day, just as they all did when Abraham of old was receiving the promises, and Homer was tuning his immortal lyre.

II.

THEIR ROCKY BEDS.

The lakes of the Wilderness, like its mountains, owe their existence to the extremely rugged, broken and corrugated strata of its old Laurentian system of underlying rocks. The extreme hardness of these primitive rocks prevents their being worn away by the action of running water, while their rough and broken surface presents many barriers, which no time can crumble, to the free passage of the rivers and streams. Meeting these obstructions, which no washing can wear away, sometimes, in many places along their channels, the rivers spread out into many lakes, and chains of lakes, in their winding courses as they run down the slopes of the Wilderness.

And now lake and lakelet sleep in their granite beds that were shaped for them when the rocky ground work of the wilderness plateau was folded into ranges and tumbled together into mountain masses, in "the making of the world."

Lake Ontario doubtless owes its great depth to the solid Laurentian barrier that crosses the bed of the St. Lawrence at the Thousand Islands. Were it not for this bar of flinty rocks, the ocean tide, instead of ceasing to be felt near Montreal, would ebb and flow up to the very foot of Niagara.

11

III.

THE LAKE BELT.

Nearly all the larger and by far the greater number of the smaller lakes of the wilderness are found in its Lake Belt. This great belt, as stated in a previous chapter, is about thirty miles in width, and extends diagonally across the center of the Wilderness from north-east to south-west, between the Level Belt on the north, and the Mountain Belt on the south.

In the Lake Belt we have at the north-east the Chazy and Upper Chateaugay lakes, the Upper and Lower Saranac, the St. Regis Lakes and Lake Placid. Centrally, we have the Raquette, the largest of all the lakes, Forked Lake, Beach's Lake, Smith's and Albany lakes, Little and Big Tupper's. To the south-west there are the eight lakes of the Fulton chain, Moose Lake, and the Red Horse chain, and the Woodhull lakes.

Cranberry Lake, Beaver Lake and Lake Francis at Number Four, Brantingham Lake, Bonaparte Lake, Chases Lake, and the Oswegatchie chain of lakes and ponds, all lie in the Level Belt of the Wilderness.

The Lake Belt seems to be a depression in or a downward fold of the rocky strata of the Wilderness, which runs parallel with the great mountain ranges. Through the whole length of this depression there is a continuous succession of lakes and streams that render its navigation possible from one end to the other. Should the hunter launch his skiff upon the waters of the Saranac river, which flow into Lake Champlain, he could pass up through the Lower and Upper Saranac Lakes, and out of their head waters into the head waters of Stoney Creek, a stream that runs into the Raquette River, by going overland only across the old Indian carry, which is but a mile in length. Once afloat upon the waters of the Raquette, he would find little difficulty in going up it into Long Lake, Forked Lake and Raquette Lake. From the Raquette he could pass up into its Brown's Tract Inlet, and then overland across another 'carry of only a mile and a quarter into the Fulton chain of eight lakes, whose waters flow through the Moose River into the Black River. Thus could he float his frail boat through the very heart of the Wilderness, and under the shadows of its highest mountain chain, without scarcely taking it from the water.

IV.

LAKES OF THE MOUNTAIN BELT.

In the eastern part of the Mountain Belt are the beautiful lakes Scarron (Schroon) and Luzerne, which are already so much frequented by summer tourists, and in the northern part are Piseco and Pleasant lakes of the Sacondaga waters. Three miles above Lake Scarron, and in the same valley, is the curious Lake Paradox. The outlet of Lake Paradox flows into Scarron River, which in times of freshet is higher than the lake. At such times the water flows from the river into the lake, instead of from the lake into the river. This apparent running up stream of these waters, one of nature's paradoxes, gave rise to the name. Similar to this is Paradox Pond, near Lake Placid. Into this pond the waters of the lake ebb and flow through its outlet, which is also its inlet, with continuous throbbing, like the ocean tide.

Lake Luzerne was named in honor of the Chevalier de la Luzerne, who was the first French minister to the United States. He was sent over by his government in 1779, and remained until 1783. He had great influence, and discharged the delicate and onerous duties of his important office with singular ability. This beautiful lake and mountain chain to which it gives its name are among the enduring monuments of our nation's gratitude to France for her priceless services in the war of the Revolution.

In the very heart's core of the Wilderness, at the foot of the old giants of the Mountain Belt, Mounts Marcy, McIntyre, Colden, Haystack, Skylight and Santanoni, are located the singular lakes Colden and Avalanche, and the lakes Sanford and Henderson, of sad memories.

Lakes Colden and Avalanche lie near each other, between Mounts Colden, Marcy and McIntyre, and are the highest lakes of any considerable size in the Wilderness. Lake Avalanche is 2,856 feet, and Lake Colden is 2,770 feet above tide. At such heights, and shut in by such mountain barriers, their still, clear, ice-cold waters glitter like mirrors in a land of shadows. In their chilly depths no living thing can exist except a species of small green lizard. Into Lake Avalanche, from time to time, vast land slides have rushed down from Mount Colden, half filling it with earth and rocks. One such avalanche came down as late as 1869, ploughing a deep gorge in the mountain's side, and nearly divided the lake into two parts.

Near the foot of these weird lakes runs the wonderful Opalescent River, the highest easterly branch of the Hudson. The Opalescent, a branch of which takes its rise in the high mountain pools Summit Water and Moss Lake, upon the sides of old *Ta-ha-was*, runs through one of the most wild and picturesque regions that can be found in the great woods. At one place it shoots through a narrow fissure in the rocks, or mountain gorge, of more than a mile in length. This gorge is called by the old hunters the "Flume of the Opalescent." The bed of the stream, which is formed of the hypersthene rock of the region, is full of crystals of opalescent feldspar. This is the exquisitely beautiful mineral Labradorite, which was first discovered by the Moravian missionaries in the Laurentian rocks in Labrador, and that when first taken by them to England brought such fabulous prices. In this wild mountain stream this brilliant gem is found in great profusion, shining through its clear waters with a marvellous play of colors.

But this is not the only gem that flashes in the dark rocks of this region. Garnets, carnelians, sapphires, agates, amethysts, jasper, chalcedony, celestine and calcite light up the old rocks with their brilliant iridescence.

The Lakes of the Wilderness, mentioned in this chapter, comprise only a few of those which are the most widely known and celebrated. The whole territory of the Wilderness is literally crowded with lakes unnumbered, and many of them still unnamed and unexplored, upon whose shores, says Colvin, there is no "mark of axe nor sign of man anywhere." Colvin, in his Adirondack survey in 1873 and in 1874, found more than two hundred and fifty lakes and ponds, that had never been laid down upon any maps, in a small part of the Wilderness,

V.

ALTITUDE OF LAKES AND FOREST STATIONS.

A table showing the height in feet above tide water of some of the lakes, summer resorts and forest stations in and near the Wilderness, mostly as computed by Verplanck Colvin in his Adirondack survey :

Name.	Height.
Adirondack Village,	1,836
Aiden Lair,	1,700
Au Sable Pond, (upper)	2,004
*Arnold's, on Brown's Tract,	1,674
Ampersand Pond,	2,078
*Albany Lake,	1,688
Beach's Lake, (Brandreth,)	1,913
Beaver Meadow Pond, (source Oswegatchie)	2,193
Blue Mountain Lake,	1,821
*Ballston Spa, (R. R. Track)	277
*Beaver Lake, (at Fenton's, Number Four)	1,409
Bog Lake,	1,755
Boquet River, (at Elizabethtown)	496
Boquet River, (Upland Valley,	2,425
*Black River, (at Watertown,)	454
*Carthage, (Black River, above Dam)	715
Calamity Pond,	2,712
Cedar Lake,	2,529
Cedar River Settlement,	1,706
*Chase's Lake, (Watson)	1,232
Caraboo Pass,	3,662
Charley Pond, (Beaver River)	1,720
Dyke Falls, (Crossing)	2,788
Elizabethtown, (river level)	496
Elk Pass,	3,302
Fairy Ladder Falls,	3,111
*Fuller Summit, Galway,	1,032
Fish House, on Sacondaga,	720
Graves's Pond,	1,795
Grasse River Ford,	1,452
Great Plains,	1,637
Harrington Pond,	1,779

*Hudson River, mouth Cedar River,............. 1,454
Indian Lake,.... 1,705
Iron Works, (Lower,)...... 1,805
Jackson's Hotel, Cedar River,............................... 1,706
*Lake Ontario,........................ 234
Lake Placid,.... 1,615
Long Lake,... 1,620
Lake Pleasant,.............................,................. 1,615
Lake Colden,....... 2,770
Lake Avalanche, ... 2,856
Lost Lake, (Oswegatchie)................................... 1,761
†Lake George,............ 243
†Lake Champlain,................... 69
Moose Lake,................................ 2,239
Moss Lake,... 4,312
North Elba Bridge,.. 1,671
†Oneida Lake,.... 369
*Piseco Lake,.. 1,648
Panther Gorge,...........,..... 3,378
Raquette Lake,.. 1,766
Red Horse Chain,.... 1,756
*Spruce Lake Summit, Hamilton county,..................... 2,392
Saranac Lake, (Upper)..................................... 1,605
Saranac Lake, (Lower)..................................... 1,556
Silver Lake,.. 1,983
Smith's Lake, Beaver River,. 1,774
Summit Water Pond,.......,... 4,326
Stillwater, Beaver River,...... 1,656
Saratoga Springs, (R. R. Track)............................ 306
Tupper's Lake,... 1,554
Tupper's Lake, (Little).... 1,737
Wells Town,... 1,016
Wilmington Village,.......,................................ 1,058

* By A. F. Edwards, Chief Engineer Sackett's Harbor and Saratoga Railroad.

† From Hough's Gazetteer.

CHAPTER X.

THE NAMING OF THE CHAZY RIVER.

And dar'st thou then
To beard the lion in his den,
The Douglass in his hall?
—*Sir Walter Scott.*

I.

The Chazy River flows from the beautiful lake of the same name, northerly and easterly, and falls into the northerly end of Lake Champlain, nearly opposite the Isle la Motte, of historic fame. The Chazy Lake sleeps at the foot of Mount Lyon, one of the central peaks of a mountain group of the Lake Belt of the Wilderness, on the rugged eastern border of Clinton county. This beautiful stream was named in memory of Sieur Chazy, a young French nobleman who was murdered on its banks, near its mouth, by the Indians, in the year 1666.

M. Chazy was a nephew of the Marquis de Tracy, Lieutenant General of Canada, and was a captain in the famous French regiment *Carignan-Salières*. This regiment was the first body of regular troops that was sent to Canada by the French king. It was raised by Prince Carignan, in Savoy, during the year 1644. Eight years after, it was conspicuous in the service of the French king, in the battles with Prince Condé in the revolt of the Fronde. But the Prince of Carignan was unable to support the regiment and gave it to the king, who attached it to the armies of France. In 1664 it took a distinguished part with the allied forces of France in the Austrian war with the Turks. The next year

it went with Tracy to Canada. Among its captains, besides
Chazy, were Sorel, Chambly, La Motte and others, whose
names are so familiar in Canadian annals. The regiment
was commanded by Colonel de Salières—hence its double
name.*

In 1665 Tracy landed at Quebec in great pomp and splendor. The Chevalier de Chaumont was at his side, and a
long line of young *noblesse*, gorgeous in lace, ribbons, and
majestic leoline wigs, followed in his train. As this splendid array of noblemen marched through the narrow streets
of the young city to the tap of drum, escorted by the Carignan-Salières, "the bronzed veterans of the Turkish wars,"
each soldier with slouched hat, nodding plume, bandolier
and shouldered fire-lock, they formed a glittering pageant
such as the New World had never seen before.

In the same year, the Captain Sieur La Motte built Fort
St. Anne upon the Isle La Motte, at the north end of Lake
Champlain, opposite the mouth of the Chazy River. Young
Chazy was stationed at this fort in the spring of 1666,
and while hunting in the woods near the mouth of the river
with a party of officers, was surprised and attacked by a
roving band of Iroquois. Chazy, with two or three others,
was killed upon the spot, and the survivors captured and
carried off prisoners to the valley of the Mohawk. For
months the war raged with unabated violence, and the old
wilderness was again drenched in blood, as it had been in
the time of Father Jogues twenty years before.

But in the August following a grand council of peace was
held with the Iroquois at Quebec. During the council,
Tracy invited some Mohawk chiefs to dine with him. At

* Parkman's Old Regimé, page 181.

12

the table some allusion was made to the murder of Chazy. A chief named *Ag-ari-ata* at once held out his arm, and boastingly said :

"This is the hand that split the head of that young man."

"You shall never kill anybody else," exclaimed the horror stricken Tracy, and ordered the insolent savage to be taken out and hanged upon the spot in sight of his comrades.*

Of course, peace was no longer thought of. Tracy made haste to march against the Mohawks with all the forces at his command. During the month of September, Quebec on the St. Lawrence, and Fort St. Anne on the Isle La Motte, on Lake Champlain, were the scenes of busy preparation.

At length Tracy and the Governor, Courcelle, set out from Quebec on the day of the Exaltation of the Cross, "for whose glory," says the *Relations*, "this expedition is undertaken." They had with them a force of thirteen hundred men and two pieces of cannon. It was the beginning of October, and the forests were putting on the gorgeous hues of an American autumn. They went up Lake Champlain, and into Lake St. Sacrament, now Lake George. As their flotilla swept gracefully over the crystal waters of this gem of the old wilderness, it formed the first of the military pageants that in after years made that fair scene famous in history.

Leaving their canoes where Fort William Henry was afterward built, they plunged boldly on foot into the southern wilderness that lay before them toward the Mohawk country. They took the old Indian trail so often trodden by the weary feet of Father Jogues, and by the war-parties

* Parkman's Old Regimé, page 192.

of savages, which led across the Hudson at the main bend
above Glens Falls, and passed across the old Indian hunting ground *Kay-ad-ros-se-ra*, through what are now the
towns of Wilton, Greenfield and Galway, in Saratoga county,
to the lower castles on the Mohawk river, near the mouth
of the Schoharie creek.   It was more than forty miles of
forests, filled with swamps, rivers, and mountains, that lay
before them.   Their path was a narrow, rugged trail, filled
with rocks and gullies, pitfalls and streams.   Their forces
consisted of six hundred regulars of the regiment Carignan-
Salières, six hundred Canadian militia, and a hundred
Christian Indians, from the missions.   "It seems to them,"
writes Mother Marie de l'Incarnation, in her letter of the
sixteenth of October, 1666, "that they are going to lay
seige to Paradise, and win it, and enter in, because they
are fighting for religion and the faith."

On they went through the tangled woods, officers as well
as men carrying heavy loads upon their backs, and dragging
their cannon "over slippery logs, tangled roots and oozy
mosses."   Before long, in the vicinity of what is now known
as Lake Desolation, their provisions gave out, and they were
almost starved.   But soon the trail led through a thick
wood of chestnut trees, full of nuts, which they eagerly
devoured, and thus stayed their hunger.

At length, after many weary days, they reached the lower
Mohawk cantons.   The names of the two lower Mohawk
castles were then *Te-hon-de-lo-ga*, which was at Fort Hunter,
at the mouth of the Schoharie creek, and *Ga-no-wa-ga*, now
Cach-na-wa-ga, which was near Tribes Hill.   The upper
castles, which were further up the Mohawk, were the *Ca-*

na-jo-ha-ie, near Fort Plain, and *Ga-ne-ga-ha-ga*, opposite
the mouth of East Canada Creek.

They marched through the fertile valley of the Mohawk,
the Indians fleeing into the forest at their approach.   Thus
the brilliant pageant of the summer that had glittered across
the somber rock of Quebec, was twice repeated by this warlike band of noblemen and soldiers, amid the crimson
glories of the autumn woods in the wild valley of the Mohawk.   They did not need the cannon which they had
brought with so much toil across the country from Lake St.
St. Sacrament.   The savages were frightened almost out of
their wits by the noise of their twenty drums.   "Let us
save ourselves, brothers," said one of the Mohawk chiefs,
as he ran away, "the whole world is coming against us."

After destroying all the cornfields in the valley, and the
last palisaded Mohawk village, they planted a cross on its
ashes, and by the side of the cross the royal arms of France.
Then an officer, by order of Tracy, advanced to the front,
and, with sword in hand, proclaimed, in a loud voice, that
he took possession in the name of the king of France of all
the country of the Mohawks.

Having thus happily accomplished their object without
the loss of a man, they returned to Canada over the route
by which they came.

The death of young Chazy was avenged.   The insolent
Iroquois were for the first time chastised and humbled in
their own country.   For twenty years afterward there was
peace in the old wilderness—peace bought by the blood of
young Chazy.   Surely was the river, on whose banks his
bones still rest, christened with his name amid a baptism
of fire at an altar upon which the villages, the wig-wams

and the cornfields of his murderers were the sacrificial offerings.

And so ended the second French and Indian war, known in colonial annals as the war of 1666.

CHAPTER XI.

RIVERS OF THE WILDERNESS.

Ah, beautiful river,
Flow onward forever!
Thou art grander than Avon, and sweeter than Ayr;
If a tree has been shaken,
If a star has been taken,
In thy bosom we look—bud and Pleiad are there!
—*Benjamin F. Taylor.*

I.

CHARACTERISTIC FEATURES.

A singular characteristic seems to mark all the rivers that flow in and around Northern New York. All of them with one exception—the Mohawk—flow from and through great chains or systems of lakes. The great river St. Lawrence, flowing from its own vast continental system of lakes, seems to be the prototype and pattern of all the others.

The Oswego river runs from and drains the Oneida, the Cayuga, and the others of the system of lakes so famous in Western New York. The River Richelieu drains Lakes George and Champlain. The Hudson and its sister streams that take their rise among its mountain masses, serve to drain the waters of the numberless lakes that lie within the shades of the Great Wilderness.

II.

THE HUDSON.

" The broadest, brightest river of the world."
—*Frances Anne Kemble.*

The Hudson is fed by a system of forest branches that spread over the whole of the Mountain Belt of the Wilderness. Its main forest branches are the Opalescent, the

Boreas, the Scarron (Schroon), the Jessups, the Indian, the
Cedar, and the Sacondaga.   The Mohawks called the Hudson *Ska-nen-ta-de*, "the river beyond the open woods."   Between the Mohawk river at Schenectady and the Hudson
at Albany was the great Indian carrying place which led
through the open pine woods.   The Hudson was therefore
"the river beyond the openings," to the Iroquois.   Its Algonquin name, however, was *Ca-ho-ta-te-a*, "the river that
comes from the mountains."   Henry Hudson, its discoverer, translating its Algonquin name, also called it the
"River of the Mountains."   The early Dutch settlers on
its banks called it "The Nassau," after the reigning family
of Holland, and sometimes "The Mauritius," from the
Stadtholder Prince Maurice.   It was first called the Hudson, in honor of its immortal explorer, by his English countrymen after they had conquered the country and wrested
it from the Dutch, in 1664.   But of all its names, none is
more significant than its old Algonquin one, "The River of
the Mountains."

The Hudson is born among the clouds on the shaggy
side of Mount McIntyre, and in the mountain meadows
and lakelets near the top of *Tahawas*, almost five thousand feet above the level of the sea.   It is cradled in
the awful chasms of the Indian Pass, the Panther Gorge,
and the Gorge of the Dial.   After thus rising upon its highest mountain peaks, it crosses in its wild course down the
southern slope of the Wilderness no less than four immense
mountain chains that all seem to give way at its approach,
as if it were some wayward, favorite child of their own.
After bursting through the Luzerne or Palmertown range,
its last forest mountain barrier, it encounters in its course

to the sea the great Apalachian system of mountains, and seems to rend them in twain from top to bottom. Or rather, old Ocean reaches up one of his throbbing arms through this Apalachian chain for a distance of one hundred and fifty miles to the city of Troy, to meet there this river, his wild forest mountain child. Thus from Troy, the head of tide-water, the mountain-born Hudson is virtually an estuary or arm of the sea, floating the navies and the commerce of the world upon its peaceful bosom.

III.

THE RIVERS THAT FALL INTO LAKE CHAMPLAIN.

Among the rivers that fall into Lake Champlain along the eastern border of the Wilderness, are the Boquet, the Au Sable, the Saranac and the Chazy.

The Boquet River rises in the deep gorge of the Hunter's Pass, which lies across the Boquet Mountain range, between Mouns Dix and Nipple Top. The bottom of this mountain gorge is 3,247 feet above the level of the sea, and in it also rises the Scarron River, that flows in a contrary direction into the Hudson.

The Boquet, which like the Scarron, gives its name to one of the five mountain ranges of the Wilderness, it is said derives its name from the French word *baquet*, a trough. This was suggested by the fancied resemblance of the con-tour of its bed and banks to a trough in the estuary at its mouth. It was in this estuary of the Boquet River that Gen. Burgoyne rested his army for some days, in the month of July, 1777, and made his celebrated treaty with his In-dian allies. It is also said that this river was first called the *Bouquet* River by William Gilliland, on account of the wonderful profusion of bright wild flowers which he found adorning its banks. Gilliland attempted to found a baronial manor on the banks of the Boquet during the last century, an account of which is given further on in these pages.

The Au Sable, the twin sister of the Hudson in the awful abyss of the Indian Pass, was named by the French in allusion to its sandy bed near its mouth, from *sable*, the French word, as the reader knows, for sand, gravel, &c.

How significant the old Indian names were of the twin sister streams, which rise together on some mountain height and separating, flow off in opposite directions to their common mother the sea, is shown in another part of the state, where we find as an example, the *Chit-te-nan-go*, meaning "the river flowing north," and the *Che-nan-go*, "the water going south."

On the head waters of the Au Sable, under the shadows of the old giants of the Adirondack range, lies the little mountain hamlet of North Elba, now so famous as the forest home of John Brown, of Ossawottamie memory.

On this river, three miles from Port Kent, is the celebrated Au Sable chasm, that is so much frequented by tourists.

The Saranac flows from the chain of lakes of that name, which are already so famous as a summer resort. The name on all the old French maps, without exception, is written, *Sa-la-sa-nac*.

The Chazy river owes its name to a tragic incident which occurred on its banks, in early colonial times, that led to important events in the history of the country.*

* See Chapter X.

13

IV.

THE RIVERS THAT FLOW INTO THE ST. LAWRENCE.

Among the rivers that flow through the Level Belt of the Wilderness and down its northern slope into the St. Lawrence, the principal are the Chateaugay, the Salmon, the St. Regis, the Raquette, the Grasse, the Oswegatchie, and the Indian river.

The Chateaugay, whose old Indian name was *O-sar-he-hon*, a narrow gorge, and which rises in the lake of the same name, runs into the St. Lawrence near Montreal. It was named from a chateau called the gay chateau, or *châ-teau-gai*, that stood on the bank of the St. Lawrence, at its mouth.

The Indian name of the Salmon River was *Gan-je-ah-go-na-ne*, " Sturgeon River."

The St. Regis River, which also rises in a lake of its name, was called by the Indians *Ah-qua-sus-ne*, " the place where the partridge drums," in allusion to the rumbling sound heard under the ice upon some parts of this stream during the winter.

The name *Raquette* is a French word, meaning snow-shoe. This name was suggested, says Dr. Hough, by the shape of a morass or wild meadow at its mouth, and was first applied to the river by a Frenchman named Parisein in the early days of the French occupancy. The Indian name of the Raquette was *Ta-na-wa-deh*, "swift water."

The Grasse River was so named by the French from the numerous wild meadows found near its mouth. It was called by the Indians *Ni-kent-si-a-ke*, " the place where many fishes live." It was among the upper branches of the

Grasse River that the tract of wild land lay which was bought on speculation at the beginning of this century, by Madame de Staël, the celebrated French author. Her tract was purchased for her in trust by her friend and agent, Gouverneur Morris. It was located in township No. Six, or Clare, which is now in the northerly part of the town of Pierrepont, St. Lawrence county. In 1846 it was sold by direction of her only heir, Ada Holstein de Staël, wife of the Duc de Broglie, to S. Pratt and John L. Russell.*

The Oswegatchie, in the Indian tongue *O-swa-gatch*, means "the river that runs around the hills." This has reference to the great bends, or " ox-bows," it forms in its course.

The Indian River is called on Morgan's map the *O-je-quack*, "the River of Nuts." It runs through Black Lake into the Oswegatchie.

V.

THE BLACK RIVER AND ITS TRIBUTARIES.

The Black River, whose Iroquois name was *Ka-hu-ah-go*, bounds the Great Wilderness plateau of Laurentian rocks, on the west, and its valley bounds the Lesser Wilderness on the east.

The principal confluents that enter the Black River from the Great Wilderness, are the Moose, the Otter Creek, the Independence, and the Beaver.

The Moose River, whose Indian name was *Te-ka-hun-di-an-do*, " clearing an opening," rises near the Raquette Lake in the centre of the wilderness, and winds through and

* Hough's Hist. St. Lawrence and Franklin counties, p. 429.

forms the celebrated Eight Lakes of the Fulton chain. The Moose passes in its course the hunting station known to all frequenters of the woods as Arnold's, or the Old Forge, on Brown's Tract. This secluded spot has long been famous in forest story as the scene of John Brown's fruitless attempt at settlement, of the failure and tragic death of his son-in-law Herreshoff, of the exploits of the Hunter Foster and his victim the Indian Drid, and of the life-long home of Otis Arnold, the hunter and guide.

The Independence River rises near the Eight Lakes of the Fulton chain and runs into Black River in the town of Watson, Lewis county, between the Moose River and the Beaver River. In its course, this river crosses the tract of wild land known to land speculators as Watson's West Triangle. The Independence River was so named in honor of our national holiday by Pierre Pharoux, the engineer and surveyor of Castorland. Near the south bank of the Independence, not far from the old Watson house, is Chase's Lake. This lake has long been a favorite resort, and is one of the most accessible in the Wilderness for the invalid or pleasure seeker. The Indian name of Otter creek is *Da-wan-net*—"the otter." It runs into the Black river between the Moose and the Independence.

The Indian name for Beaver River is *Ne-ha-sa-ne*, "crossing on a log." It rises in the heart of the wilderness to the north of Raquette lake, and running in its course through Smith's lake, Albany lake, and Beaver lake, waters the territory of ancient Castorland, the seat of French influence on the Black river. Beaver lake, an expansion of this river at Number Four, a famous summer resort, is one of the most charming lakes in the wilderness.

VI.

WILDERNESS TRIBUTARIES OF THE MOHAWK.

The Mohawk River, whose Indian name was *Te-uge-ga*, runs along the whole southern border of the Great Wilderness, but rises in the Lesser Wilderness, to the north of Oneida lake. Its principal tributaries from the north, however, take their rise in the heart of the Great Wilderness, in the region of the Raquette lake. They are the East and West Canada creeks. Upon the West Canada creek are the famous Trenton Falls, one of the principal attractions of Northern New York, so often visited by summer tourists. The Indian name for Trenton Falls was *Date-wa-sunt-ha-go* —"Great Falls," and for Canada creek was *Kan-a-ta*, meaning "Amber River," in allusion to the color of its waters.

This completes the list of the principal rivers which flow in and around Northern New York and its Great Wilderness.

CHAPTER XII.

LA FAMINE AND THE LESSER WILDERNESS.

By *la Riviere de la Famine*, ocean tried and travel sore,
They upreared a rustic altar, tapestried with mosses o'er,
Crucifix they set upon it where the oak tree's shadow fell
Lightly o'er the lighted taper, 'mid the sweet *Te Deum's* swell.

Never *Dominus Vobiscum* falling upon human ears
Made so many heart-strings quiver, filled so many eyes with tears,
The Good Shepherd gave his blessing—even red men gathered there,
Felt the sacrifice of Jesus in his first thanksgiving prayer.
                                    —*Caleb Lyon of Lyonsdale.*

I.

ITS LOCATION.

Among the problematical places of the olden time in Northern New York, whose names were once familiar in European circles but are seldom heard in modern story, no one was once more famous than *La Famine*.

Two hundred years ago, La Famine was a well-known stopping-place upon the eastern shore of Lake Ontario for the weary hunter and the bold explorer, and the spot where even armies encamped, and the ambassadors of hostile nations met in solemn council. To-day its name can only be found on the historic page, and in old maps and musty records, while its locality is often a matter of controversy. The ancient Indian landing-place and camping-ground known to the French as La Famine, was situated on the shore of Famine Bay, now called Mexico Bay, in the southeast corner of Lake Ontario, at the mouth of La Famine River, now known as Salmon River.

The Salmon River, the ancient French *La Famine* and the Indian *Ga-hen-wa-ga*, rises in the central part of the plateau of the Lesser Wilderness, in the south-west corner of Lewis county, and runs westerly through the northern part of Oswego county into Lake Ontario.

The Lesser Wilderness, like *Couch-sach-ra-ge*, the Greater Wilderness, was one of the beaver hunting countries of the Iroquois. The key to this hunting ground of the Lesser Wilderness from the west was the Salmon river. On their way to the hunting ground through Lake Ontario, the western Indians landed at the mouth of this river, and their trail then led up its banks.

La Famine then was the ancient seaport of this famous hunting ground of the Lesser Wilderness, and was situated near what is now the village of Mexico. The Indian name for this entre-pot of theirs was *Ga-hen-wa-ga*. Hence we find on a map of New France, published by Marco Vincenzo Coronelli, in 1688, this place put down at the mouth of what is now known as the Salmon River, but in his map it is called *la Famine Rivere*. It bears the following inscription : " Cah-ihon-oiia-ghe ou la Famine, lieu ou la plus part des Iroquois des barquent pour aller en traitte du Castor," which may be translated thus : *Ga-hen-wa-ga*, or La Famine, the place where the greater part of the Iroquois embarked to go upon the trail of the beaver.

II.

THE LESSER WILDERNESS.

The Lesser Wilderness of Northern New York is situated upon the long narrow plateau which stretches first westerly and then northerly from the Upper Mohawk valley and the Oneida Lake almost to the city of Watertown. It lies between Lake Ontario on the west and the valley of the

Black River on the east. The rocky ground work of this plateau is composed of level strata of limestone and slate which rise in a series of terraces of a mile or two in width from its borders into a high level table land. Upon the central part of this table land, which has an elevation of near two thousand feet above the level of the sea, are situated the forests, swamps, marshes and wild meadows of the Lesser Wilderness.

Numerous streams take their rise in the swamps and wild meadows of this region. Down the southern slope of this ridge of highlands the Mohawk, which rises in the Lesser Wilderness, flows first southerly and then easterly toward the Hudson. The Fish Creek and other streams run into Oneida Lake.

On its western border, the Salmon River, once La Famine, the Sandy Creek, once the Au Sable, and other streams, run into Lake Ontario.

Down the more regular terraces of its western slope, locally called Tug Hill, the streams which rise in the swamps of the Lesser Wilderness hurry in a series of falls and cascades into the Black River, wearing deep chasms in the yielding rocks along their courses. Among these streams are the Deer River, which is the Indian *Ga-ne-ga-to-da*, (pounding corn) the Silvermine, the Martins, the Whetstone and other Creeks.

This Lesser Wilderness was one of the most famous hunting grounds of the Indian. Its woods were literally filled with game, and its streams with fish. La Hontan says that there were so many salmon in La Famine River that they often brought up a hundred at one cast of the net.

The deer came across the valley of the Black River from

the Great Wilderness, every spring, in droves to feed upon the luxuriant summer herbage, and returned every autumn to escape the deep snows of the Lesser Wilderness. Their runways were along the valleys of the Deer River, the Sugar River and other streams, which as before stated run down the eastern slope of the Lesser Wilderness into the Black River. The deer were caught in great numbers by the early settlers of the Black River valley, during this half-yearly migration.

The forests of the Lesser Wilderness have always been favorite nesting places for the wild pigeons. Even now-a-days these birds often build their nests in these woods, in countless myriads, over miles in extent. The Lesser Wilderness has always been celebrated for its deep snows. The snow in March and April is almost always six or seven feet in depth. The present season, 1876, the snow was three feet in depth over the Lesser Wilderness on the first day of May.

III.

ORIGINAL BIRTH PLACE OF THE IROQUOIS.

It is an old tradition of the Iroquois that the Lesser Wilderness was the original birth place or Eden of their race. It is a well known mythical story of the Iroquois that their race once dwelt in a subterranean world, which was at first a vast chaos, but which by degrees came to be a solid area of sea and land, like the upper earth.

In the course of time their great sachem *Hi-a-wat-ha* came to their relief, and enabled them to crawl up out of their dark abode into the bright sunshine and pleasant

14

hunting grounds of the world in which we now live. After coming into their new abode, *Hi-a-wat-ha* made for them bows and arrows and taught them how to hunt their game. He gave them corn, squashes, beans and tobacco, and showed them how to raise their crops.

According to their traditions, the place of their people's birth, or where they came out of the ground, was in the Lesser Wilderness, somewhere between the head waters of the Salmon River—*La Famine*, and those of Sandy Creek —*Au Sable*.

The French author Pouchot, in his memoirs, after minutely describing the shores of Lake Ontario and its tributaries, coming to Sandy Creek, makes the following curious statement in regard to its head waters.

" Between the River Au Sable and La Famine is a little stream called by the Indians *Canogatiron*. The River Au Sable, in Indian *Eteataragarence*, is remarkable in this that at the head of its south branch, called *Tecanononouaronesi*, is the place where the traditions of the Iroquois fix as the spot from whence they all issued, or rather according to their ideas, where they were born." His remarks confirm the existence of this òld tradition.

IV.

THE COUNCIL OF DE LA BARRE AND THE IROQUOIS.

But La Famine derives its chief historical importance from its having been the scene of the celebrated council held in the month of September, 1684, by Le Febru de la Barre, the Governor General of Canada, with the embassadors of the Five Nations.

The Senecas had been lately attacking and pillaging the French canoes in the far western waters, and to obtain redress De la Barre raised an army and set out from Quebec on the 9th day of July in that year, by way of the St. Lawrence River and Lake Ontario, to make war upon the offending savages. His forces consisted of five hundred forest rangers and three hundred christian Iroquois. He reached Montreal on the 16th of July, and after a toilsome journey by land around the rapids, he arrived at La Galette, which was at the rapid and portage on the St. Lawrence next below Ogdensburgh, on the 15th of August. On the 21st he proceeded on his voyage. In his report he says : " Finally on the 21st my canoes arrived with what I sent them for. I set to work immediately with all possible diligence to have bread and biscuit baked, and sent off forthwith the king's troops, D'Orvillier's and Dugués' two brigades and two hundred christian savages to encamp at La Famine, a port favorable for fishing and hunting, four leagues from Onontagué, so as to be nearer the enemy and to be able to refresh ourselves by fishing and the chase."

Further on in his report he continues: "After having been beaten by bad weather and high wind, we arrived in two days at La Famine. I found there tertian and double tertian fever, which broke out among our people, so that more than one hundred and fifty men were attacked by it. I had also left some of them at the fort,* which caused me to despatch, on arriving, a christian savage to Onontagué to M. Lemoine, to request him to cause the instant departure of those who were to come to meet me, which he did with so much diligence, though he and his children were sick,

* Fort Frontenac, at Catarocuoi, now Kingston.

that he arrived as early as the 3d of September, with fourteen deputies, nine from Onontagué, three from Oneida,
and two Cayugas, who paid me their respects, and whom I
entertained the best manner I was able, postponing until
to-morrow the talk about business, at which matters were
fully discussed and peace concluded after six hour's deliberation, three in the morning and as many after dinner,
Father Brias speaking for us and *Ha-ta-wa-te* and *Gara-*
gon-kier for the Iroquois; *Te-gan-cout*, a Seneca, was present, the other Senecas not daring to come, in order not to
displease Col. Dongan, (the English governor,) who sent to
promise them a reinforcement of four hundred horse and
four hundred foot if we attacked. The treaty was concluded in the evening, on the conditions annexed, and I
promised to decamp the next day, and withdraw my troops
from this vicinity, which I was indeed obliged to do by the
number of sick which had augmented to such a degree
that it was with difficulty I found enough of persons in
health to remove the sick to the canoes, besides the scarcity
of provisions, having no more than the trifle of bread that
I brought them."*

But to continue my narrative : Two days after the arrival
of the Iroquois at La Famine they gave notice to M. de la
Barre that they were ready for the council. De la Barre
sat in his chair of state, with his officers on either hand.
To the eastward of him sat *Ha-ta-wa-te*, the *Grangula*, the
orator of the Indians, clad in his rich robes of beaver and
otter furs, at the head of his men. His pipe was in his
mouth and the great calumet of peace lay before him.

The Grangula was very attentive to the interpreter as he

* Doc. Hist. of New York, vol. I, p. 114.

delivered the speech of M. de la Barre. In his speech, M. de la Barre, in a haughty way, told the Iroquois that his king had sent him to smoke with them the pipe of peace, but on the condition that they make reparation for past offences, and give assurance of future good conduct; otherwise war was positively proclaimed. After the French speech was finished, the Grangula arose, walked slowly five or six times around the ring formed by the council, and returned to his place. Then standing erect, he looked up to the sun for a moment, as if by way of invocation. He then spoke to the Governor-General as follows :

"Onnontio, I honor you, and all the warriors that are with me do the same. Your interpreter has made an end of his discourse, and now I come to begin mine. My voice glides to your ear; pray listen to my words.

"Onnontio, in setting out from Quebec you must needs have fancied that the scorching beams of the sun had burnt down the forests which render our country unaccessible to the French, or else that the inundations of the lake had surrounded our castles and confined us as prisoners. This certainly was your thought; and it could be nothing else but the curiosity of seeing a burnt or drowned country that moved you to undertake a journey hither. But now you have an opportunity of being undeceived, for I and my warlike retinue come to assure you that the Senecas, Cayugas, Onondagas, Oneidas and Mohawks are not yet destroyed. I return you thanks in their name for bringing into their country the calumet of peace that your predecessor received from their hands. At the same time, I congratulate your happiness in having left underground the

bloody axe that has so often been dyed with the blood of
the French.

"I must tell you, Onnontio, I am not asleep; my eyes
are open, and the sun that vouchsafes the light gives me a
clear view of a great captain at the head of a troop of soldiers who speaks as if he were asleep. He pretends that
he does not approach to this lake with any other view than
to smoke with the Onondagas in the great calumet; but
the Grangula knows better things; he sees plainly that the
Onnontio meant to knock them on the head if the French
arms had not been so much weakened.

"I perceive that the Onnontio raves in a camp of sick
people, whose lives the Great Spirit has saved by visiting
them with infirmities. Do you hear, Onnontio, our women had taken up their clubs, and the children and the old
men had visited your camp with their bows and arrows, if
our warriors had not stopped and disarmed them when *Ak-
oues-san*, your messenger, appeared before our village? But
I have done; I will talk no more of that.   *   *

" This Belt comprehends my words.

"We have conducted the English to our lakes in order
to traffic with the Ottawas, just as the Algonquins conducted the French to our five cantons to carry on a commerce
that the English lay claim to as their right. We are born
freemen, and have no dependence either upon the Onnontio or the Corlear. We have a power to go where we
please, to conduct who we will to the places we resort to,
and to buy and sell where we think fit. If your allies are
your slaves or children, you may even treat them as such.

" This Belt comprehends my words.

"We fell upon the Illinois and the Miamis because they

cut down the trees of peace that served for limits or boundaries to our frontiers.   They came to hunt beavers upon our lands, and contrary to the custom of all the Indians, have carried off whole stocks both male and female.   We have done less than the English and the French, who without any right have usurped the grounds they are now possessed of.

" This Belt contains my words.

" I give you to know, Onnontio, that my voice is the voice of the five Iroquois cantons.   This is their answer; pray incline your ear and listen to what they present.   The Senecas, Cayugas, Onondagas, Oneidas and Mohawks declare that they buried the axe at Catarocoui, in the presence of your predecessor, in the very centre of the fort, and planted the tree of peace in the same place that it might be carefully preserved; that it was then stipulated that the fort should be used as a place of retreat for merchants and not a refuge for soldiers; and that instead of arms and ammunition it should be made a receptacle of only beaver skins and merchandise goods.   Be it known to you, Onnontio, that for the future you ought to take care that so great a number of martial men as I now see, being shut up in so small a fort, do not stifle and choke the tree of peace.   Since it took root so easily it must needs be of pernicious consequence to stop its growth, and hinder it to shade both your country and ours with its leaves.

"I do assure you in the name of the Five Nations, that our warriors shall dance the calumet dance under its branches; that they shall rest in tranquility upon their mats, and will never dig up the axe to cut down the tree of peace until such time as Onnontio or Corlear do either jointly or

separately offer to invade the country that the Great Spirit
has disposed of in the favor of our ancestors.

" This Belt contains my word, and the other comprehends
the power granted to me by the Five Nations."[*]

The treaty of peace being concluded, M. de la Barre re-
embarked in haste, and returned with his sick and famished
army to Quebec. The feathered and painted Iroquois
jumped into their canoes, and soon appeared like mere
specks on the bounding waves of Lake Ontario, as they
sped on their way to the mouth of the Oswego River that
led to their castles on the shores of the beautiful lakes of
Western New York.

V.

VISIT OF CHARLEVOIX.

In the year 1720, Pierre François Xavier de Charlevoix,
the celebrated French traveller, and historian of New
France, while on a voyage through the great lakes was
storm-bound for several days at La Famine. From this
place he dates one of his letters to Madame de Lesdiguières, from which I make an extract below. The reader
must bear in mind that from Fort Frontenac at *Catarocoui*,
now Kingston, as the old explorers dare not venture in
their frail canoes far out into the open lake, Father Charlevoix's route was along the coast, first down the British
channel and around Wolfe Island and then up the American
channel to the *Isle aux Chevreuils*, now Carleton Island.
From Carleton Island he went around Stony Point in Hen-

* Letter of Baron La Hontan, of the 2d Nov., 1684, in Pinkerton,
vol. XIII, page 271.

derson, called by him *Point de la Traverse*, to Famine Bay, now Mexico Bay.

"FAMINE BAY, 16th May, 1720.

" *Madame :*   I have the misfortune to be detained here by a contrary wind which in appearance will last a long time and keep me in one of the worst places in the world. I shall amuse myself with writing to you.   Whole armies of those pigeons they call *Tourtes* pass by here continually. If one of them could carry my letter you would perhaps have news of me before I leave this place.   But the Indians never thought of bringing up pigeons for this purpose, as they say the Arabs and many other nations formerly did. I embarked the 14th, exactly at the same hour I arrived at *Catarocoui* [Kingston] the evening before.   I had but six leagues to go to the *Isle aux Chevreuils* [Roe-Bucks, now Carleton Island,] where there is a pretty port that can receive large barques, but my Canadians had not examined their canoe, and the sun had melted the gum of it in many places.   It took water everywhere, and I was forced to lose two whole hours to repair it in one of the islands at the entrance of Lake Ontario.   After that we sailed till ten o'clock at night without being able to reach the *Isle aux Chevreuils*, and we were obliged to pass the rest of the night in the corner of the forest.

" This was the first time I perceived some vines in the wood.   There were almost as many as trees, to the top of which they rise.   I had not yet made this remark because I had always till then stopped in open places, but they assure me it is the same everywhere, quite to Mexico.   The stocks of these vines are very large, and they bear many bunches of grapes, but the grapes are scarcely so big as a pea ; and

15

this must be so, as the vines are not cut nor cultivated.
When they are ripe it is a good manna for the bears, who
seek them at the top of the highest trees. They have,
nevertheless, but the leavings of the birds, who have soon
gathered the vintage of whole forests. I set out early
the next morning, and at eleven o'clock I stopped at the
Isle aux Gallots [now Gallop Island,] three leagues beyond
the *Isle aux Chevres* [now Grenadier Island] in latitude
43° 30'.

"I re-embarked about noon, and made a traverse of a
league and a half to gain the *Point de la Traverse* [now
Stony Point]. If to come hither from the place where I
passed the night I had been obliged to coast the continent,
I should have had above forty leagues to make; and we must
do this when the lake is very calm, for if it is the least agi-
tated the waves are as high as in the open sea. It is not
even possible to sail under the coast when the wind blows
hard from the lake.

"From the point of the *Isle aux Gallots* we see to the
west the river *Chouguen* [Oswego], otherwise called the
River *d'Onnontague* which is fourteen leagues off. As the
lake was calm and there was no appearance of bad weather,
and we had a little wind at east, which was but just enough
to carry a sail, I resolved to make directly for this river,
[the Oswego,] that I might save fifteen or twenty leagues in
going round. My conductors, who had more experience
than myself, judged it a dangerous attempt, but out of com-
plaisance they yielded to my opinion.

"The beauty of the country which I quitted on the left hand
did not tempt me any more than the salmon and numbers
of other excellent fish which they take in six fine rivers,

which are two or three leagues distant one from the other.*
We took to the open lake, and till four o'clock we had no
cause to repent of it, but then the wind rose suddenly, and
we would willingly have been nearer shore.   We made toward the nearest, from which we were then three leagues
off, and we had much trouble to make it.

"At length, at seven at night, we landed at Famine Bay,
thus named since the M. de la Barre, Governor General of
New France, had like to have lost all his army here by hunger and disease, going to make war with the Iroquois."†

Almost two hundred years have passed away since M. de
la Barre and Father Charlevoix enlivened the then savage
scene by their presence.   The summer tourist of to-day, as
he passes by steamer near the site of the ancient La Famine
(now Port Ontario), on his way from Niagara to the Thousand Islands will perhaps read with interest these reminiscences of the olden time relating to the St. Lawrence River,
the ancient *Ho-che-la-ga*, and to the shores of Lake Ontario,
the " Beautiful Lake " of the Iroquois.

* Note to original :   " The River of the *Assumtion* [now Stony Creek
in Henderson] a league from the point of Traverse ; that of *Sables* [now
Sandy Creek], three leagues further ; that of *la Planche* [now Little Sandy Creek], two leagues further ; that of *la grand Famine* [now Salmon
River,] two leagues more."

† Charlevoix's Voyage to North America, vol. I, p. 173, Dublin edition
of 1756.

CHAPTER XIII.

TRYON COUNTY.

"Still in your prostrate land there shall be some
Proud hearts, the shrines of Freedom's vestal flame.
Long trains of ill may pass unheeded dumb,
But Vengeance is behind and Justice is to come."

I.

BOUNDARIES.

In the crowded annals of the state of New York there floats another almost mythical name which, like La Famine, for nearly a century has had no "local habitation." That name is Tryon county, whose story during the long and weary twelve years of its actual existence, is a story that is written in characters of blood.

For a long period previous to the year 1772, which was the birth year of Tryon county, the whole northern and western part of what is now the state of New York, that lay to the north and west of the county of Ulster, was included in the county of Albany. In the spring of that year the county of Albany was divided by the Colonial Government. In the first place they set off the county of Tryon, naming it in honor of William Tryon, who was then Governor of the province. They then set off the county of Charlotte, which was named in honor of the Princess Charlotte, the eldest daughter of George III.

The bounds of Tryon county were fixed as follows: The easterly line began at a point on the Canadian border, near the Indian mission of St. Regis, and ran due south through the Upper Saranac Lake, and along the westerly

bounds of what are now Essex, Warren and Saratoga counties, until it struck the Mohawk river about ten miles west of the city of Schenectady. From the Mohawk it turned south-westerly around what is now Schenectady county, and then again southerly through the center of what is now Schoharie county to the Mohawk branch of the Delaware River. Thence down that stream to the north-east corner of Pennsylvania. Tryon county included the whole of the province of New York that lay to the west of this line. It was two hundred miles wide along this eastern border, and stretched out westward three hundred miles to Lake Erie. Better had it been called an empire.

The county of Charlotte included all the northern part of the state of New York that lies easterly of the Tryon county line, and northerly of what are now Saratoga and Rensselaer counties. Charlotte county also included the westerly half of the disputed territory which is now in the state of Vermont, then known as the New Hampshire Grants.

II.

SIR WILLIAM JOHNSON.

The shire-town of this immense county of Tryon was Johnstown, near the Mohawk, the residence of Sir William Johnson, Bart.

Sir William was then living in baronial splendor at Johnson Hall, with the Mohawk Princess, Molly Brandt, who was his Indian wife, and their eight dusky children. He was then His Brittanic Majesty's Superintendent General of Indian affairs in North America, Colonel of the Six Nations, and a Major General in the British service.

Thirty-five years before this, he had come over from Ireland a poor young man, and settled in the Mohawk valley, then a wilderness, to take care of a large tract of land that was located there and owned by his uncle, Sir Peter Warren. Sir Peter Warren was an Admiral of the British navy, who while a commodore distinguished himself by the capture of Louisburgh from the French in 1745. Sir Peter married a daughter of Etienne De Lancey of New York, and with her received as a dowry this large tract of land in the Mohawk valley. It was situated in the eastern angle between the Mohawk River and the Schoharie Creek.

Sir William Johnson, upon his first taking up his residence in the Mohawk valley became a fur trader with the Indians, and kept for many years a country store for the accommodation of the scattered settlers of the region. Rising by degrees, through dint of industry and fair dealing, and by the faithful performance of the public trusts imposed upon him, he had become the proprietor of immense landed estates, the acknowledged lord of a princely manor, and high in the confidence of his sovereign. His victory over the French and Indians under Baron Dieskau, at Lake George in 1755, had won for him his title of nobility. His wonderful influence, the most remarkable on record, over the Indian tribes, had given him an importance in the affairs of state second to no American then living. He was surrounded by a numerous tenantry and by followers that were loyal to him and his family even unto death.

Sir William married in the more humble days of his early life a poor, modest gentle-hearted German girl, whom he found living with her parents in the Mohawk valley, whose maiden name was Catherine Weisenberg. She died young, leaving three children, a son, Sir John Johnson, and two daughters who married respectively Col. Claus and Col. Guy Johnson.

Sir William's Indian wife was Molly Brandt a sister of the celebrated Mohawk war-chief, *Ta-en-da-ne-ga*, or Joseph Brandt, who was afterward so long the terror of the border. After the death of his first wife he became enamored of Molly at a general muster of the Mohawk Valley militia held at or near Johnstown. Among the spectators at the training was a beautiful Indian maiden. One of the mounted officers, in sport, dared the maiden to ride on the bare-back of his horse behind his saddle three times around the parade ground, little thinking she would accept the challenge. Bounding from the ground, like a deer, upon his horse behind him, she encircled his waist with her arms, and over the ground they flew like the wind, her red mantle and luxuriant raven tresses streaming behind her, her beautiful face lighted up with the pleasurable excitement of the novel adventure.

Sir William was an admiring witness of the scene, and was smitten with the charms of the dusky forest maiden. He inquired her name, and was told that she was the Indian Princess, Molly Brandt. He sought her at once, and made her his Indian bride. He married her after the true Indian style, by them considered binding, but never acknowledged her as his lawful wife. In his will he remembered her, calling her his "housekeeper, Molly Brandt," and left a large tract of land to his children by her, which lay in Herkimer county, between the East and West Canada creeks, and was long known to the early settlers as the Royal Grants.

In the height of his power, Sir William Johnson at his
seat near the Mohawk, on the border of a howling wilderness that stretched away to the Pacific, dispensed a right
royal hospitality. Many a scion of the English nobility sat
at his generous board, or, like the Lady Susan O'Brien,
wandered through the woods with Sir William's accomplished Indian wife, in search of the strange wild flowers of the
New World. The Lady Susan passed considerable time at
Johnson Hall. She was a neice of the first Lord Holland,
and the sister of Lady Harriet Ackland, who as well as the
Baroness Riedesel, the wife of the Hessian general, accompanied her husband, under General Burgoyne, to the
battle-field of Saratoga.

In the summer, Sir William spent much of his time at
the Fish House, his hunting lodge on the Sacondaga River,
and at his cottage on Summer House Point, on the great
Vlaie, which is one of the mountain meadows of the wilderness.

Once every year the sachems of the Six Nations renewed
their council fire at the Manor house, to talk with Sir
William, the agent of their white father, who lived across
the big water. On such occasions Sir William was himself
painted and plumed and dressed like an Indian chief.

Such was Sir William Johnson, at the time of the formation of Tryon county, and such was he two years later at the
time of his death in 1774. He seems to have been merci-
fully taken away just before the slumbering fires of the
Revolution were to burst forth, which were so soon destined
to stain the fair valley of his home with blood, to send his
family and followers fugitives across the Canadian border,

and to scatter his princely possessions like chaff before the wind.*

II.

THE DUTCH SETTLERS OF THE MOHAWK VALLEY.

Among Sir William's nearer neighbors were several Dutch families whose descendants still live in the valley. They had left their less adventurous friends on the Hudson to become themselves the pioneers in the settlement of the wilderness of the Mohawk valley.

They carried with them to their new homes that love of liberty which they had inherited from their ancestors of the glorious little Republic of Holland, at the mouth of the Rhine, the birth-place of civil and religious freedom. They had not forgotten their national humiliation at the British conquest of New Amsterdam, at the mouth of the Hudson in 1664. In short, in a war for independence, there was but one side for the Dutch settlers of the Mohawk valley to take—the side of freedom.

III.

THE PALATINES.

A few miles further up the valley of the Mohawk, at German Flats, now Herkimer, were other neighbors of Sir William. They were the Palatines, who were emigrants from the Lower Palatinate of the Rhine, one of the states of ancient Germany, adjoining Alsace and Lorraine.

Connected with the French court under the Merovingian kings, the first Frankish dynasty in Gaul, who reigned from

* See Life and Times of Sir William Johnson, by Wm. L. Stone; Trappers of New York, by Jeptha R. Simms.

16

the fifth to the eighth centuries, was a high judicial officer called the *comes palatii*. This officer was a master of the royal household, and had supreme authority in a large class of causes that came before the king for decision. Whenever the king wished to confer a particular favor upon the ruler of a province, he granted to him the same powers within his province as the *comes palatii* exercised in the royal palace. With the power also went the title *Comes Palatinus*, or Count Palatine. From this ruler the province was called a palatinate.

The Lower Palatinate was situated upon both sides of the Rhine, its area being about sixteen hundred square miles. Its chief cities were Mannheim and Heidelberg. For long centuries this little state and its neighboring provinces of the Rhine were in the pathway and formed the battle-ground of the devastating armies of Europe. In the beginning of the last century, Queen Anne of England took under her protection a large number of its homeless, war-stricken people. In the year 1709 she sent over three thousand Palatines to America to help settle the virgin wilderness. For a dozen years or more they were quartered at the expense of the British crown upon the Livingston Manor, on the banks of the Hudson. But Robert, the first lord of the Livingston Manor, it is said, was grasping and avaricious, and while he laid broad and deep the foundations of his house, since rendered so illustrious by his gentle descendants, the Palatines murmured and became discontented under his rule. So in the year 1722 a number of families of these Palatines pushed their way from the Livingston Manor up the wild valley of the Mohawk, and began a settlement at German Flats, while others settled in Cherry Valley and on the Schoharie kill.

The Palatines had left their vineyards of the dear old Rhineland, so often laid waste by cruel war, for a still more savage home in the American wilds of a hundred and fifty years ago.

At the formation of Tryon county, just fifty years after its early settlement, German Flats had grown into a large and flourishing settlement, under the hands of these industrious, frugal, painstaking Germans. With the Dutch settlers, they formed an important element in the politics of the new county. Like them, too, there was but one side for the Palatines to take in the coming contest.

IV.

THE IROQUOIS.

But there was another element in the heated, seething politics of Tryon county, of more importance than all the others.

Chief among the powers of Tryon county, previous to the war of the Revolution, was the remarkable Indian league or confederacy, known as the Six Nations. During all the long and bloody French and Indian wars, from their first encounter with Champlain and his Algonquin allies, in the summer of 1609, to the final conquest of Canada, in 1763, these people of the Iroquois family of nations had been the firm friends and allies of the English. Throughout the whole length of Tryon county, from the manor house of Sir William Johnson, at Johnstown, to the falls of Niagara, lay the castles of these fierce savages like so many dens of ravening wolves.

They were, as I have before stated, the most powerful, the most crafty, the most cruel, the most savage, the most politic, the most enlightened, of all the Indian tribes of North America. They were subject to no power on earth but their own fierce wills, yet were under the almost complete control of Sir William Johnson. In a war with Great Britain, it could not have been expected that the people of the Six Nations would desert their ancient ally.

Such were the slumbering elements of discord that lay contiguous to each other, in seeming peace, within the limits of Tryon county at the date of its formation, on the eve of the Revolution.

V.

THE CONFLICT.

In the spring of 1774, Sir William held his last grand council with his Iroquois neighbors, the people of the Six Nations, at his manor house in Johnstown. It was an occasion of more than ordinary pomp and ceremony. Delegations of sachems, chiefs, warriors and women, from all the castles of the Six Nations, were entertained for days at Sir William's expense. On the last day of the council Sir William made a speech of more than usual eloquence and power. But the terrors of the impending conflict which he knew must soon come, seemed to cast an unwonted gloom over his spirit. Exhausted by his effort, he was carried to his bed to die, before the smoke had ceased to rise from the council fires.

In less than two years after Sir William's death the war-cloud, which had been so long gathering, burst like a whirl-wind over the valley of the Mohawk. Tryon county be-

came a scene of desolation and blood, such as even the old
Wilderness, with all its savage horrors, had never seen before. It would weary us all to follow the fortunes of the
several peoples who made up the inhabitants of Tryon
county through those terrible seven years of war. The
history of the twelve years of the existence of Tryon county would fill a volume. A mere glance at what occurred
during the war must suffice for these pages.

In pursuing this history, we should listen to the story of
the first vigorous uprising, and the flight of Sir John Johnson and his father's numerous tenantry and loyal adher-
ents, together with his ever faithful allies, the Mohawks,
to Canada, in the summer of 1775. Our blood would cur-
dle at the relation of the cruel butchery of Cherry Valley,
on the 11th of October, 1778, which is second only in tragic
interest to that of the far-famed valley of Wyoming, which
occurred a few months earlier in the same year. The
narrative would reveal the sickening horrors of the several
raids made by Sir John Johnson's men and their savage
allies, as they from time to time swooped down from their
secure retreat beyond the St. Lawrence, upon the homes of
their former neighbors in the valley of the Mohawk, leaving in their track nothing but blackened corpses and the
ashes of ruined firesides.

We should stand in imagination by the side of the gallant Herkimer, the Palatine general, in the bloody ambuscade at Oriskany on the 5th day of August, 1777, when
Brandt and his Mohawks, and Butler with his Tory rangers
met their old neighbors, with whom they had been reared
as children together on the banks of the Mohawk, in a

hand-to-hand conflict, each dying in the other's arms in the terrible rage of battle.

In the long recital of stirring events, perhaps nothing would interest us more than the details of Gen. Sullivan's avenging march with his army, in August, 1779, into the country of the far-off Senecas, in the Genesee valley, leaving nothing on his return but the ashes of villages and cornfields, and the scattered remnants of the once powerful confederacy.

And when the glad tidings of peace once more should come, we should see in Tryon county nothing but a desolate blood-stained wilderness. We should learn that when the war broke out in 1775, Gov. Tryon reported ten thousand whites and two thousand Indian warriors as comprising the population of Tryon county. Two years before the end of the war, the Indian tribes were broken and scattered. Of the ten thousand white inhabitants, one-third had espoused the royal cause and fled to Canada, one-third had been driven from their homes or slain in battle, and of the remaining third, three hundred were widows and two thousand were orphan children.*

Then, when peace was declared, we should see the old Dutch settlers of the valley and their neighbors, the Palatines, coming back to find the places of their old hearthstones overgrown with bushes, and fast reverting to the original forests. But they were now the masters of the valley, the true lords of Tryon county. And smiling through their tears, in 1784, they dropped the now odious name of Tryon, and called their county in honor of the lamented Montgomery.

* See Campbell's annals of Tryon county.

The name of the county of Charlotte was at the same time changed to Washington, and the two names, Tryon and Charlotte, have long since fallen out of human speech, and can now only be found in musty records or on the historian's page.

To-day the traveller, as he whirls along through the fertile valley of the Mohawk, in the palatial cars of the modern railroad which is built over the old Indian trail, perchance gets a glimpse of the old mansion called Fort Johnson, on the north bank of the river, which is one of the few remaining historical landmarks connected with the memory of Sir William, while Tribes Hill, Canajoharie, and other Indian names still suggest the old Mohawk occupancy, and Palatine Bridge connects the present with the long chain of historic circumstances which run back in unbroken course to the old homes of a people in the Rhineland of two hundred years ago. But he will hear nothing in all his journeyings of Tryon county.

CHAPTER XIV.

THE MANOR OF WILLSBORO.

" Life hath its harvest moons,
Its tasselled corn and purple weighted vine,
Its gathered sheaves of grain, the blessed sign
Of plenteous reaping, bread, and pure rich wine,
Full hearts for harvest tunes.

" Life hath its barren years
When blossoms fall untimely down ;
When ripened fruitage fails to crown
The summer toil ; when nature's frown
Looks only on our tears."

I.

SEIGNEURIES.

Of the many attempts in colonial times to follow in the New World the old order of things, the Dutch and English baronial manors founded upon the Hudson, and the French *seigneuries* on the St. Lawrence, were in a measure successful ones, but in the rugged soil of the Wilderness, all such efforts proved abortive. Among such unsuccessful efforts there is none which possesses a more melancholy interest than the now forgotten Manor of Willsboro, which was located near the mouth of the Boquet River, on Lake Champlain.

During the French occupancy of the Champlain valley, the Governor-General of Canada granted large tracts of land lying on both sides of the lake to several persons holding office under the French king. These grants were seigneuries over which the proprietors could exercise certain minor executive and judicial powers, after the manner of the feudal lords of the Old World. On two only of their seigneuries lying within the territory of Northern New York were settlements made by the French proprietors.

One settlement was commenced on the seigneurie of Sieur Pean, major of the castle and town of Quebec, at the mouth of the Chazy, granted in 1733, and another on the Seigneurie of Alainville, granted to Michael Chartier de Lotbiniere by the Marquis de Vaudreuil, Governor-General, in November, 1758. The Seigneurie of Alainville lay partly on Lake George, and partly on Lake Champlain, between the outlet of Lake George and Crown Point. It was four leagues front by five in depth. After the conquest of Canada in 1763 the title to all the French seigneuries became vested in the British crown.

II.

WILLIAM GILLILAND.

Soon after the conquest, William Gilliland, then a rich and prosperous merchant of New York, purchased several large tracts of these lands that lay along the western border of Lake Champlain and near the mouth of the Boquet River. The tracts first purchased by Gilliland were parts of the seigneurie of Sieur Robart, king's storekeeper at Montreal. Sieur Robart's tract embraced "three leagues front by two leagues in depth on the west side of Lake Champlain, taking in going down one league below the River Boquet, and in going up two and a half above said river," as described in the grant. Sieur Robart's seigneurie was granted in 1737. It was surveyed, but he failed to effect a settlement upon it. Upon these tracts Gilliland made an unsuccessful attempt to found a magnificent baronial manor in imitation of the Van Rensselaers, the Livingstons, the Phillipses, and the Van Cortlandts on the

17

Hudson. His first tract extended about six miles in front
on the lake, and from three to four miles in depth, and contained 3,500 acres. About one-half mile of the front lay
north of the Boquet, and the remainder south of the river.
He afterwards located another tract of 4,500 acres in the
modern town of Westport, which he called Bessboro, after
his daughter, and several thousand acres more on the Salmon River, which he called Jamesboro, after his brother;
and still another tract at Cumberland Head, which he
called Charlottesboro, from another daughter. The town
of Willsboro commemorates his own name. William Gilliland was born near the city of Armagh, in Ireland, about
the year 1734. At the schools of Armagh he received a
liberal education. His culture, his intelligence, his polished
manners and fine person soon made him a favorite in its
best society. A mutual and warm attachment followed his
acquaintance with a young lady of noble birth and great fortune, the Lady Betsey Eckles. But the disparity of their birth
and fortune was an insuperable barrier to their marriage.
Her family, interposing its powerful arm, secluded her and
banished her lover from his country. He enlisted in the
thirty-fifth regiment of the line, and after four years' service was discharged alone and friendless in the city of
Philadelphia. He soon after went to the city of New York,
and entered a mercantile house, in which he shortly became
a partner. Before a year elapsed he won the affections of
Elizabeth Phagan, the beautiful and accomplished daughter
of his wealthy partner. They were married on the eighth
day of February, 1759. He received with her hand the
large sum, for the time, of fifteen hundred pounds, as her
dowry.

But the ambition of young Gilliland was not satisfied by his brilliant and successful career as a merchant. He was charmed by the baronial estates on the lower Hudson, and resolved to be himself the founder of a manor of equal magnificence. In his dreams of the future he saw himself in the exalted station of a great landholder, ruling over a subservient tenantry with the power of the old feudal authority that had once so effectually spurned his presence in his native country. Would not his triumph in the New World make amends for his too severe rebuke in the Old ? So in 1764, he purchased his tract on the Boquet River, and began the settlement of his manor under the most auspicious circumstances. A little flourishing settlement soon sprang up around him in the wilderness, and his wildest dreams seemed likely to be realized. His plan of settlement was similar to that of the manors on the Hudson. He held the land in fee, and leased to settlers at a small annual rent.

But after twelve short prosperous years had passed by, the war of the Revolution broke out, and his growing manorial estate lying in the great northern valley, through which ran the old war-trail of the Indian, and being in the long-trodden pathway of devastating armies, it was doomed to destruction. The Americans under Arnold in 1776 commenced, and the British under Burgoyne in 1777 completed the ruin of his possessions. He fled to New York, and did not visit his property for seven long years. After the war he returned to find his tenantry scattered, his buildings in ashes, and the wild forest fast encroaching upon the once fair fields of his now desolate domain.

But hope still gilded the scene, and he made fruitless attempts to retrieve his shattered fortunes. He petitioned

Congress for redress on account of the damage sustained in the war, but Congress, although willing, had no money to repay him his losses. At length, being unable to surmount his financial difficulties, and heavy judgments having been filed against him, in September, 1786, he was placed upon the jail limits of New York for debt, at the suit of his creditors, he having already disposed of all his interest in his landed estates. He was not released until 1791. After this six years involuntary exile, he again returned to his former home on the banks of the Boquet.

But his accumulated misfortunes were too much for even his strong intellect, and his mind partially gave way beneath the constant strain. No longer able to make further effort to retrieve his fallen fortunes, he was employed, on account of his intimate acquaintance with such matters, by an association in which he had some interest, formed for the purchase and location of wild lands, in looking up the corners of their lots, and in tracing the lines of their lands through the forest. Finally, in the year 1796, in the month of February, while travelling in the woods on foot and alone, for the purpose of locating some lots of wild land, he wandered from his path, and perished from cold and exposure. He had evidently been stricken by some sudden attack that deprived him of the power of walking. His bleeding hands and knees, worn to the muscles and nerves, showed his unavailing struggles.

> " Found dead ! dead and alone !
> Nobody near with love to greet,
> Nobody heard his last faint groan,
> Or knew when his sad heart ceased to beat ;
> No mourner lingered with tears or sighs,
> But the stars looked down with pitying eyes,

And the chill winds passed with a wailing sound
O'er the lonely spot where his form was found.

" Found dead ! dead and alone !
There was somebody near, somebody near,
To claim the wanderer as His own,
And find a home for the homeless here ;
One, when every human door
Is closed to His children scorned and poor,
Who opens the heavenly portals wide ;
Ah ! God was near when the wanderer died."

"Such," says Winslow C. Watson, "was the last sad and tragic scene in a singularly variegated drama of a remarkable life. The career of Gilliland was a romance. Its strange vicissitudes not only invoke sympathy and compassion, but are calculated to impart solemn and salutary admonition. The pioneer of the Champlain valley thus piteously perished in what should have been the ripeness of his years and the plenitude of his powers and usefulness— for his age was scarcely three-score. The former lord of a vast domain, the generous patron and tender father, the dispenser of magnificent hospitalities, the associate and counsellor of vice-royalty, died, far away from human care, of cold and famine, with no voice of love to soothe his sufferings, and no kind hand to close his dying eyes."

Gilliland for several years kept a diary of the transactions relating to the settlement of his manor. In this diary he carefully noted many of the details and the more important incidents of his attempts to settle his lands. It is an interesting story of energetic effort and fruitless endeavor. It has been published by Joel Munsell, of Albany, with a Memoir by Winslow C. Watson, under the title of "The Pioneer History of the Champlain Valley."

A touching account is given in Mr. Gilliland's diary of

the drowning of his little daughter Jane, aged six years, near Half Moon, now Waterford, on the 10th of May, 1776. With his mother and brothers, his wife and family, he was going up the river in batteaux, on his way from Albany to his manor on the Boquet. The batteau in which his daughter was sitting was carelessly run upon a fallen tree top that lay extended from the bank into the stream, and capsized. Her body was found the next day near the spot where she fell into the water, and was buried on the shore of the river in the burial place of a Mr. Coleman at Stillwater, not far from the battle ground made famous the year after, called Bemis Heights.

Some of Gilliland's numerous descendants still own and occupy parts of his patrimonial estate in Northern New York, while others are scattered in various parts of the United States and Canada, all occupying the highest social positions. Elizabethtown, the shire-town of Essex county, was named in honor of his accomplished wife. And now the old seigneuries and the Manor of Willsboro on Lake Champlain,. like Tryon county, and like the ancient La Famine on Lake Ontario, have long been forgotten.

CHAPTER XV.

NORTH ELBA.

The tomb of him who would have made
The world too glad and free.
—*Hervey*.

I.

ITS SITUATION.

The little mountain hamlet of North Elba, now of world-wide fame, was for ten years the forest home of John Brown of Ossawottamie memory. It is situated in the township of the same name, on the western border of Essex county, in the very heart of the Great Wilderness, It is about forty miles west of Lake Champlain, and seven miles north of the Indian Pass. It is surrounded on all sides save its western by an ampitheatre of mountain ranges. To the westward it stretches off into the great wilderness plateau that lies beyond, filled to the brim with gleaming lakes, towering mountain peaks, and numberless wild meadows. At different points near this wild hamlet, the forms of the giant mountains which surround it, their gorges and landslides, are brought clearly into view, as they tower in their sublime and awful grandeur above an unseen world of woods and waters.

II.

AN INDIAN VILLAGE.

North Elba has had a checkered history. Before and during the colonial period it was the summer home of the Adirondack hunting bands. In all the old maps an Indian

village is located near the spot. According to a tradition
still lingering in this region, the bold partizan Capt. Robert
Rogers, with his rangers, once attacked and destroyed this
Indian village in the absence of the warriors. Upon their
return, the infuriated braves pursued him, and gave him
battle when he reached, upon his retreat, the banks of the
Boquet River.

There was also another Indian village not far away, near
the Indian carry between the waters of the Saranac and the
Raquette. The remains of this last-named village, with its
burying ground, may still be traced.

III.

THE PLAINS OF ABRAHAM.

About the beginning of the present century, a little band
of pioneer settlers strayed off into this secluded valley,
made small clearings, and built their rude cabins. These
pioneers, being separated from the outer world by impassible mountain barriers, except by a long and circuitous
trail up the valley of the Au Sable, subsisted mostly by
hunting and fishing. In time they became almost as wild
as the Indians that preceded them in the occupancy of their
forest home. The place was then known as the "Plains of
Abraham."

At length in the year 1810, Archibald McIntyre, of Albany, and his associates founded the North Elba iron works,
on the Au Sable, near the Plains of Abraham, and broke
in with their new industry upon the seclusion of these
pioneers. New life was thus infused into this little half-wild
community. But McIntyre's enterprise was finally abandon-

ed about the year 1826, and nothing soon remained of it but a few decaying buildings and broken water-wheels. At length, in that year the old Indian Sabelle led David Henderson, the son-in-law and associate of McIntyre, from the abandoned works at North Elba, through the Indian Pass to the iron dam on the Hudson. The Adirondack Iron Works springing up in consequence of this discovery, cast another gleam of ruddy light across the mountain shadows of the Plains of Abraham.

Then, with the decay of the Adirondack village, new and strange characters appeared upon the scene. The careless pioneer settlers of the Plains of Abraham had squatted upon their lands, and had never acquired the title to them from the state. About the year 1840, a land speculator swooped down upon their possessions, and they were in their turn, like the Indians, driven from their homes. It was about this time that Gerrit Smith bought the Plains of Abraham, with miles of the land contiguous to them, and made his attempt to colonize the grim old northern wilderness with the free colored people of the state. He made to each family a gift of forty acres of land on condition of settlement. He hoped thereby to found in that secluded spot, among their own people, a secure asylum for the many fugitive slaves who were then fleeing toward Canada from the southern plantations.

IV.

JOHN BROWN OF OSSAWOTTAMIE.

In the year 1849, Smith deeded to John Brown, as a free gift, a farm of three hundred and fifty acres, situate on the western slope of the valley of the Au Sable, at North Elba,

18

and he at once became the leading spirit in the enterprise.
John Brown had but just before made a journey to Europe.
While there he admired the superb stock upon the English
estates, and his martial spirit was aroused by the splendid
equipments and elaborate evolutions of the vast armies of
continental Europe. He moved his family of stalwart sons
into his forest home, and with the aid of his colored brethren he cleared his fields. He stocked his mountain pas-
tures with imported British cattle, and under his management the little hamlet among the mountains, for a while,
seemed to prosper. But the mutterings of the "irrepressible conflict" reached him in his secluded retreat. His
spirit was as turbulent and wild as the torrents that dashed
around his home. His stormy soul was filled with prophetic
visions of the vast armies that were destined then so soon
to march on throughout the length and breadth of our
land to their fratricidal struggle. When the troubles about
slavery broke out in Kansas they at once attracted his attention, and, with his sons, he hastened into the thickest of
the fight. Conspicuous in almost every contest therein,
his name is intimately associated with this stormy period in
our country's annals.

While engaged in this anti-slavery controversy, for ten
years he was seldom seen at his home in North Elba,
but he made it his head-quarters, and paid.it an occasional
visit, until, in the year 1859, his life was ended upon the
scaffold, in Virginia, in consequence of his insane attempt
to liberate the southern slaves by force of arms, an act
which seemed to precipitate the Great Rebellion. After
his death, his body was brought by the remaining members

of his family, and buried in front of the house in which he had lived at North Elba.

"The house," says a writer in *Old and New* for September, 1870, "is unpainted and plain, though equal to the ordinary farm houses of the region. It stands well up the hills, separated from the wilderness by a few cleared fields, commanding a majestic view of the mountain world. A few rods in front, a huge boulder, surrounded by a plain board fence, is the fit monument of the fierce old apostle of liberty. At its foot is the grave. The headstone was brought from an old grave yard in New England, where it stood over the grave of his father, Capt. John Brown, who died in New York in 1776. The whole stone is covered with the family inscriptions: John Brown, executed at Charlestown, Va., Dec. 2, 1859. Oliver and Watson, his sons, both killed at Harper's Ferry, the same year; and his son Frederick, murdered in Kansas by border ruffians in 1856. Above the little grassy enclosure, towers the mighty rock, almost as high as the house, and on its summit is cut in massive granite characters the inscription 'John Brown, 1859.' Standing on the top of this monumental rock, for the first time I felt that I comprehended the character of the man whose name it commemorates. I could well understand how such a man, formed in the mould of the old Scotch Covenanters and English Puritans, brooding over the horrors of slavery, foreseeing the impending struggle for liberty, maddened by the murder of his son and friends in Kansas, with the mighty northern hills looking down upon him, the rush of strong rivers, and the songs of resounding tempests, and the mystery of the illimitable wilderness all about him, should easily come to think himself inspired to descend like a mountain torrent, and sweep the black curse from out the land. I reverently raised my hat, and sung 'John Brown's body lies a-mouldering in the grave; His soul is marching on.' "

The attempt of Gerrit Smith to found a colony of colored people at North Elba, proved an utter failure. The children of the sunny south could not tame the old north wilderness. The surviving members of John Brown's family sought elsewhere more congenial homes, and now the little forest hamlet, after its eventful career, sits almost deserted among its sheltering mountains, inhabited by a few families only, and affording a transient stopping place for the curious summer tourist, and the wandering hunter.

CHAPTER XVI.

THE ADIRONDACK VILLAGE.

From the ground
Comes up the laugh of children, the soft voice
Of maidens, and the sweet and solemn hymn
Of Sabbath worshippers. The low of herds
Blends with the rustling of the heavy grain
Over the dark brown furrows. All at once
A fresher wind sweeps by and breaks my dream,
And I am in the Wilderness alone.
—*Bryant.*

I.

In the depths of the limitless forest, and surrounded by the towering peaks of the old giants of the mountain belt, now sleeps, like a strong man after his labors are ended, the little decaying and deserted hamlet known as Adirondack Village, or the Upper Iron Works. Its story is a tale of almost superhuman effort, crowned with partial success, but finally ending in fruitless endeavor, disaster and death.

Six or seven miles below, and to the south of the old Indian Pass in the valley of the infant Hudson, and fed by its waters, which there run through them, are the lakes Sanford and Henderson, lying about a mile apart.

Between these two lakes, upon the right bank of the Hudson, the connecting river, this famous village is situated. To the west of it rises Santanoni, to the north yawns the awful gorge of the Indian Pass, and to the east of it old Tahawas towers up above the clouds.

II.

About the year 1826, Archibald McIntyre, of Albany, David Henderson, his son-in-law, of Jersey City, and Duncan McMartin, with others, were or had been proprietors of iron works at North Elba, on the Au Sable. One day in that year, Mr. Henderson, while standing near his works, was approached by an old Indian, of the St. Francis tribe, named Sabelle, who often hunted near that wild region. The Indian took from under his blanket a lump of rich iron ore, and showing it to Mr. Henderson, said to him :

"You want to see 'um ore? Me find plenty all same."

"Where ?" said Mr. Henderson, eagerly.

"Me hunt beaver all 'lone," replied old Sabelle, "and find 'um where water run pom, pom, pom, over *iron dam*, 'way off there," pointing toward the southern woods beyond the Indian Pass.

The next day an exploring party, guided by old Sabelle, set out in search of this wonderful bed of iron ore, and boldly plunged into the then unknown wilderness. They spent the first night within the gorge of the Indian Pass, at the fountain head of the infant Hudson. The day after, following the course of the stream, they reached lakes Sanford and Henderson, and found the iron dam across the bed of the Hudson between the two lakes. The old Indian had not misled them. There was " plenty " of ore—there were mountains of ore all around them. There was ore enough there apparently to supply the world with iron for ages.

Mr. Henderson and his associates hastened to Albany, purchased of the State a large tract of land, and formed a company to be called the "Adirondack Iron and Steel Company," with a capital of one million dollars, to operate these inexhaustible mines. A clearing was soon made near the "iron dam" of old Sabelle. A road was cut into it with great labor, winding around the mountain masses a distance

of fifty miles from Crown Point, on Lake Champlain. Then
a little mountain hamlet sprung up, as if by magic, in the
wild, secluded valley. Forges, boarding houses, store
houses, cottages, mills, and a school house were built. The
mountain shadows were soon lighted up with the ruddy glow
of furnace fires, and the howling wilderness was made vocal
with the roar of ponderous machinery, with the hum of
many industries, and the songs of labor. The busy house-
wives spun and wove, and plied their daily toil ; the children laughed, and frolicked, and loitered on their way to and
from their school, and from many a stumpy pasture round
about came the drowsy tinkle of the cow bells.

III.

But a sad calamity awaited Mr. Henderson, the man
whose tireless energy helped so much to build up this little
oasis in the wilderness. In the month of September, 1845,
he was one day exploring the woods near the foot of Mount
Marcy. He was accompanied only by his little son, ten
years old, and the famous hunter John Cheney as their
guide. They stopped to rest upon a rock that lay on the
border of a little mountain pond, since known as Calamity
Pond. Mr. Henderson, thinking their guide had laid his
knapsack, in which was a loaded pistol, in a damp place,
took it up to remove it to a dryer one. When putting it
down again the hammer of the pistol struck, in some way,
the solid rock. The pistol exploded, its ball entering Mr.
Henderson's heart. "To die in such an awful place as
this," moaned the fallen man. "Take care, my son, of your
mother when I am gone," were his last words.

Upon the wild spot where he fell his children afterward
erected a beautiful monument of Nova Scotia freestone,
carved with exquisite taste, in the highest style of art. It
was brought in pieces to the spot by the hands of the sor-
rowing workmen of the forge. Upon it is this touching inscription : " ERECTED BY FILIAL AFFECTION TO THE MEM-
ORY OF OUR DEAR FATHER, WHO ACCIDENTALLY LOST HIS
LIFE ON THIS SPOT 3D SEPTEMBER, 1845."

" How often," says Street, " has the wild wolf made his
lair beside it ; how often the savage panther glared at its
beautiful proportions, and wondered what object met his
blazing eye-balls."

After the death of Mr. Henderson, the industries of the
little village flagged. Its distance from market over almost
impassable roads proved to be an insuperable hindrance to
its further progress. In a few years the Adirondack village,
as a business enterprise, was entirely abandoned. For nearly a quarter of a century it has been left to decay, and has
been the abode of solitary fishermen and hunters. Nature,
always aggressive, is fast re-asserting her stern dominion
over the once busy scene—once busy, but now desolate and
forsaken—

> " Where the owl still hooting sits,
> Where the bat incessant flits."

CHAPTER XVII.

VISCOUNT DE CHATEAUBRIAND.

> " I planted in my heart one seed of love
> Watered with tears and watched with tenderest care,
> It grew, but when I look'd that it might prove
> A glorious tree, and precious fruit might bear,
> Blossoms nor fruit were there to crown my pain,
> Tears, care, and labor had been all in vain,
> Yet now I dare not pluck it from my heart,
> Lest with the deep-struck root, my life depart."
> —*Quoted from memory.*

I.

HIS " SYLPHIDE."

Among the many distinguished European travelers who, like Peter Kalm, Tom. Moore, the Duc de la Rochefoucauld, and the Prince de Talleyrand, visited Northern New York while it was still nearly all clothed in the wild splendor of its primeval forests, was Châteaubriand, the eminent author and statesman of France. Seventy years ago his works were read and admired by every one. They were dramatized and acted upon the stage, and translated into other tongues. They were then the best interpreters of the spirit of the age—the spirit of reviving Christianity. To-day he is almost forgotten.

François Auguste, Viscount de Châteaubriand, was born of a noble family on the 14th of September, 1768, at St. Malo, the birthplace of the old mariner Jacques Cartier, the discoverer of the river St. Lawrence. St. Malo, as before stated in these pages, is a quaint old seaport town of Brittany, built in mediæval times upon a rock then forming a part of the mainland. In 1709 an earthquake turned it into an island, and it is now a huge rock standing in the

19

middle of a salt marsh, which is covered by the sea at high
tide.

Many a strange old superstition still flourishes among its
simple people. Its quaint mediæval customs were carried
to the New World by its old mariners, and the songs heard
in its streets found a wild echo among the Thousand Islands
of the St. Lawrence and along the mountain shores of Lake
Champlain. Thus, too, in the wilds of the New World were
introduced by these mariners the stories of the dwarfs and
giants of the fairy mythology which the Northmen of the
tenth century brought from their ancient home when they
invaded Brittany.

The family of Châteaubriand, like many of the old *noblesse*, had, in his youth, fallen into decay. His early days
were passed in squalid poverty, his father saving all his in-
come to buy back the family possessions. With shirt in
rags, his stockings full of holes, and his slippers down at
the heel, the proud, sensitive, romantic boy would shrink
from his better dressed companions, and wander for days
on the shore of some lonely bay among the rocks, watching
the waves of the storm-beaten Atlantic, as they came in,
freighted with wild tales of the wonderful land beyond it in
the New World. It was here in his moody, brooding boyhood, while studying Rousseau, that he conceived the idea
of a romance founded upon savage life, and pictured to his
imagination a beautiful creature, clothed with every virtue
and girlish charm, whom he called his *Sylphide*. This fairy
creature of his boyish fancy, this "vision beautiful," haunted his dreams until after he had become familiar with the
dusky maidens of the American forests, it grew at length
into his "Atala," the heroine of his most famous story.

Finally he was sent to school, and growing up to manhood, wandered to Paris just as the delirium of the French Revolution was at its height.   In Paris he found every one living in the wildest excitement at balls, theatres, clubs, political meetings, gaming houses, and the old order of things in state, in religious and in social life, completely reversed.

II.

HIS JOURNEYINGS.

We now come to the second phase of his life.   Out of the turmoil of the Revolution, Châteaubriand, in the year 1791, sailed for America.   After visiting Philadelphia, and being presented to Gen. Washington, to whom he had letters of introduction, he went to New York, and then to Albany. Westward of Albany even, in those days, the whole country lay spreading out in its aboriginal wildness, save a few feeble settlements up the Hudson and along the valley of the Mohawk.   Châteaubriand now dressed himself in the garb of an Indian hunter, and plunged at once into the wilderness.   Sometimes alone, sometimes in company with an Indian band of hunters, he wandered through the sublime scenes of primeval nature that he afterward painted so glowingly in his romances.   Sometimes he would spend weeks together at an Indian village, studying the strange characters around him, and witnessing the wild gambols of the Indian children, saw in the perfect forms of the dusky forest maidens the physical ideal of his beauteous *Sylphide*. Sometimes in his travels he found the friendly shelter of a hut and a bed of bear skins.   Oftener his bed was made "upon the dead leaves of a thousand years," under the shelter of some mighty tree, beside a lonely camp-fire, "locked in the arms of a limitless moon-lit silence, broken only by the cries of wild animals, or the stir of the wind-swept leaves, or the distant roar of eternal Niagara."

After he had thus wandered for more than a year in these northern wilds, he found in a Canadian cabin an English newspaper, in which was an account of the arrest of Louis XVI. He hastened back to France to find his family in dungeons and his estates confiscated. The next eight years he spent in poverty and exile, composing in the meantime his immortal romances, that upon his return to France under the Consulate and the first Empire, were destined to create so deep and wide spread a sensation.

III.

HIS "ATALA."

During the French Revolution the Voltaire school of thought accomplished its mission and reduced all its wild theories to practice. Liberty, Equality, Fraternity and Atheism were established, and failed to satisfy the wants of the people. Upon the establishment of the Consulate and the first Empire, when society began to move in its old channels, the people began to tire of the hopeless world of scepticism, and to long for the old belief. The sons of the men who had considered Christianity an absurd and nox-ious thing, were now longing ardently for its re-establish-ment. Châteaubriand was the first one to put these long-ings after the old belief into language, and his christian ro-mances struck the popular heart of France with wonderful power, and made it thrill with joy.

In 1801 he published his " Atala, a Christian Romance."
In September of that year Napoleon re-established the
right of public worship, and the Christian religion. In
1803, Châteaubriand published his "*Génie du Christianisme,*"
the object of which was to show forth the beauties of the
christian faith in the garb of romance. Thus he struck the
spirit of his age, the " spirit of reviving Christianity," and
he shone like a meteor, under the Consulate, the Empire,
and the Restoration. He made Christianity lovely by asso-
ciating it with poetry and music, with majesty and peace.
He brought back to the mind of the people the solemn
chant of the processional, the glorious roofs of grand cathe-
drals, the tenderness of charity, the valor of the crusaders,
the devotion of the missionary. He illustrated it all by the
charms of the wild exuberance of nature among which he
had wandered in the forest wilds of the New World. His
romances were filled with dazzling descriptions of the glory
of the autumn woods, the odor of the violet and the rose,
the music of running brooks, the awful majesty of mountain ranges and the thunder of the cataract.

The heroine of his best romance was "Atala," an Indian
maiden who had become a Christian, and who took upon herself a vow of perpetual virginity. She falls passionately in
love, however, with an Indian brave named René, who is a
captive in her tribe, and whose escape she contrives. She
follows him alone through the forest, and finding her love
for him overcoming her, kills herself rather than break her
christian vows. Around this simple plot he weaves a story
full of christian fervor, hope and love.

IV.

HIS IDEAL.

But I can not take leave of Châteaubriand without saying something of his friendship, his love in his declining years for Madame Julie Récamier. Like Abelard and his Heloise, like Petrarch and his Laura, like Dante and his Beatrice, like Tasso and his Eleonora, like Goethe and his Minna, we find Châteaubriand and his Julie bound together by the links of a spiritual chain, and joined by that mysterious sympathy which seems in some measure to satisfy the infinite longings of us poor mortals, which helps somehow to compensate us for our small acquirings, and to give us here on earth some slight foretaste of the eternal joy of heaven. In the inviting *salon* of Madame Récamier were daily congregated the wit, the intellect, and the beauty that were left of the old *régime*, and what was best of the new, all attracted by her matchless beauty and wonderful goodness. Of this fascinating woman, Châteaubriand was also, during all the last years of his life, a constant daily visitor. Thus at length, after all his wanderings, he found in her loving presence a haven of sweet rest, and there at her feet he sat in perpetual adoration of her charms. In her at last did he not find, when it was all too late, the spiritual ideal of his beautiful "Sylphide," the "vision beautiful" of his boyish fancy? Is not this the old, old story with us all? "Do we ever find our ideals before it is too late?" Do we ever find them at all except in our waking or in our sleeping dreams?

In 1848 Châteaubriand died, and was buried on a little island near his birth-place, St. Malo. I said that to-day he was almost forgotten, yet on the 14th of September, 1875, which was the one hundred and seventeenth anniversary of his birth, the best men and women of France made a pilgrimage to his tomb, and as they gathered around it, a statue was raised to his memory on the old sea-girt rock of St. Malo. Thus at last a somewhat tardy justice has been done to the memory of him whom Sainte-Beuve has called the "poetical advocate of Christianity."

CHAPTER XVIII.

CASTORLAND.

On an hundred thousand acres, never trod by foot of men,
He had mapped out farms and vineyards, roads o'er precipice and glen,
And like scenes of an enchanter rose a city wondrous fair.
With its colleges, its churches, and its castles in the air.

Then was struck a classic medal by this visionary band,
Cybele was on the silver, and beneath was CASTORLAND,
The reverse a tree of maple, yielding forth its precious store,
Salve magna parens frugum was the legend that it bore.
                                    —*Caleb Lyon of Lyonsdale.*

I.

CASTORLAND STATION.

 The summer tourist, on his way from Trenton Falls to the Thousand Islands, may pass through the beautiful and flourishing valley of the Black River, over the Utica and Black River Railroad. As the train draws near to the first station north of the village of Lowville, he will hear the sharp voice of the brakeman crying out "Cas-tor-land." He will look out of the car window and see a wide level clearing of pasture land and meadow, skirted by forests, one side of which is bounded by the river. In the middle of this clearing he will see only the small station house, and three or four scattered buildings surrounding it, and will doubtless wonder whence comes the high-sounding name for such meagre surroundings.

The story of Castorland is the often repeated tale of frustrated settlements in the old wilderness. It is the story of an attempt of the exiled nobility and clergy of the old *régime* in France to found a settlement in the wilds of the the New World, where they could find a secure retreat from the horrors of Revolution in the Old.

This attempt was made at the close of the last century in the valley of the Black River, on the western slope of the Great Wilderness. But, like the settlement of the first Catholics on the Patuxent, the Jacobites with Flora Mc-Donald at Cape Fear, the Huguenots with Jean Ribault at Port Royal; like New Amsterdam on the Hudson, New Sweden on the Delaware; like Acadie in Nova Scotia, Castorland on the Black River lives now only in poetry and history. Its story is one of brilliant promises all unfulfilled, of hopes deferred, of man's tireless but fruitless endeavor, of woman's tears.

To rescue this name so fraught with historical associations from oblivion, it was applied to the railroad station which is nearest to the site of the largest projected city of ancient Castorland. That city was laid out on the Beaver River, which flows into the Black River from the Wilderness nearly opposite this station.

II.

ANCIENT CASTORLAND.

For the purpose of effecting the settlement of Castorland a company was formed in Paris, under the laws of France, in the month of August, 1792, and styled *La Compagnie de New York*. On the 31st day of the same month the Company, by its agent, Pierre Chassanis, bought a large tract of land lying in the valley of. the Black River, of William

20

Constable, who was the owner of Macomb's Purchase. This tract lay along both sides of the Black River below the High Falls, and extended westerly through the counties of Lewis and Jefferson to Lake Ontario, and easterly into the heart of the Great Wilderness. The Castorland purchase at first comprised the whole of Great Lot No. 5 of Macomb's Purchase, and contained six hundred and ten thousand acres. But subsequently all south and west of the Black River, being the part which now constitutes the richest towns of Lewis and Jefferson counties, was given up, and only that lying to the north and east of the river retained. The portion so retained contained only two hundred and ten thousand acres. This was the Castorland of the olden time.

The name Castorland, that is to say, the Land of Beavers, is doubtless a literal translation of the old Indian *Couch-sach-ra-ge*, which means in the Iroquois tongue, the " Beaver Hunting Country," Castorland being taken out of the western half of this old Indian hunting ground.

During the negotiations between Constable and Chassanis for this tract, the Revolution that had been so long smouldering, burst forth in all its savage fury, and the streets of Paris were slippery with human gore. Constable locked the door of the apartment in which they met, with the remark that, " if they parted before the purchase was completed they might never meet again." The Palace of the Tuilleries was already surrounded by the bloodthirsty mob. The attendants of the royal family were butchered, and the feeble king cast into a dungeon. In comparison with such awful scenes as these in the very heart of the highest civilization the world had ever seen, the savage wildness of the old American forests was a scene of peaceful rest. To the fugitive *noblesse* of France, the former possessors of titles, rank, wealth and culture, the quiet shades of Castorland afforded a secure asylum from the horrors of the Reign of Terror.

III.

SCHEME OF SETTLEMENT.

A romantic scheme was at once conceived and perfected by the company in Paris for the settlement of Castorland. In pursuance of this scheme a pamphlet was printed in Paris and issued by the Company, containing a programme of colonization under its auspices. This pamphlet was entitled "Association for the purchase and settlement of six hundred thousand acres of land, granted by the State of New York, and situated within that state, between the 43d and 44th degrees of latitude, upon Lake Ontario, and thirty-five leagues from the city and port of Albany where vessels land from Europe." It set forth, among other things, in glowing colors, the wealth of agriculture presented by its fertile soil, the fine distribution of its waters, its facilities for an extended commerce on account of its location in the vicinity of a dense population, and above all the security afforded to its inhabitants by the laws of a people who were independent and rich with their own capital, thus extending to the immigrant all the benefits of liberty with none of its drawbacks. It was stated that the object of the proprietors was to form of the colony a sort of family, in some way united by common interests and common wants, and that to maintain this union of interests a plan had been devised that rendered each member directly interested in the

whole property.   It was all to be done by and in the name
of Sieur Chassanis, in whose name they had purchased the
estate, and who alone had power to issue certificates of
ownership.

There were six thousand certificates to be issued, each
entitling the holder thereof to ownership in manner following :   The whole tract at that time consisted of six hundred and thirty thousand acres.   Of this, six hundred
thousand acres were divided into twelve thousand lots of
fifty acres each, and the price of each share fixed at eight
hundred livres ($152.38.)   In the beginning six thousand
lots were set apart for individual properties, and the other
six thousand lots were to belong to a common stock which
was to be divided at some future time, after improvements
had been made thereon by the Company.   Each holder of
a certificate was to receive at once a deed for a separate lot
of fifty acres, to be drawn by lot, and also a lot of fifty
acres in the common undivided stock.

Of the thirty thousand remaining acres, two thousand
were set apart for a city to be formed on the great river in
the interior, and two thousand more for another city on
Lake Ontario, at the mouth of the river, which was to form
a port and *entre-pot* of commerce.   Among artizans six
thousand acres were to be divided, and rented to them at
twelve sous per acre.   The proceeds of the twenty thousand
acres remaining were to be expended by the Company in
the construction of roads, bridges and other improvements.

The two cities were divided into fourteen thousand lots
each. Of these lots, two thousand were set apart for churches,
schools, markets, &c.   The remaining twelve thousand lots
were to be divided among the six thousand holders of cer-

tificates in the same manner as the large tract. Each holding one separate lot and one in common.

The affairs of the Company were to be managed by five trustees,. three to remain in Paris and two upon the tract. Such was the scheme matured in the *salons* of Paris for the settlement of Castorland. Beautiful and promising beyond measure upon paper, as an ideal, but utterly impracticable and bitterly disappointing as a reality. Yet many shares were eagerly taken.

IV.

ORGANIZATION.

On the 28th of June, 1793, it being the second year of the French Republic, the actual holders of certificates convertible into shares of *La Compagnie de New York* met in the rooms of citizen Chassanis, in Paris, to organize their society upon the basis already established, and to regulate the division, survey and settlement of their lands. There were present at that meeting forty-one shareholders in all, who represented one thousand eight hundred and eight shares. They perfected and completed their organization ; they adopted a long and elaborate constitution; they chose a seal for their corporation, and appointed five commissaries to manage its affairs, three for Paris and two for Castorland. In the meantime the tract had been re-conveyed, and the large part lying west and south of the Black River given up, the part retained being that lying east and north of the river, and containing only two hundred and ten thousand acres, as before stated. To accord with this fact the number of shares was reduced from six thousand to two thou-

sand. It was at this meeting that a silver piece was ordered to be struck, termed a *Jetton de presence*, one of which
was to be given at every meeting to each Commissary as an
attendance fee.*

The Commissaries appointed for America were Simon
Desjardines and Pierre Pharoux, who lost no time in proceeding to America to execute their important trust. Desjardines had been a Chamberlain of Louis XVI. He was of
middle age, an accomplished scholar and gentleman, but
knew not a word of English when he arrived. He had
with him his wife and three children, and his younger
brother, Geoffrey Desjardines, who shared his labors and

OBVERSE.   REVERSE.

*These pieces occur in coin cabinets, and have been erroneously called
" Castorland half-dollars." A *Jetton* is a piece of metal struck with a
device, and distributed to be kept in commemoration of some event, or
to be used as a counter in games of chance. The one here noticed was
termed a *Jetton de presence*, or piece "given in certain societies or companies to each of the members at a session or meeting." (*Dic. de
l'Acad. Francaise.*) It was engraved by one of the Duvivier brothers,
eminent coin and metal artists of Paris. The design represents on the
obverse the head of *Cybele*, who personified the earth as inhabited or
cultivated, while on the reverse *Ceres* has just tapped a maple tree.

The Latin legend on the reverse is a quotation from Virgil, which,
with its context, reads:

> " Salve magna parens frugum, Saturnia tellus
>   Magna virum   *   *   *   *   *Geor.* ii, 173.
>   —*Hough's History of Lewis County.*

trials. He also brought with him his library of two thousand volumes. Pierre Pharoux, as before mentioned in these pages, was a distinguished young architect and engineer of Paris, of high scientific attainments and marked ability. He was earnestly and faithfully devoted to his duties; and his love of science, his honesty, his good sense, and genial and ardent friendship were manifested in all his doings. He left behind him in France an aged father to mourn his untimely death.

They sailed from Havre on the fourth day of July, 1793, in the American ship Liberty, but did not arrive in New York until the 7th of September following. There came over in the same vessel with them a young French refugee named Mark Isambart Brunel, who afterward filled the world with his fame as an engineer in England. Brunel had been in the French navy, and was driven from home on account of his royalistic proclivities. He went with them in all their journeys through the wilderness, and shared in all their hardships during the first year, but does not seem to have been employed by them in Castorland.

One of their duties was to keep a daily journal and record of all their doings for the information of the Company in Paris. This journal was lately discovered, by some one who appreciated its value, among a lot of old rags exposed for sale upon the Seine in Paris, and was brought to this country. It is now in the possession of Dr. F. B. Hough, the learned historian. This journal throws a flood of light upon the settlement of Castorland. "This journal," says Dr. Hough, "gives, with the greatest minuteness, the facts and incidents of their operations, their plans and failures, hopes and fears, gains and losses, with the most scrupulous exactness, while there runs through the whole a vein of humor that proves the authors to have been men who keenly enjoyed the ludicrous, and who closely observed both men and things."

But I fear I shall weary the patience of the reader if I go much into detail upon the subject, and shall therefore endeavor to be brief.

V.

THEIR FIRST EXPLORATIONS.

Soon after their arrival in this country, Desjardines and Pharoux, with their friend Brunel, set out on a voyage of exploration to their " promised land " in the wild valley of the Black River. To realize the difficulties of the undertaking, the reader must bear in mind that the country they were in quest of lay far away from Albany in the depths of a howling wilderness, which had then never been visited by white men, except around its border, or when carried across it as prisoners in savage hands; that the only route to it was up the Mohawk, in batteaux, to Fort Stanwix, now the city of Rome; thence by the way of Wood Creek, the Oneida Lake, and the Oswego River to Lake Ontario, and from Lake Ontario up the unexplored route of the Black River. It was over the old Indian trail, the savage warpath of the French and Indian and of the Revolutionary wars, and even then there was threatened a general Indian war by all the tribes around our borders. But in the face of all these difficulties our explorers, in the autumn of 1793, set out for Castorland.

In describing their passage over the carrying place from Fort Stanwix to Wood Creek, near where the four busy tracks of the New York Central Railroad now run, they write in their journal, under date of October 10th: "Upon taking a walk into the woods a short distance we saw on every hand it was a fearful solitude. You are stopped sometimes by impassable swamps, and at other times by heaps of trees that have fallen from age or have been overthrown by storms, and among which an infinite number of insects and many squirrels find a retreat. On every hand we see the skeletons of trees overgrown with moss and in every stage of decay. The Capillaire and other plants and shrubs spring out of these trunks, presenting at once the images of life and death."

The fort at Oswego was still held by a British garrison. Jealous of Frenchmen, the commander at first refused to allow them to pàss into Lake Ontario, but it was finally arranged that Brunel should remain as a hostage for the good conduct and safe return of the others. Brunel, however, was refused access to the fort, and was ordered to encamp alone in the woods on the opposite side of the river. Considering that such treatment invalidated his parole, he escaped from Oswego disguised as a common sailor and proceeded with his friends on their expedition. They proceeded cautiously along the shore of the lake over the route that had become historic by the presence of M. de la Barre and his army in their visit to La Famine in 1684, and of Father Charlevoix in 1720, and which had so often been traversed by their countrymen in the palmy days of the old French occupancy, until their arrival at *Niaoure Bay*, now called Black River Bay. Here after a long search they discovered the mouth of the Black River, the great river that watered Castorland. But it was already so late in the sea-

21

son that they only explored the river up to a point some
five or six miles above the falls at Watertown, and then returned to Albany to complete their preparations for the
next year's journey.

VI.

THE SETTLEMENT OF CASTORLAND.

The next spring, being in the year 1794, the Desjardines
brothers and Pharoux, with a large company of men, with
their surveyors and assistants, took up their toilsome journey
from Schenectady to their forest possessions, being this time
fully equipped to begin their settlement. Their route this
year was up the Mohawk in batteaux to Fort Schuyler, now
Utica, thence overland across the Deerfield hills sixteen
miles, to the log house of Baron Steuben, who had then just
commenced his improvements upon his tract of sixteen
thousand acres given him by the state. From Steuben's
it was twenty-four miles further through the trackless forest
to the high falls on the Black River in Castorland.

At Fort Schuyler they found a small tavern surrounded
by a few other buildings, then constituting the whole of
what is now the city of Utica. In one of these buildings
there lived Peter Smith, the father of Gerrit Smith. This
tavern, which occupied the site of Bagg's hotel of to-day,
was kept by John Post. Our refined and sensitive Frenchmen do not speak in their journal in very complimentary
terms of the entertaiment they found there. But by
Baron Steuben they were received with all the gentle-
manly courtesy which so distinguished him, and by all the
marks of favor to which their rank and accomplishments
entitled them.

Upon the heights near Steuben's they obtained the first grand view of the Level Belt of the Northern Wilderness, that lay stretched out from their feet to the dimly distant border of the St. Lawrence. "Like Moses from Pisgah's summit," says Dr. Hough, "so they from the highest crest of the Steuben hills could see the level blue horizon of the distant Castorland, while the dusky lines of deeper shadows and brighter spots basking in the sunlight, spoke of happy valleys and sunny slopes in their future homes."*

The difficulties of the journey then still before them can scarcely be imagined by the reader of to-day. At length they reached their tract on the welcome banks of the Black River, and began their labors. But there is no space in these pages to follow them in all their operations, in their sore trials and their bitter disappointments, their final discomfiture and utter failure.

Suffice it to say that they began a little settlement on the banks of the Black River, at the place now called Lyons Falls. That they surveyed their lands and laid out one of their cities, Castorville, on the Beaver River, at a place now called Beaverton, opposite the little station now called Castorland, in memory of their enterprise. That they laid out their other city, the lake port, which they named "City of Basle," at what is now Dexter, below Watertown, and in 1795 they founded the present village of Carthage. That Pharoux was accidentally drowned in the river at Watertown in the fall of 1795. That Desjardines gave up the agency in despair in 1797, and was succeeded by Rodolphe Tillier, "Member of the Sovereign Council of Berne," who in turn gave place to Gouverneur Morris in 1800, and that

* Lecture at Lowville Academy, 1868.

the lands finally became the property of James Donatien,
Le Ray de Chaumont, his associates and grantees.

" After toils and many troubles, self-exile for many years,
 Long delays and sad misfortunes, man's regrets and woman's tears,
 Unfulfilled the brilliant outset, broken as a chain of sand,
 Were the golden expectations by *Grande Rapides'* promised land."

VII.

DEATH OF PIERRE PHAROUX.

One of the saddest incidents in the story of Castorland is
the death of Pharoux at the falls of Watertown, in 1795.
In September of that year, after the river had been swollen
by heavy rains, Pharoux set out with Brodhead, Tassart
and others, on a journey to Kingston, on the St. Lawrence.
In passing down the river upon a raft, they were drawn over
the falls.   Mr. Brodhead and three men were saved, but
Pharoux and all the others were drowned.   The survivors
made unremitting search for Pharoux's body, but it was not
found until the following spring.   It was washed ashore
upon an island at the mouth of the Black River, where it
was found by Benjamin Wright, the surveyor, and by him
decently buried there.   M. Le Ray de Chaumont many
years afterward caused a marble tablet to be set in the rock
near his grave, bearing this inscription:

To the Memory of
PETER PHAROUX,
This Island is Consecrated.

The reader will remember that the year before his death,
Pharoux had discovered and named the river Independence
in Castorland, and had selected a beautiful spot at its
mouth on the Black River, near a large flat granite rock, for

his residence. This spot, called by the Desjardines brothers Independence Rock, was ever afterward regarded by them with melancholy interest. They could not pass it without shedding tears to the memory of their long-tried and trusted friend. Under date of May 28th, 1796, Simon Desjardines, the elder brother, recorded in his journal: "Landed at half-past two at Independence Rock, and visited once more this charming spot which had been so beautifully chosen by our friend Pharoux as the site for his house. The azaleas in full bloom loaded the air with their perfume, and the wild birds sang sweetly around their nests, but nature has no longer any pleasant sights, nor fragrance, nor music, for me."

And now ancient Castorland may be added to the long list of names once famous in the cities of Europe, and long celebrated in the forest annals of Northern New York, but now forgotten, and found only in history and song.

CHAPTER XIX.

SISTERSFIELD.

That best portion of a good man's life,
His little, nameless, unremembered acts
Of kindness and of love.
—*Wordsworth*.

In ancient Castorland, about six miles above the village of Carthage, and on the easterly side of the Black River, there has long been a small deserted clearing, that is now, or but lately was, mostly overgrown with low scrubby pines, sweet ferns, and wild blackberry briars. This little clearing is situated directly opposite the mouth of the Deer River, a western branch of the Black River, which there enters it after tumbling down in a series of beautiful falls and cascades the limestone and slaty terraced hills of the eastern slope of the plateau of the Lesser Wilderness, in whose swamps and wild meadows it takes its rise.

Of the falls on the Deer River, the High Falls, about five miles above its mouth, near the village of Copenhagen, in the town of Denmark, are of exceptional height and beauty. The stream there plunges over a perpendicular precipice of one hundred and sixty-six feet in height into a deep, yawning chasm of more than a mile in length, whose perpendicular walls rise, upon one side, to the giddy height of two hundred and twenty-five feet. Two miles below the High Falls are the celebrated King's Falls, so named from the visit of Joseph Bonaparte, the ex-king of Spain, by whom they were much admired. The King's Falls are only about fifty feet in height, but they excel even the High Falls in their wild picturesque beauty.

Like many a similar place in the old Wilderness and around its borders, this little old deserted clearing has a long-forgotten history. It was once known as Sistersfield, and was for many years, at the beginning of the present century, the home of a French nobleman who was a refugee from the Reign of Terror in France, and whose name was Louis François de Saint-Michel.

Saint-Michel had been forester to Louis XVI. He was a tall, spare man of noble presence and courtly bearing, his dress, his manner, his whole appearance, indicating that he had been bred in the most polished society of Europe. His eye flashed a keen intelligence, but his French vivacity was tempered and softened down by a most fervent piety and a deep thoughtfulness. But his manners, though elegant, were not disdainful, and among his neighbors of the Black River valley, of New England lineage, he had many warm friends. Among them he never exhibited the ostentatious bearing and haughty speech, so often among the characteristics of the old nobility of France. Of those who represented that ancient but dissolving order, Saint-Michel, in an eminent degree, like Le Ray de Chaumont, displayed their virtues and graces unalloyed by their vices. Born and bred among the dazzling splendors of the French Court of the old *régime*, himself a participator in its most gorgeous pageants and imposing ceremonies, at the palace of the Tuilleries, in Paris, in the forests of Fontainebleau, and at the castles of Blois, the favorite homes of French royalty, it was the strange fortune of Saint-Michel to pass his declining years in the deep seclusion of this little clearing of Sis-

tersfield, in Castorland, that has been so long forgotten, on
the borders of the old Wilderness.

He was accompanied in his exile by an only daughter,
Sophie de Saint-Michel, who had been tenderly reared in
the schools of Paris. His wife had died in early woman-
hood, leaving this daughter an only child. After the death
of his wife, Saint-Michel placed his daughter at a convent
school in Paris. When the Revolution broke out he was
obliged to flee from France to save his life. On the eve
of his flight he called at the convent gate for his daughter.
She was brought to him in disguise, and with her he made
his escape from France and came to Castorland. In their
secluded forest home she applied herself to the duties of her
father's household with a self-sacrificing spirit that did
much to enliven the gloom of their solitude and to lighten
the sorrows of their situation.

Saint-Michel arrived in New York in 1798, and under-
took the management of Sistersfield, which was a tract of
twelve hundred acres belonging to three sisters, one named
Renée Jeane Louise, another Reine Marguerite, and the
third a Mrs. Blake, who were the daughters of Sieur Lam-
bot of Paris. On this tract of land called Sisterfield Saint-
Michel built an humble log cabin, on the bank of the Black
River, where he and his daughter lived for several years in
the greatest seclusion. His lonely hut was often the temporary resting place for the hunters and trappers of the
region, who were charmed with the exquisite grace and
beauty of his daughter, who, in spite of the tenderness with
which she had been reared, performed the menial duties of
her exiled father's household with a cheerfulness and resignation remarkable for one of her years. After awhile his

daughter married a Frenchman named Louis Marsile. Upon the marriage of his daughter, Saint-Michel accompanied her to her new home, which was a little south of the present village of Deer River, where he died about the year 1830.

But Sieur Saint-Michel found near him in his exile many congenial spirits, and many of the friends of his better days. Among his near neighbors in Castorland were several retired French army officers, and a few miles below Carthage, at Le Rayville, on the Black River, was the elegant château of James Donatien, Le Ray de Chaumont, another French nobleman, who was, as it before appears in these pages, largely identified with the landed interests of Northern New York. At Champion, a village five miles west of Carthage, lived Samuel A. Tallcott, who was afterward the eminent lawyer, and the Attorney General of the State for several years. At Le Rayville was Moss Kent, the brother of the Chancellor, and Father Pierre Joulin, the curé of Chaumont in France, who refused to take the constitutional oath, and was sent to America by M. de Chaumont, to save him from the guillotine. At the hospitable board of Sieur de Chaumont, Saint-Michel was always a most welcome guest, and there he often met many of the old *noblesse* of France, who were the cherished friends of his early years, and whom fickle fortune had, like himself, thrown in exile.

I have said that Saint-Michel was a man of fervent piety. He was so devout that he passed much of his time on his knees in prayer. After he was dead, the skin upon his knees was found to be callous—it was hardened to the bone by almost constant kneeling. But just before his death, he forgot his Latin, the language in which all his prayers

22

were said, and he mournfully told his attendants that he
could no longer pray.

And now, reader, as you pass on northerly from Castorland station, on the Utica and Black River Railroad, you
will soon come to the little station called Deer River.
When you arrive there, look to the eastward across the wide
interval meadows, and across the Black River, and about
half a mile from you, you will see the gently rising slope of
the old clearing in Sistersfield that was so long the forest
home of the noble Frenchman, the exiled Louis François
de Saint-Michel, one of the early settlers of Castorland.

CHAPTER XX.

JOHN BROWN'S TRACT.

The sounding cataract
Haunted me like a passion ; the tall rock,
The mountain and the deep and gloomy wood,
Their colors and their forms, were then to me
An appetite, a feeling and a love.
—*Wordsworth.*

I.

JOHN BROWN OF PROVIDENCE.

"John Brown's Tract" has long been a familiar generic name for the whole of the Great Wilderness, but John Brown's Tract proper comprises only a small part of the wilderness, lying on its western slope, near the head waters of the streams that flow into the Black River.

John Brown was one of the richest merchants and belonged to one of the oldest and most noted families of Providence, Rhode Island. He was born in the year 1736, and was a descendant of Rev. Chadd Brown, who was driven into Providence with Roger Williams in 1636. In 1772, John Brown led the party that destroyed the British schooner Gaspee in Narragansett Bay. For twenty years he was the treasurer of Brown University, named in honor of his family, and he laid the corner-stone of its edifice. In 1779 he was elected to the Continental Congress, and served therein two years. He is described as "a man of magnificent projects, and extraordinary enterprise." He was the first merchant in Providence who traded with China and the east. But even he failed to subdue the old wilderness.

In November, 1794, James Greenleaf, of New York

bought of Samuel Ward, then with William Constable, the
owner of the greater part of Macomb's Purchase, the tract
of land containing two hundred and ten thousand acres,
since known as John Brown's Tract.   It stretched entirely across the northern part of Herkimer county into
Hamilton on the east and into Lewis on the west.   The year
after his purchase, Greenleaf mortgaged the tract to Philip
Livingston, for the sum of $38,000.   He also gave a second
mortgage to John Brown and others, for large sums of
money.   Aaron Burr and John Julius Angerstein, the famous
Russian merchant and patron of the fine arts, of London,
also had some interest in this tract.   But Greenleaf failed
to keep up the payments, and in 1798 Livingston was obliged to foreclose his mortgage.   The whole tract was bid in
at the sale by John Brown for the sum of $33,000.

The next year, 1799, John Brown visited his tract, and
remained a part of the summer.   He caused it to be surveyed, and divided it into eight townships.   Number 1 he
called Industry; No. 2, Enterprise; No. 3, Perseverance;
No. 4, Unanimity; No. 5, Frugality; No. 6, Sobriety; No.
7, Economy; No. 8, Regularity.   He made a clearing on
No. 7, cut a road into it, built a grist-mill, saw-mill, and
several log houses.   In that year also, his agent, James
Sheldon, moved with his family on to the tract.   For two or
three years after, John Brown made toilsome journeys to his
forest possessions, but he died in 1803, leaving his tract a
wilderness.   In the expressive language of Thomas Sheldon,
a son of James, who was giving his testimony in open court,
in Lewis county, Justice Bacon presiding, in relation to this
tract, in a suit recently pending in the Supreme Court, in

which it was the subject in dispute :* "The tract was then a wilderness, and is now." These few words tell the whole story of Brown's Tract.

II.

THE HERRESHOFF MANOR.

Charles Frederick Herreshoff was a son-in-law of John Brown. He married a daughter of John Brown, the widow Francis, the mother of John Brown Francis, afterward Governor of Rhode Island.

About the year 1812 Herreshoff went on to this tract. He cleared over two thousand acres, built thirty or forty new buildings, drove in cattle and a flock of three hundred merino sheep. He built a forge and opened and worked a mine of iron ore. He spent his own fortune there and all the money that he could borrow from his friends. But the rugged old Wilderness would not be subdued. When he entered the forest he made this declaration to a friend : " I will settle the tract or settle myself." He settled himself. In December, 1819, his money was all gone and his friends had deserted him. One day, in a fit of utter despondency, he went out of his dwelling to a lonely spot on the tract that had been so long the scene of his fruitless endeavors, and ended his life by a pistol shot.

Herreshoff was a Prussian by birth. He was over six feet in height, well-formed, and of commanding presence. He was a man of great energy and perseverance, of high culture, and the most engaging manners, but extremely

*John Brown Francis vs. Marshal Shedd, Jr., and others. Edward A. Brown, of counsel for plaintiff: Charles D. Adams, of counsel for defendants.

proud and aristocratic. He was somewhat visionary in his
schemes, and not so well adapted to the settlement of a new
country as many men of less enterprise. After all his
efforts he made but one ton of iron at his forge. Every
pound of it cost him more than a dollar in gold. His wife
did not approve of his forest undertaking, and never went
on to the tract. Herreshoff was fond of calling his settlement "The Manor." Like Gilliland, he had dreams of a
magnificent baronial estate rising in feudal grandeur in the
wild American forest, like those more favored ones along
the Hudson—himself its princely lord. At his grave in
Boonville, Oneida county, is a modest marble slab, bearing
this inscription :

CHARLES

FREDERICK

HERRESHOFF.

OBIIT DEC. 19,

1819,

ÆTAT 50.

III.

ARNOLD'S.

After the failure and death of Herreshoff, his little settlement was soon deserted by his tenantry, and went swiftly
into decay and ruin. The deserted dwellings were sometimes the temporary resting places of the wandering hunter
or trapper, and sometimes the homes of the wild beasts and
birds of the forest. It was not until about the year 1832
that the premises were again more permanently occupied.
In that year the old Herreshoff manor was leased to the
famous hunter and trapper, Nathaniel Foster, who moved

on with his family, and took possession of the wild forest retreat. But Foster's unfortunate affair with the Indian Drid rendered it unsafe, in his opinion, for him to remain thus exposed to the vengeful rifles of Drid's relatives, and so he removed from the tract, after remaining but three or four years. The tourist is now shown the grave of Drid, not far from the old forge, and the point at the bend of the river where he was shot by Foster is known as Indian Point.

After Foster had retired from the scene another hunter went in with his family, to reside there, whose name was Otis Arnold. Arnold moved in about the year 1837, with his wife and one child, and took possession of the old Herreshoff house. Here he lived and raised a large family of children, keeping a sort of forest hostelry, until his death in 1868.

In the autumn of 1855, the Hon. Amelia M. Murray, maid of honor to Queen Victoria, while making a tour of the United States and Canada, went through the lake belt of the wilderness, over the route described in a former chapter. Her companions were Gov. Horatio Seymour, the Governor's neice, and other friends. On their way they stopped, of course, at Arnold's. But I will let the Lady Amelia tell the story in her own words, as written in her diary, under date of September 20th, 1855 : "Mr. Seymour remained to make arrangements with the guides, while his neice and I walked on to Arnold's farm. There we found Mrs. Arnold and six daughters. These girls, aged from twelve to twenty, were placed in a row against one wall of the shanty, with looks so expressive of astonishment, that I felt puzzled to account for their manner, till their mother informed us they had never before seen any other woman than herself! I could not elicit a word from them, but, at last, when I begged for a little milk, the eldest went and brought me a glass. I then remembered that we had met a single hunter rowing himself on the Moose River, who called out, 'Where on 'arth do they women come from?' And our after experience fully explained why ladies are such rare birds in that locality."

But Arnold's life went out in a dark tragedy that stained the old wilderness with human blood once more. In September, 1868, in a fit of uncontrollable anger, occasioned by a quarrel with him about a dog collar, he shot and killed a guide named James Short, of Warrensburgh, Essex Co., who was resting at the forge. But instant remorse succeeded his anger. Proceeding to Nick's Lake, a favorite resort of his near by, he filled his pockets with stones, and tied a large one to his neck. He then stepped into his hunting boat, and paddling out into the middle of the lake, plunged into its clear, cold waters to rise no more. In view of Otis Arnold's long and blameless life, and of his thousand acts of kindness to many a wanderer in the forest, who can help but wish it were possible to throw, in some way, the mantle of charity over his dreadful crime.

And now, after writing all this of the famous John Brown's Tract, in this our country's Centennial year, all that can be said of it may still be summed up in the expressive words of Sheldon on the witness stand: "The tract was then a wilderness, and is now."

CHAPTER XXI.

THE HUNTER FOSTER AND THE INDIAN DRID.

The hunting tribes of air and earth
Respect the brethren of their birth;
Nature, who loves the claim of kind
Less cruel chase to each assigned.
The falcon poised on soaring wing
Watches the wild-duck by the spring;
The slow-hound wakes the fox's lair,
The greyhound presses on the hare;
The eagle pounces on the lamb,
The wolf devours the fleecy dam;
E'en tiger fell, and sullen bear
Their likeness and their lineage spare.
Man, only, mars kind nature's plan,
And turns the fierce pursuit on man.
                              —*Sir Walter Scott.*

I.

NATHANIEL FOSTER.

Nathaniel Foster has long been known in forest story as one of the most famous hunters and trappers of the Great Wilderness. Like Nicholas Stoner and Jonathan Wright, Foster belonged to a race of hunters and trappers that has long since passed away. They were men of iron mould who had survived the savage Indian warfare of the Revolution with bitter remembrance of its cruel massacres and burning dwellings. They frequented the forest partly to obtain a subsistence, but more from that wild love of it which is the sure out-come of a familiarity with its trials and dangers in its savage state. The Indians left their famous beaver hunting country, their old *Couch-sach-ra-ge*, with the greatest reluctance. Long after the Revolution, and for many of the early years of the present century, they made, singly or in bands, annual visits to their ancient hunting grounds. Although not always hostile, they disputed the favorite haunts of the beaver, the moose and the deer

23

inch by inch with the white hunters. And in the secluded depths of the old forest there was many a desperate encounter between the single white hunter and the lone Indian, in which only one lived to tell the tale, or more often to die afterward with the awful secret in his bosom.

Like the forest ranger of the Canadian woods and waters, the hunter of the olden time, by his years of "bush-ranging," had become spoiled for civilization, and, like him, had become in a great measure the adopted child of nature. For him the voice of Nature, as she has for us all, had a wild, sweet charm that drew him irresistibly into her savage haunts. "Rude as he was," says Parkman, of the Canadian forest ranger—the *coureur de bois*—" her voice [Nature's,] may not always have been meaningless for one who knew her haunts so well ; deep recesses where, veiled in foliage, some wild shy rivulet steals with timid music through breathless caves of verdure, * * or the stern depths of immemorial forests, dim and silent as a cavern columned with innumerable trunks, each like an Atlas, upholding its world of leaves and sweating perpetual moisture down its dark and channelled rind; some strong in youth, some grisly with decrepit age, nightmares of strange distortion, gnarled and knotted with wens and goitres ; roots intertwined beneath, like serpents petrified in an agony of distorted strife ; green and glistening mosses carpeting the rough ground mantling the rocks, turning pulpy stumps to mounds of verdure, and swathing fallen trunks, as bent in the impotence of rottenness they lie outstretched over knoll and hollow, like mouldering reptiles of the primeval world, while around and on and through them springs the young growth that fattens on their decay,—the forest devouring its own dead." Such were the forest scenes with which the old hunters were the most familiar in their daily vocation.

Nathaniel Foster was born in what is now Vernon, Windham county, Vt., in 1767. At the age of twenty-four he married Miss Jemima, the daughter of Amos Streeter, of New Hampshire, and emigrated to Salisbury, Herkimer county, then nearly surrounded by the old wilderness. Wild game was exceedingly plentiful there at that time, and being eager in the pursuit of it, he soon became a famous hunter and trapper. Volumes almost have been written of his daring exploits in the forest. He was nearly six feet in height, his frame was well-knit, large and muscular. His features were strongly marked, his eyes dark, his hair a sandy brown, and his countenance sallow. From the days of his boyhood Foster had nursed a deadly hatred of the Indian, and marvelous stories are told of the numbers slain by him during his long career in the forest.

In the year 1832, game becoming scarce around his home in the Mohawk valley, Foster removed with his family to the long deserted Herreshoff Manor, where he could be nearer his congenial haunts.

II.

DRID.

Foster's only neighbors on the tract were three bachelor hunters, named William S. Wood, David Chase and Willard Johnson, and a St. Regis Indian, whose real name was Peter Waters, but who always, in the forest, went by the name of Drid. Drid was a morose, quarrelsome Indian, who often threatened Foster's life, although Foster and his family had

done him many acts of kindness.   Upon one occasion, when
they had been debating about something, Drid said to
Foster:

"There is no law here.   If I kill you, I kill you, and if
you kill me, you kill me."

"I will not make any such bargain as that," replied Foster.   "I do not wish to harm you, and you have no reason
to feel like that toward me."

On another occasion Drid was heard to say, "Me got a
bad heart.   Me put a bullet through old Foster."

At length, on the morning of the 17th day of September,
1833, Foster and Drid had another encounter, in which
Drid attempted to take Foster's life.   They were separated
by the hunters present, but not until Drid had severely cut
Foster's arm with his knife in attempting to stab him to the
heart.

In the course of an hour after this, Drid started up the
river in his canoe, bound for the lakes, in the company of
two white hunters, who were in their own boat.   After Drid
had left, Foster took down his trusty rifle, and taking an
overland course on foot across a bend in the river, reached
a point on the stream about two miles above the Forge, before Drid arrived there.   Stepping down to the edge of the
bank, and pointing his rifle through the bushes that thickly
lined the shore, Foster shot Drid through the heart as Drid
was paddling his canoe past the spot where Foster stood.
In killing Drid, Foster shot between the two white hunters
as they passed along between him and the Indian, one
sitting in each end of their boat.   But Foster made no mis-
takes with his unerring rifle.   Foster then hastened homeward by the way he came.   The two hunters also returned

at once in their boat to the Forge, and when they arrived
at Foster's home they found Foster lying quietly in his bed
as if nothing had happened..

But Foster was arrested, indicted, and tried for the murder of Drid.   His trial came on at the Herkimer Oyer and
Terminer in September, 1834, Justice Hiram Denio of the
Circuit Court, presiding, and Jonas Cleland, John B. Dygert, Abijah Osborn, and Richard Herendeen, Judges of the
Common Pleas, sitting to form the court.   James B. Hunt,
the District Attorney, and Simeon Ford, were for the
people, and E. P. Hurlbut, Joshua A. Spencer, A. Hack-
ley, and Lauren Ford of counsel for the defence.   The trial
excited unusual interest, and the court room was crowded
from day to day as it progressed.   The prosecution proved
to the jury the facts of the killing as above set forth, and
rested the case.   The counsel for the prisoner offered in
evidence the several previous threats made by Drid against
the life of Foster.   His Honor the presiding judge and
Judge Dygert were of the opinion that the threats made
previous to the homicide were not admissable.   But, for the
first time in his life, Judge Denio found himself over-ruled
by the Judges of the Common Pleas.   The other three
judges, being a majority of the court, admitted the evidence,
and the case was given to the jury.   After but two hours'
deliberation, the jury returned into court with a verdict of
not guilty.

Foster, overcome by the excitement, when the jury came
in, was almost insensible.   But when the words *not guilty*
fairly struck his senses, he rose to his full height, and
stretching out his arms wide over the heads of the silent
spectators, exclaimed "God bless you all!   God bless the

people!" Then rushing out of the court room, he bestrode his well-known hunter's pony, and rode away to his home in the forest.

But Foster dare not remain long on Brown's Tract, lest the relatives of Drid should seek to revenge his death. Yet the friends of Drid never troubled Foster. They came down from St. Regis and took Drid's widow and children back with them to their home on the St. Lawrence. As for Drid, they said "He was a bad Indian. Let him go."

Foster removed with his family to Boonville, Oneida Co., and from there to the forest wilds of Northern Pennsylvania, where he again for a time followed his favorite pursuits. But his mind never seemed quite at rest after killing Drid. He at length returned from Pennsylvania to Boonville, but he dare not venture out of doors in the dark. Foster died in Boonville, in March, 1841, aged 74 years.*

* Trappers of New York, by Jeptha R. Simms.

CHAPTER XXII.

SMITH'S LAKE.

Since in each scheme of life I've failed,
And disappointment seems entail'd;
Since all on earth I valu'd most,
My guide, my stay, my friend is lost.
O Solitude, now give me rest,
And hush the tempest in my breast;
O gently deign to guide my feet
To your hermit-trodden seat;
Where I may live at last my own,
Where I may die at last unknown.
—*Grainger.*

In most countries, and in all ages of the world there have been men who, actuated by some motive or other, have lived apart from the society of their fellows, and led lonely lives in desert places. In tracing from memory and tradition what little is known of the solitary lives of the hermit hunters of the Great Wilderness, it will be seen that our own country is no exception to this rule. Of some of these hermit hunters, traditions still remain along the borders of their exploits in the chase, of the motives which incited them to abandon the world, of their manner of life, of their sufferings and death.

One of the most charming lakes in the Lake Belt of the Wilderness is Smith's Lake. It lies at the head waters of the Beaver River, in the county of Hamilton, about ten miles as the crow flies north of Raquette Lake, and four miles to the west of Little Tupper's Lake. Ten miles to the north of it, lies Cranberry Lake, on the Oswegatchie, in St. Lawrence county, and ten miles westerly are the lakes of the Red Horse chain, while between it and the Raquette is Beach's Lake. Smith's Lake is now frequented mostly by hunting parties that approach it from Lowville, a station on the Utica and Black River Railroad, on the western side of the wilderness. On the borders of this lake are several hunting lodges. Deer are still abundant in its vicinity, and brook trout abound in all the waters near it. There is no place in the whole wilderness more secluded than this, and none where more game can be found.

Some time about the year 1830, a hunter named David Smith took up his abode on the shore of this lake in what was then and for many years afterward an unfrequented and pathless forest. Smith was one of those brooding "problematic characters," whom we sometimes meet and who we often think belong to that land which borders on the realms of insanity. This border land is, I fear, broader than we think for, and is more thickly peopled than many of us will readily admit. It is said that in early life Smith married a wife whom he tenderly loved and cared for, but who died shortly after their marriage. Her untimely death sent him a hermit into the depths of this forest, where he could brood in solitude and silence over his great grief. About the year 1820, while the first settlers at Number Four were beginning their little clearings near Beaver Lake, Smith pushed on up the river twelve miles further and built his first rude shanty at Stillwater, which became long afterward the hermitage of James O'Kane. At Stillwater, for some ten years, Smith lived a solitary life, being its first inhabitant, and followed his occupation as a hunter and trapper. At length, about 1830, Stillwater became too much frequented by hunting and fishing parties, and Smith again went further up the river, and settled at the lake which has since borne his name. Stillwater was then without a per-

manent occupant until James O'Kane took up his abode
there. Smith made on the border of this wild lake a little
clearing, wherein he raised a few potatoes, and in which he
built a rude log shanty for his habitation. In this secluded
spot he spent much of his time in hunting and fishing, and
in fitting up a sort of rude museum of the stuffed skins of
the wild animals and birds which he had contrived to catch.
In the Summer he would sometimes take his little collec-
tion into the back settlements for exhibition. On such occasions his appearance was wild and grotesque in the extreme. Clad in skins with the fur outward, and hardly to
be distinguished from a wild animal himself, he often exhibited with much skill, on a sort of revolving framework
which he had made, his well preserved specimens of moose,
deer, bears, foxes, wolves, wildcats and birds. During the
extreme cold of winter, when game was scarce and it was
difficult to reach the settlements through the deep snows,
he sometimes suffered from the want of provisions and
other necessaries. On one occasion he accidentally choked
himself while eating a piece of moose meat, and being unable to remove the obstruction, went out, with infinite pain
and labor, a distance of forty miles, to Fenton's at Number
Four, before he found relief. He could breathe, but could
not swallow, and nearly perished from hunger.

For fifteen years he lived this wild hermit life, pursuing
his favorite vocation as a hunter and trapper, unmolested
in his far away forest home. But when the fishing and
hunting parties from the outer world began to find their
way in to his lake, Smith left his no longer secluded hiding
place in disgust at what he considered their intrusion upon
his solitude. It is said that he sought another congenial
24

home in the far west, and has never since been heard
of. His little clearing is now thickly covered with a luxuriant growth of young forest trees, among which his lonely
deserted hearthstone is crumbling into ruins. But the
beautiful lake on whose shores he spent so many years, still
commemorates his name. If the heart-history of this
brooding lover of solitude, this hermit hunter of the wilderness, could be written, it would doubtless move us to
pity his sorrows and to drop the mantle of charity over his
eccentricities.

CHAPTER XXIII.

NUMBER FOUR.

How the sacred calm that breathes around
  Bids every fierce tumultuous passion cease,
In still small accents whispering from the ground
  A grateful earnest of eternal peace.

There scattered oft, the earliest of the year,
  By hands unseen, are showers of violets found,
The red-breast loves to build and warble there,
  And little footsteps lightly print the ground.
        —Rejected verses of Gray's Elegy.

I.

One of the oldest and most frequented places of forest resort in the Great Wilderness, on its western border, is Number Four, in Brown's Tract.

The Beaver River, which flows from Smith's Lake, near the Raquette, passes in its course through Brown's Tract, and on township Number Four spreads out into Beaver Lake, which lies within a mile of Lake Francis. Lake Francis was so called in honor of Gov. John Brown Francis, a proprietor of the tract.

There is not a lake in the whole wilderness more beautiful than Beaver Lake, as seen from Fenton's, near by, in the soft hazy light of a sultry August day. Surrounded by its deeply indented, thickly wooded shores, it then appears like a pool of liquid amber, sleeping in an emerald basin. It is a sweet picture of repose, typifying that sense of perfect rest which steals over us nowhere else but in the deep stillness of the woods and fields, far away from the ceaseless din of crowded cities.

Since the settlement of the Black River valley, at the beginning of the present century, Number Four at Beaver

Lake has been one of the favorite resorts of hunters and fishermen and summer pleasure-seekers. In the month of June, 1818, the first fishing party visited Beaver Lake. This party consisted of Charles Dayan, Cornelius Low, Russell Parish, Heman Stickney, Otis Whipple and Samuel Rogers, with Thomas Puffer as guide. Some of these men afterward became distinguished in the councils of the state and nation. They encamped for eight days at the " Fish Hole," near the inlet of the lake at the mouth of a little stream which they named Sunday Brook, in memory of the first day of their encampment there. The next year Ziba Knox, Alexander W. Stow and James T. Watson encamped for a week at Beaver Lake. These were the pioneers of the long succession of visitors, who, for nearly fifty years have every summer sought relief from cankering care in the innocent abandon of this wild forest retreat.

But Number Four, like many another place in the old wilderness, has been the scene of a fruitless attempt at settlement. The first settler at Number Four was Ephraim Craft, who followed in the trail of the first fishing parties in the year 1820, and began his clearing on the west side of Beaver River beyond Fenton's, on what is now called the Champlain road. No signs of this early clearing now remain.

In the year 1822, Gov. John Brown Francis, of Rhode Island, had succeeded his grandfather, John Brown, in the ownership of township Number Four. For the purpose of effecting a settlement of his lands, Gov. Francis offered a deed of one hundred acres each as a gift to the first ten settlers on township Number Four near Beaver Lake. Attracted by this inducement, ten men accepted his offer, and ten families soon moved in, began their clearings, built their log houses, planted their first crops, and commenced in earnest the life of pioneers in the wilderness. Saw-mills were soon built, various improvements were made, and in a few years more than a thousand acres were cleared and fenced off into farms and gardens. A schoolhouse was built, and a little school of more than sixty scholars gathered in. Within ten years after the first clearing was made some seventy-five settlers were trying their fortunes at Number Four.

But it is the old sad story of the wilderness that will not be tamed by man. The soil was none of the best; the climate was cold, the summers were short, and the winters were long; the markets were distant, and the roads to them through the forest were almost impassible during much of the year. One by one the settlers, growing weary of the undertaking, sold out their improvements or abandoned them, and with their families left the forest hamlet, to seek other homes, until within twenty-five years after the first house was built, only three families were left at Number Four. These three remaining families were those of Isaac Wetmore, Chauncey Smith and Orrin Fenton. Chauncey Smith has long been a famous hunter and trapper, and is still living there at an advanced age. Isaac Wetmore died there in 1853, and was buried in the little burial place now overgrown with bushes and brambles near his former home. And now the old dwellings, with two or three exceptions, have all disappeared, the schoolhouse and its children are no longer to be seen there. The fences are gone, and the once cleared fields are fast reverting to their original forest state.

II.

No one of the many settlers of Number Four became so identified with its history as Orrin Fenton. Fenton moved to Number Four with his family in the year 1826, and lived there nearly forty years. For many years Fenton's house became, from necessity, there being few other accommodations, a forest hostelry, open for the entertainment of the hunters and pleasure seekers who so often visited the region. Many a tired and half famished traveller remembers with gratitude how, after a day's tramp in the woods, he received the kindly attentions of Fenton's welcome fireside, presided over so gracefully by his busy wife. Should this page meet the eye of any who visited "Fenton's" in days gone by, many a pleasing reminiscence will be called up, and many a savory repast of delicious trout and venison, cooked and served as no one but Mrs. Fenton could cook and serve them, will be remembered.

But Fenton at length, like the other settlers at Number Four, sold out his forest home and reluctantly left it to reside there no more. The person to whom he sold it, however, kept the place but a few years, and now it is owned by Mr. Fenton's son Charles, who, as his father did, now keeps there a famous forest hostelry, overlooking Beaver Lake in its wild enchanting beauty.

"Fenton—who shall or can," says W. Hudson Stephens in his *Historical Notes*, "chronicle the experiences of his heart-life of forty years in the wilderness. In the memory of how many a laborer and wanderer is his cheerful, tidy home treasured, and the kindly attention of his forest resort recalled with grateful recollections. Amid such scenes of wild beauty the genius of a Wordsworth was roused into active utterance of the melody of 'a heart grown holier as it traced the beauty of the world below.' The silence and solitude of the northern forest has had its charms for him. Who will say his heart's earlier aspirations have not been as effectually satisfied in the solitudes of the uncultivated forest as if he had moved amid the busy haunts of the crowded city? This sportsman by land and stream, this forest farmer, looks back upon woodland scene and experience with sighs. How true that while hope writes the poetry of the boy, memory writes that of the man,"

CHAPTER XXIV.

JAMES O'KANE.

O Solitude, romantic maid !
Whether by nodding towers you tread,
Or haunt the desert's trackless gloom,
Or hover o'er the yawning tomb ;
Or climb the Andes' clifted side,
Or by the Nile's coy source abide ;
Or, starting from your half-year's sleep,
From Hecla view the thawing deep ;
Or at the purple dawn of day,
Tadmor's marble waste survey ;
    You, recluse again I woo,
    And again your steps pursue.
            —*Grainger.*

On the Beaver River, in the depths of the forest, twelve miles above Number Four, is a hunter's shantying ground, long known as Stillwater, but sometimes now called Wardwell's.

The first occupant of this old hunting station was David Smith, afterward known as the hermit of Smith's Lake, many miles further up the river. The first ten years of Smith's hermit life were passed in this spot, but the early fishing parties coming in, disturbed his seclusion, and he went further up the river, where he could find a still deeper solitude.

Ten years or more after Smith left Stillwater, about the year 1844, another hermit of the woods took up his abode there, named James, or as he was always familiarly called Jimmy O'Kane. For twelve years his shanty stood on the banks of Twitchell Creek, a confluent of the Beaver River at Stillwater, near the old Champlain road that leads from Number Four past Raquette Lake. In solitude and alone lived Jimmy all these weary years amid the dreary scene.

Jimmy lived mostly by hunting and fishing, but as he grew old and feeble he was too clumsy a hunter to take many deer, although they were numerous on his hunting-ground, and so he depended mostly on smaller game and fish. His method of preserving game and laying in supplies was a model one, in its way, for convenience and economy. He kept in his shanty what he called his "poultry barrel." In this he salted down indiscriminately all the small animals and birds he could catch. In times of scarcity his poultry barrel was his never-failing resource. He was, however, generally well supplied with better food, and was always hospitably inclined to all the passing hunters.

Why Jimmy thus absented himself from "the haunts and the converse of men" and voluntarily chose this mode of life, still remains a mystery. Whether he became disgusted with the trials and vexations always incident to this poor life of ours, with the perfidy of man or the frailty of woman, or whether he sought in the retirement and seclusion of the wilderness the opportunity for that meditation on things spiritual and eternal which he deemed necessary for his soul's repose, or whether he was an ardent student of nature, and loved to gaze upon the brightness of silver waters, the loveliness of the wild flower, or upon the grandeur of forest scenery, rocks, hills, mountains, lakes and streams stretching afar off from his solitary home, or whether the sports of the chase were his only solace, must be left to the conjecture of the curious observer of the changing vagaries of the human heart. A worn copy of "The Gospels" and a work on the "Piscatory Art" constituted his scanty library. His only constant companions were his dog and gun. He was the owner of several small boats that he

25

would sometimes let to passing hunters on their way to Smith's Lake, and many a frequenter of the wilderness remembers with pleasure the night spent under Jimmy's protecting roof.

But at length he grew so old and feeble that he was no longer able to hunt and fish, and he depended for his subsistence mostly upon the generosity of passing sportsmen, who always kept him well supplied with food.

In the month of May, 1857, I passed his hermitage on my way to the lakes beyond. He was then quite feeble from disease and exposure. It was the first day of the spring in which he had been able to crawl out to the bridge across the creek, and set his poles for fish. In December following he grew worse, and on the first day of the new year he died, aged about seventy years. His body was found lying on his rude bed, near the fire-place, his head and shoulders somewhat elevated, his cap drawn over his eyes, and his hands crossed upon his breast.

> " He passed from earth, breathing a prayer,
>   Far from the world's rude voices, far away ;
>   Oh ! hear and judge him gently ; 't was his last.

> " I come alone, and faint I come,
>   To Nature's arms I flee ;
>   The green woods take their wanderer home,
>   But Thou, O Father ! may I turn to Thee ?"

While the busy throngs of crowded cities were reveling in the gay festivities which ushered in the " glad New Year," Jimmy, sick and alone upon his couch in the far-off forest wilds heard a footstep upon the threshold of his shanty door, and the " King of Terrors" stood before him. He pulled his cap down over his face, and was softly carried across the dark waters.

The incoming of the New Year was followed by one of those terriffic storms of wind and snow so common in the wilderness. When the storm cleared away, some passing hunters, seeing no smoke issuing from Jimmy's chimney, opened his shanty door and found him "Dead, dead and alone."

On the 5th day of the month a party of men waded through the deep snow from Watson, near thirty miles away, to bury the dead hunter. They laid him to rest upon a bluff near his cabin which he had himself selected, the year before, for his burial place. To mark the spot they erected a rude wooden monument at the head and a boat paddle at the foot of his solitary grave. For this kindly deed, their names are worthy of remembrance. The men who thus buried him were Elder Elihu Robinson, Ex-Sheriff Peter Kirley, Joseph Garmon, William Glenn, E. Harvey, Thomas Kirley, F. Robinson and Aretas Wetmore. Thus lived, died, and was buried one of the hermit hunters of the Great Wilderness.

CHAPTER XXV.

JAMES T. WATSON.

It suffices. What suffices?
  All suffices reckoned rightly;
Spring shall bloom where now the ice is,
  Roses make the bramble sightly,
  And the quickened sun shine brightly,
  And the latter wind blow lightly,
And my garden teem with spices.
                —*Christina Rossetti.*

I.

At the close of the last century and the beginning of the present, large grants of land, from time to time, were made by the state to speculators in wild lands. The largest of these grants in Northern New York was Macomb's Purchase. This vast tract lay in the angle between the St. Lawrence River and Lake Ontario. It embraced almost the whole of Franklin, St. Lawrence, Jefferson and Lewis counties, with a part of Herkimer. It contained 3,816,660 acres. The purchase was made on the 10th of January, 1792, and the price was eight pence an acre. Alexander Macomb, Daniel McCormick and William Constable were equally interested in this purchase. But soon after the purchase Macomb became insolvent, and Constable became the principal owner of the tract. William Constable served honorably in the war of the Revolution as the aid-de-camp of Gen. La Fayette. After the war he was extensively engaged in commercial pursuits in New York, London and Paris. Since Macomb's purchase fell into his hands, he and his family have been largely identified with the landed interests of Northern New York.

Of these grants, another of the largest and best known is Totten and Crossfield's Purchase. This great purchase was made before the Revolution, and comprises a large part of the mountain and lake belts of the wilderness. Among the numerous ones that lie between the borders of Totten and Crossfield's Purchase and the settlements, but still mostly in the virgin wilderness, are two tracts of land lying on its western border, known as Watson's East and West Triangles, which were a part of Macomb's Purchase.

These two large tracts of land lie on the western slope of the Level Belt of the Wilderness, in the counties of Lewis and Herkimer. The East Triangle lies in the extreme northern part of Herkimer county, near the Oswegatchie Ponds, and borders on the Totten and Crossfield Purchase. It is one of the wildest and most unfrequented regions of the whole wilderness. The West Triangle lies in the eastern part of Lewis county, on the border of the settlement, and westerly of township number four of Brown's Tract. The two tracts are not contiguous, but are connected by a narrow tongue of land that extends between them. The westerly corner of the West Triangle has much of it been cleared and settled, and lies not far from the Black River.

II.

No sadder story is to be found in forest annals than that of James Talcott Watson, the owner of these tracts. His father, James Watson, who was a rich merchant of New York at the time of and after the Revolution, purchased of William Constable, the owner of Macomb's Purchase, in the year 1796, the tracts above described, containing sixty-one

thousand four hundred and thirty-three acres. It was the
West Triangle which is mostly watered by the Independence
River and its branches, that his only son, the James T.
Watson above named, made an attempt to settle. His
father dying in 1809, left him the sole heir to these large
tracts of land in the old wilderness.

Like Gilliland on the Boquet River, like Herreshoff on
the Moose River, like Arthur Noble on the head waters of
the East Canada Creek, young Watson attempted to found
a great landed estate on the River Independence, in what
is now the town of Watson, where he could live in something like the old baronial splendor, surrounded by numerous dependents, and dispensing in his mansion house a
generous hospitality. Like his father, in early life, Watson
was a wealthy merchant of New York, being a member of
the firm of Thomas L. Smith & Co., East India traders, in
which capacity he once made a voyage to China.

He was a man of high culture, of poetic fancy, and of
wonderful conversational powers. To these were added a
playful wit, the most engaging manners, and a kind and
tender heart. But over all this was cast a deep shadow that
blasted at once his hopes and his life. " The death of a
Miss Livingston," says Dr. Hough, "with whom he was
engaged to be married, induced a mental aberration which
continued through life, being more aggravated at certain
seasons of the year, while at others it was scarcely percepti-
ble. In after life, the image of the loved and lost often
came back to his memory, like the sunbeam from a broken
mirror, and in his waking reveries he was heard to speak of
her as present in the spirit, and a confidant of his inmost
thoughts." Laboring thus under this mild type of insanity,

in his social life and business transactions he often evinced strange caprices. At one time he planted a large vegetable garden at his mansion house, not far from the banks of the Independence, so late in the season that no mature crop could be expected from it. His remark was "that if the seeds sprouted well he should be satisfied, as that would prove the capacity of his land." He sometimes gave the most brilliant entertainments at his country seat above referred to, and was always a most welcome guest in the cultivated and refined social circles of the neighboring villages of the valley of the Black River.

But the memory of the loved and lost haunted him continually like a wild sweet passion, and his life was spent in violent fluctuations between the most lively and pleasurable excitement and the deepest despair. At length, in the year 1839, in a fit of the deepest melancholy, in which his gentle spirit seemed utterly beyond relief from any human sympathy, he ended his own life at the age of fifty years. Let us hope that he found his soul's idol on the other side of the river he so rashly crossed. His large tracts of land are still mostly covered by their original woods.

CHAPTER XXVI.

LAKE BONAPARTE.

By sinuous shore the baying hound
Tells the stag seeks on silver sands
Diana's mirror ; here is found
One of *Endymion's* haunted lands.

The lilies that on thy glowing breast
Loll languidly in crowns of gold,
Were pure Evangels speaking rest
Unto an Exile's heart of old.
—*Caleb Lyon of Lyonsdale.*

I.

ITS SITUATION.

Upon the north-western border of the Level Belt of the Wilderness in the town of Diana, Lewis county, and near the St. Lawrence county line is the beautiful Lake Bonaparte. It covers about twelve hundred acres of surface ; its shores are rugged and picturesque ; it is studded with wild rocky islands, and its waters are as clear and bright as those of the Loch Lomond or the Loch Katrine so famous in Scottish story. This lake was named in honor of Joseph Bonaparte, ex-king of Naples and of Spain, the brother of the great Napoleon.

In the year 1815, Joseph, under the assumed name of Count de Survilliers, purchased a large tract of wild land of his friend Le Ray de Chaumont, for a summer hunting park, lying around and including this lake. The tract so purchased contained 150,260 acres. It is said that Napoleon at the time of the purchase intended to accompany his brother Joseph in his flight to America, and to settle upon these lands. The scheme of the Bonapartes was to found large manufacturing establishments in the valley of the Black River, and thus become England's rival in her most important interests. This subject was once discussed at a dinner given by M. de Chaumont, at his château near the Black River, in honor of a son of Marshal Murat, then M. de Chaumont's guest. But Napoleon concluded to remain, and the valley of the Black River lost the honor of receiving an imperial visitor.

II.

COUNT DE CHAUMONT.

No man in its annals is more intimately associated with the settlement and development of Northern New York, except perhaps William Constable, than James Donatien Le Ray, Comte de Chaumont, of whom Joseph Bonaparte made this purchase. Le Ray de Chaumont belonged to the old nobility of France. When the war of the American Revolution broke out his father espoused the cause of the colonists with such ardor that he devoted the most of his large fortune to their interests. It was at the elegant château of the elder Count de Chaumont in his park at Passy that Franklin so long resided while he was our commissioner at the French Court.

Soon after the war James D. Le Ray de Chamount came to America to settle his father's accounts. While here he was induced by his friend, Gouverneur Morris, to purchase large tracts of land in Northern New York. M. de Chamount also bought, with his associate, the Count de la Forest, the Consul General of France, a smaller tract in Otsego county, to which they sent Judge Cooper, the father of J. Fennimore Cooper, the novelist, to be their agent.

26

At one time M. de Chamount owned thirty thousand seven hundred and fifty-eight acres of land in Franklin county, seventy-three thousand nine hundred and forty seven in St. Lawrence, one hundred and forty-three thousand five hundred in Jefferson, and one hundred thousand in Lewis county. About the year 1808 he came with his family to reside at his château at Le Rayville, near the Black River, some ten miles easterly of Watertown. This château, which may still be seen standing, was for many years the seat of a most refined and elegant hospitality. Kings, princes, courtiers and noblemen were his frequent guests. Thus a ray of sunshine from the most polished court in Europe had fallen suddenly among the shadowy pines of the old American forest. It was while traveling in France in the year 1815, that M. de Chamount heard that Joseph Bonaparte had arrived in his flight at the city of Blois. M. de Chaumont, who had known him intimately in his better days hastened to pay his respects to the fugitive king. He was invited by Joseph to dine with him. While at the table Joseph said suddenly to M. de Chaumont :

" Well I remember you spoke to me formerly of your great possessions in the United States. If you have them still, I should like very much to have some in exchange for a part of that silver I have there in those wagons, and which may be pillaged at any moment. Take four or five hundred thousand francs and give me the equivalent in land."

" I can not do so," replied M. de Chaumont. " It is impossible to make a bargain when only one party knows what he is about."

" Oh," said the prince, " I know you well, and I rely more on your word than my own judgment."

This conversation led to the conditional purchase of a large tract of wild land. The tract so purchased lay much of it in the town of Diana, and included the lake within its boundaries. In December, 1818, a deed of this tract was executed to Pierre S. Duponceau, his confidential agent, in trust for Joseph.

III.

DIANA.

The name of Diana, the goddess of huntsmen, was conferred upon the town at Joseph's request. In Roman mythology, the Diana Venatrix, or goddess of the chase, is represented in painting and statuary as a huntress, tall and nimble, with hair partly tied up and partly flowing, with light flowing robe, legs bare to the knees, and feet in buskins, such as were worn by the huntresses of old. Sometimes she rode in a chariot drawn by two white stags with golden antlers, and sometimes upon a stag cross-legged. Her attributes were the spear, the bow, the quiver and arrows. Her attendants were Dryads, the nymphs of the woods and hunting hounds. She had a three-fold divinity, being styled Diana on earth, Luna, or the moon, in heaven, and Hecate, or Proserpine, in hell. She is the same as the Artemis of the Greeks, the daughter of Zeus and Leto, and twin sister of Apollo. The Arcadian Artemis was a goddess of the nymphs who hunted on the Taygetan mountains, and was drawn in a chariot by four stags with golden antlers.

The favorite pastime of the ex-king was hunting. With poetic fancy he imagined the goddess Diana herself might covet this sylvan retreat in the wilds of the American forest as her favorite home, and he so named it in her honor.

IV.

JOSEPH BONAPARTE.

In 1828, Joseph Bonaparte, under the assumed name of Count de Survilliers, built a hunting lodge on the bank of the lake. The same year he made a small clearing and built a summer house on the outlet where the village of Alpina now stands. He also built a summer house, with bullet-proof sleeping rooms, at Natural Bridge on the Indian River, seven miles south of the lake, which is still standing. For several summers in succession he visited his forest possessions. Joseph was living during this time in great splendor at Point Breeze, near Bordentown, New Jersey. In going from Bordentown up the banks of the Hudson, and through the Mohawk valley, to his summer retreat in the forest wilds of the Black River country he went in great state, accompanied by a large retinue of friends and attendants. His journeys on such occasions were not unlike those made by the French kings from Fontainebleau to Blois during the last century under the old *régime*. When on his way, he cut a road through the forest and often went in to his lake in his coach drawn by six horses, with great pomp and ceremony. Dressed in his elegant green velvet hunting suit with gilded trappings to match, he seemed indeed a prince among the hunters.

Upon these excursions he was often accompanied by the

friends of his better days, who, like himself, were then in exile. Sometimes in going and returning, he would stop by the wayside to dine under the shade of the primeval pines, and his sumptuous repasts were served on golden dishes with regal splendor.

In his journeys Joseph often stopped at Carthage, on the Black River, where a long reach of still water extends up the river for forty miles, which is navigable for small steamers. On this part of the stream Joseph would launch an elegant six-oared gondola, such as he had been accustomed to use on the waters of Italy when he was king of Naples. This gondola he transported overland and also launched it upon his beautiful lake of the wilderness, where, with liveried gondoliers and gay trappings it floated gracefully upon its waters.

Joseph was the favorite brother of Napoleon, and resembled him in person more than the others. By his courtly but pleasing manners he won the esteem and respect of all the neighboring hunters and settlers, and became endeared to many of them by his uniform kindness and timely generosity. In 1835 he sold his wild lands to John La Farge, the rich merchant of New York. As the forest home of exiled royalty in the New World a romantic interest now attaches to this enchanting lake.

> " Brother of him whose charmed sword
>   Clove or created kingdoms fair,
> Whose faith in him was as the word
>   Writ in the Memlook's scimeter.
>
> Here he forgot La Granja's glades,
>   Escurial's dark and gloomy dome,
> And sweet Sorrento's deathless shades,
>   In his far-off secluded home."

CHAPTER XXVII.

THE LEGEND OF THE DIAMOND ROCK.

" He that sounds them has pierced the heart's hollows,
The place where tears are and sleep,
For the foam flakes that dance in life's shallows
Are wrung from life's deep."
—Fugitive Poem.

I.

The village of Lansingburgh is pleasantly situated upon
the east bank of the Hudson directly opposite the point
where the Mohawk, coming in from the westward and striking the valley of the Hudson, separates into three or four
" sprouts," and soon mingling its troubled waters with the
more placid tide of the larger river, rests from its labors.
The valley of the Hudson at this point, along its easterly
bank, is not more than half a mile in width, and terminates
in a range of hills running parallel with the river, which
rise somewhat abruptly to the height of two or three hundred feet. Between this range of high hills and the river
our village nestles in a complete forest of shade trees.
Troy, its younger sister, but three miles below it, swelling
into the pomp and pride of a city, long since absorbed the
business growth of our village, and left it a retreat for quiet
homes. The city has drawn away from the village its
counting-houses, its warehouses,—in a word its more sordid
interests, but has left to the village its schools, its churches,
its firesides, around which cluster, after all, life's dearest
hopes and most enduring joys.

II.

High up on the brow of the hill overlooking the village, a huge mass of calciferous sand rock of the Quebec group crops out near the bordering strata of Hudson River slate and shale, and terminates in a peak rising some sixty feet above the surrounding surface, with jagged, sloping sides, extending over an area of half an acre or more of ground. This rock, throughout its whole structure, is filled with beautiful shining quartzose crystals, and its surface glitters in the sunlight as if it were covered all over with sparkling gems.   Hence it is known far and near as the Diamond Rock.

This rock can be seen from every part of the village, rising up against the eastern sky like a miniature mountain peak, and is often pointed out by the villagers to the tourist and stranger as an object of interest well worthy of a visit. From its summit can be seen the whole upper valley of the Hudson, from the Catskills on the south to the Adirondacks on the north—a sweep of view extending more than a hundred miles along the river.   No fairer scene anywhere on earth greets the human vision.

While this valley was under the dominion of the red man, so prominent a natural object as this rock was, of course, regarded as a land-mark.   Situated as it was, overlooking the confluence of two important rivers, which then, as well as now, marked out the great highways of travel westward to the great lakes, and northward to the great river leading from them to the ocean, this rock was a beacon to the wanderer.   From its top could be seen far off in the distance the camp-fire of the northern invader, as well as the welcome signal of the western ally coming to the rescue.

III.

In the summer of 1858, while spending a few weeks in the great northern wilderness of New York, in company with some friends,* I heard from the lips of an old Indian, a legend of this Diamond Rock. We were encamped upon a little island on the northern shore of the Raquette Lake, opposite the mouth of the Marian River. From this point it was our practice to make excursions to the different points of interest around the lake. Upon a sultry day in August we all started upon a trip to the summit of the Blue Mountain, which lies twenty miles to the eastward, and can be seen from all parts of the lake, looming grandly up against the sky.

Our course was up the Marian River, and through the Eckford chain of lakes, the last one of which, its waters clear as crystal, sleeps at the mountain's base. We expected to be absent from our camp two or three days, so we proceeded leisurely upon our journey. In the skiff with myself were two others of the party, and our little craft, for some reason or other, was far in advance of all the rest. Toward night-fall we entered a small lake, and while pad-

* Prof. Samuel W. Johnson, of New Haven, Rev. William H. Lockwood of Eau Claire, Wis., Leonard C. Davenport and W. Hudson Stephens of Lowville, were of this party, with Amos Spofford and Al. Higby as guides. While at the Raquette we encamped on Osprey Island, since then the camping ground of Rev. Mr. Murray, of Adirondack fame. While we were there, Prof. Agassiz, Prof. Benedict, Mr. Longfellow, and Mr. Thoreau were occupying the "Philosopher's Camp," on the Saranac.

dling slowly along so that the others might the more readily overtake us, we saw a deer at the distance of a mile ahead of us, standing in the edge of the water, quietly feeding among the lily-pads.   Bright visions of venison steaks steaming hot from the embers of our camp-fire for supper and breakfast instantly arose before us, and we at once determined to secure the game if it were possible, and thus be able to realize our ideal in that particular.

My companions soon landed me upon the shore, which was covered with a dense mass of evergreens reaching almost down to the water's edge.   With rifle in hand I walked noiselessly along the bank to the point directly opposite the place where we had seen the deer standing.   Carefully separating the overhanging boughs so as to obtain a view of the lake, much to my disappointment I discovered that the deer was no longer visible.

Those visions of venison steaks began to appear wonderfully like dissolving views.   Determined, however, to investigate the matter further, I stepped down the bank into the lake, and waded out a little distance in the shallow water. Turning toward the shore, I saw the deer skulking just above the water's edge, partially hidden by the foliage, not ten rods distant from where I stood.   In another instant the sharp crack of my rifle reverberated round the shores of the peaceful lake, and a splendid doe lay sprawling before me upon the bright sandy beach.   As I approached the dying deer, she raised her head with a piteous, pleading look, that stung me with remorse for the ruin I had wrought.

The dying deer sheds tears.   Soon those pleading eyes began to fill with tears, and the bright drops to trickle down

27

upon the sand.　They seemed to me like human·eyes, like those deep spiritual eyes sometimes seen in woman that haunt our dreams forever after.

IV.

While I stood half entranced by those tearful eyes, I was startled from my reverie by a slight movement of the bushes on the bank.　In a moment they parted, and an aged Indian emerged from the forest.　Giving me a grunt of recognition, he stopped short, and stood for a moment gazing at the dying deer.　Then shrugging his shoulders, he broke the silence, saying in broken English : "White man, you good shot.　Deer very much plenty round here.　Me Indian kill two yesterday.　Deer always cry so like squaw when me kill um."*

As the tears were falling fast upon the beach, the old Indian stooped down and gathered a handful of the coarse sand wet with their flow.　Pointing out to me some crystals that were brightened by the moisture of the tears, he again spoke :

"Pale face, look here.　See how tears make pretty stones

* Hark ! the hunter's piercing cry !
See the shafts unerring fly !
Ah ! the dappled fool is stricken—
See him tremble—see him sicken.
All his worldly comrades flying,
See him bleeding, panting, dying ;
From his eye-lids wan and hollow,
How the big tears follow—follow
　　Down his face in piteous chase :
How they follow—follow, follow
　　Without stop, drop by drop,
How they follow drop by drop.
　　　　　　　　Gen. John Burgoyne.

to shine very much.   White man, come to Indian's wigwam to-night.   Me tell white man good story."

Our whole party soon came up to where we stood, and as it was already time to look out for a camping ground for the night, we concluded to accept the Indian's kindly proffered hospitality.

He said his wigwam was half a mile further up the lake, and we took our deer into the skiff, and proceeded thither. As we paddled quietly along, the sun was setting behind us. We saw before us the departing sunlight, followed by the evening shadows, crawl gradually up the mountain side, and disappear on its summit.   Then the soft blue haze that all day long had lingered round the mountain, soon assumed purple and golden hues, until the whole atmosphere in which we moved seemed saturated with a thousand nameless tints of wondrous beauty.   Not a breath of wind ruffled the surface of the lake.   All the glowing splendors of the firmament above the waters were reflected in the firmament beneath the waters.   It seemed as if we had at last found the charmed spot where the rainbow touches the earth.   But the shadows of evening soon obscured the radiant picture.

In a short time we reached the Indian's shanty.   It was situated at the head of a small bay or cove that indented the shore, and in the valley of a little brook that there runs into the lake.   It was a rude, frail structure, made after the fashion of the wilderness.   There were two upright posts, some six feet in height and ten apart, with crotches at the top, across which a pole was laid.   From this pole others extended, upon one side only, in a slanting direction to the ground, some eight feet distant.   This frame-work was covered with large pieces of spruce bark, peeled from some neighboring trees, upon the slanting roof and ends only, leaving the front side open to the weather. The earth under the shanty was thickly strewn with freshly-cut hemlock boughs to the depth of a foot or more. These fragrant boughs, with a couple of bear-skins for a covering, served for a bed.

Directly in front of the shanty a cheerful fire was burning when we arrived. Over the fire a steaming pot was hanging, sustained by a small pole resting upon two upright crotched sticks. The Indian was cooking a venison stew for his supper, and while thus engaged had heard the report of my rifle.

With our hatchets we soon added to his scanty supply of wood sufficient for the night, and, dressing the deer, soon had our own savory steaks smoking over the bright coals of the fire. One of our party had shot a pair of young black ducks, and these, whizzing away in a frying-pan, promised no mean addition to our fare. To these we added some brook trout, cooked in true backwoods style—a fish that is so exquisitely delicate, that, like the ripe strawberry, it will bear neither keeping nor transportation, but, to be enjoyed in its perfection, must be cooked and eaten when but just dripping from its native element. The old Indian's mess of pottage and some potatoes roasted in the ashes, completed our sumptuous repast.

After supper we piled brush and huge logs upon the fire, and, lighting our pipes, reclined upon the fragrant bed of boughs to rest our limbs, weary with the days' tramp and excitement.

The flames lit up the forest around us, the nearer trees standing out in bright relief against the somber shadows beyond. Above the trees, the stars looked down from out their awful depths. The night winds sighing through the pines filled the air with gentle murmurs, the brook answering with its prattle, gurgling over its stony bed. We were within the great heart of Nature. Her pulses were throbbing all around us. We could hear the perpetual hum of her myriad voices. We could feel the magnetism of her all-pervading presence.

V.

Thus engaged, and with such surroundings, we were in just the mood to hear and enjoy the old Indian's tale. I will not trouble the reader with his broken English, but give the substance of it in my own words. Taking three or four strong whiffs from his pipe, he began :

You must know that I belong to the Mohawks, one of the Five Nations. Our tribe, in ancient days, built its lodges along the valley of the Mohawk, and upon both sides of the Hudson, near the junction of the two rivers. It is a tradition of our fathers that the Five Nations first came out of the ground from their subterranean home at some place south-easterly of the Oswego River, in the Lesser Wilderness, and from thence spread out into the different parts of the country they afterward inhabited. The Five Nations called themselves *Ho-de-no-sau-nee*, which means, in the Indian tongue, "The People of the Long House." The Mohawks guarded the eastern door of the long house, and the Senecas the western door; while the Oneidas, Onondagas and Cayugas took care of the interior, the great central council fire being always kept brightly burning in the country of the Onondagas.

Before the union of the nations was accomplished by the exertions of the great sachem Hi-a-wat-ha, the Mohawks wandered away up the Hudson into the valley of the St. Lawrence, and built their lodges and planted their corn-fields, near where Montreal now stands. To the north and west of them dwelt a powerful nation called by our people Adirondacks, and afterward named by the French Algon-quins. The Adirondacks soon became jealous of our growing strength, and seeking a pretence for war, drove our people back again to the valley of the Mohawk. Our tribe not long after united their fortunes with their sister tribes, and became a part of the mighty people called by the English the Five Nations, by the French the Iroquois, and by themselves the *Ho-de-no-sau-nee.*

While our people were in the land of the Adirondacks they were governed by an old sachem named Ho-ha-do-ra. His wife, Mo-ne-ta, was young, and one of the most beautiful women of her tribe. She bore him two sons, whom he called Ta-en-da-ra and O-nos-qua.

It so happened that in an attack upon their village, before our people were overpowered and driven from the St. Lawrence, a band of Adirondack warriors took O-nos-qua, the sachem's youngest son, captive and hurried him off into their own country, where he was saved from torture by be-ing adopted by an Adirondack woman who had lost her own son upon the war-path. Ho-ha-do-ra made many attempts to recapture O-nos-qua, but they all proved unavailing.

With a heavy heart the old sachem, with his wife and re-maining son, led his people back to their former home upon the Mohawk and Hudson, leaving his darling boy in hope-less captivity in the land of his enemies. The old sachem soon sank beneath the heavy blow, and when near his end, called his son Ta-en-da-ra to his side and said :

"Ta-en-da-ra, my son, your father will soon go to the happy hunting grounds, while your brother O-nos-qua is still a slave in the land of the Adirondacks. Swear by the Great Spirit that O-nos-qua's bones shall rest by the side of Ho-ha-do-ra's, Mo-ne-ta's and Ta-en-da-ra's on the banks of the Mohawk."

"I swear!" said Ta-en-da-ra, "but who will take care of Mo-ne-ta, my mother, while I am gone for my brother?"

"My people shall do it," replied the dying sachem, "Mo-ne-ta shall be their queen until her sons come back."

In a little while the old sachem died, and Mo-ne-ta, after the custom of her people, sat up four nights by a fire lighted upon the river bank to guide his soul into the spirit world. As she sat and mourned by the fire through the dismal nights, she sang a low, sweet dirge for the dead, and the soft cadences of her melodious voice rose and fell through the recesses of the tangled forest like the wail of some wild bird mourning for its lost mate.

After the days of her mourning were ended she called her son to her. "Ta-en-da-ra," she said, "your father's bones cannot rest alone. His soul cannot be happy while O-nos-qua is a slave. Go and find your brother in the land of the Adirondacks. Mo-ne-ta will kindle a fire upon the beacon rock and watch until her sons come to her. When you are coming back with your brother from toward the setting sun, or from under the moveless star, you will see the light of my beacon fire from afar, and will know that Mo-ne-ta is still waiting for her children. Go."

Ta-en-da-ra then went to a lonely spot in the forest and

fasted seven days to invoke his guardian spirit. He then painted his face, struck his tomahawk into the war-post, and put on his plumes for the war-path. With his quiver full of arrows and his trusty bow, he set out in his bark canoe up the Hudson. When he came to the end of his first day's journey, he looked back toward his home and saw the faint glimmer of Mo-ne-ta's beacon light appearing like a rising star upon the horizon.

It was long, weary years before he saw it again. He went away a youthful, valiant brave. He came back after many sufferings had bowed his frame, an old man, tottering beneath the weight of his brother's bones, which he bore with him in solemn triumph, as his life's great trophy.

Of his journeys, of his bold exploits, of his captivity, of his adoption by the Adirondacks, his meeting with his long lost brother, his brother's death, of his escape at last and his journey home from the St. Lawrence, I shall not now speak. My story is of Mo-ne-ta.

The clan to which Mo-ne-ta belonged had its lodges on the plain which lies on the east bank of the Hudson, directly opposite the mouths of the Mohawk. In the rear of the plain was a tangled swamp. Beyond the swamp was a high hill, upon the top of which was the beacon rock, overlooking a vast country up and down the river. From the wigwams near the river a trail led through the swamp and up the hill to the beacon rock.

When the shades of night were falling, upon the day of Ta-en-da-ra's departure, Mo-ne-ta wended her way through the swamp and up the hill to the beacon rock. She gathered some sticks, and rubbing two dry ones together, kindled a fire upon the highest point of the rock and sat down beside it. She was then just in the first sweet prime of woman-hood, and scarcely forty summers had passed over her faultless form and features. Her raven tresses hung loosely down her shoulders and rested on the rock around her. Thus she sat and mourned. Her heart was far away in the wilderness with her wandering son and his captive brother, —in the great wilderness that lies beneath the moveless star.

Moon after moon waxed and waned, and still they came not. Then summer after summer tipped the fir trees with fresh green, and called back the birds, but Ta-en-da-ra and O-nos-qua, where were they? Still she lighted the fire upon the beacon rock, and sat and mourned. Her people did not forget the words of their dying chief. They filled her wigwam with venison and corn.

As the seasons glided by she grew old, and was no longer able to find sticks sufficient for her beacon fire, and the young women of her clan gathered them for her, and kept her signal fire brightly burning.

It is said that the Indian never weeps. This is true of him while upon the war-path—while enduring torture and while in the presence of the stranger. But by the side of his dying kindred and his own fire, his tears come out of their pent-up fountains like those of other men.

Each night, just before Mo-ne-ta left the rock to return to sleep in her wigwam, she would repeat her low sweet funeral dirge, and then tears would come to her relief, and save her heart from breaking. Thus tears, blessed tears, dropped upon the beacon rock night after night for year after year. At length Mo-ne-ta's mind began to wander—began to give way beneath the constant strain. Her people

28

then had to lead her up to her place upon the rock and light her fire for her. Yet each night the dirge was sung and the rock watered with her tears. Thus passed five hundred moons and Ta-en-da-ra had not come.

At last, upon a sultry evening of the green corn moon, Mo-ne-ta had been led to the rock and her fire lighted. There she sat just as she did forty years before, but now she was old and gray, and crazed with ceaseless watching.

As the sun went down, long banks of heavy clouds in the south-west betokened a coming storm. As the evening advanced, the sky became overcast, the wind came up in sudden gusts, and the lightning began to play vividly with that incessant glare that sometimes accompanies such storms in the valley of the Hudson.

From the lodges near the river, the beacon light could be seen faintly glowing in the darkness between the flashes. When the flashes came, the beacon rock, with Mo-ne-ta sitting on its summit, stood out in sharp relief against the dark clouds beyond.

Moved by some strange impulse, Mo-ne-ta struck up an Indian song, wild and sweet, that floated out upon the troubled elements, and while the wind would lull, filled the valley with its strange melodies. Had the wild tokens of the coming tempest stirred up the latent fires in Mo-ne-ta's bosom and brought back her wandering reason? Or had some spirit-bird fanned her face with its wings and warned the mother's heart of the coming of her returning son? It was the spirit-bird.

Weary and worn with travel, Ta-en-da-ra was even then going up the trail to the beacon rock. He catches the wild snatches of his mother's song, and in an instant the vigor

of youth returns to his limbs. In a moment more he is
standing by her side.   A wild shriek of tumultous joy
from Mo-ne-ta rings through the valley high above the
voices of the storm, and awakens the very echoes of the
forest.

The people rushed out from their wigwams. In the bright
glare of the lightning they beheld in *tableau vivant* upon
the beacon rock, Ta-en-da-ra standing upon its summit,
with Mo-ne-ta bowing her head upon his bosom—mother
and son in loving embrace.   But such unutterable rapture
is not for mortals.   In an instant more a bolt came down
from heaven jarring the earth with its violence, and shak-
ing the beacon rock to its very foundations.   The people,
trembling, saw in the lightning the manifest presence of
the Great Spirit.   They heard His terrible voice in the
thunder, and struck with unutterable awe they shrank back
to their wigwams.

In the morning the people gathered again around the
beacon rock.   Its surface was riven and shattered by the
bolt.   O-nos-qua's scattered bones were there, but no trace
of Mo-ne-ta nor of Ta-en-da-ra was to be seen.   Then it
was that the people believed that that mother and her son
had so consecrated their souls by a life-long sacrifice upon
the altar of true affection that in the moment of their supreme felicity they had become too pure for earth and were
absorbed—translated into the presence of the Great Spirit
by the power of His lightnings, which they thought were
but sparks struck with awful thunderings from the eternal
fire of His glory.   And while they stood gazing upon this
strange scene in awe and wonder, the sun came up over the
eastern hills and shed his beams upon it, when lo ! they for

the first time saw that the rock was glittering all over with sparkling gems.

"See, see!" they cried with one accord, "See Mo-ne-ta's tears," "Mo-ne-ta's tears."

So free from earthly dross had been that mother's tears shed for her children, that the Great Spirit, by the refining fire of His glory, had changed them into crystals—into glittering immortelles such as cover forever the shining trees in the hunting grounds of the blessed, and to this day those crystalized tears are still to be seen imbedded in the solid rock, there to remain while the earth shall last as bright mementoes of a mother's changeless love.

When the pale-face came across the big water and saw them he exclaimed, "See! see! a diamond rock! a diamond rock!"

The tears of the dying deer falling upon the bright sands of the beach had suggested the old Indian's story.

CHAPTER XXVIII.

THE TWO WATER WHEELS.

" Be good, my friend, and let who will be clever;
    Do noble things, not dream them all day long ;
So making life, death, and that vast forever,
    One grand, sweet song."

I.

THE DREAMER.

" Thou hast me a dreamer styled,
    I have gazed on thy wakefulness and smiled."

Twenty years ago this morning, that is to say, on the 23d day of September, 18—, I left the old homestead farm and went to the village of Lowville, to enter upon the untried field of another vocation.

And now it seems to me but yesterday since I arose early on that bright autumn morning twenty years ago, took a last look at the sheep and lambs, the pigs and chickens, and saw the cows driven away to the river pasture. It seems but yesterday since I bade the oxen and horses, my fellow-workers in many a hard day's toil, good-bye, and laid away the pitchfork and plough to take them up no more.

Since then I have often said, and now I say, Alas the day! There is a world of drudgery upon the farm, but there is nowhere else such sweet rest.

These personal reminiscences may not interest the reader, but at the thought of those old familiar fields on this, to me, an anniversary morning, they rush into consciousness all unbidden from the chambers of memory, and my pen records them against the promptings of my better judgment.

The village of Lowville is situated upon a little stream at the foot of the terraced hills which skirt the western limits of the valley of the Black River in Northern New York. The village is surrounded on every side save that which faces the river with high hills, and nestles in groves of sugar maples and stately elms, which serve, when clothed with the exuberance of June, or decked in the more brilliant hues of October, to render it one of the earth's fairest bowers of beauty. In this quiet, unpretending, lovely village, thus situated about midway between the rush of traffic and travel that surges along the valley of the Mohawk on the one hand, and the St. Lawrence upon the other, yet far removed from the influence of either, I took up my abode.

But twenty years have wrought great changes in the village of Lowville. Its elms have grown taller and its maples cast a wider breadth of shade. Stately blocks of stores and elegant mansions now adorn its streets, taking the places of the more humble structures of earlier days.

But more than this. The telegraph and railroad have recently invaded the secluded valley of the Black River, bringing in their train the spirit of modern progress. The quiet village of twenty years ago has become a busy mart of trade, and now rivals in importance its more favored sisters upon the Mohawk and the St. Lawrence.

The little stream above mentioned is formed by the junction of three branches near the village. These three branches come tumbling down the terraced slope of the plateau of the Lesser Wilderness from the westward in a series of beautiful rapids and cascades, and have worn deep gorges for their beds through the soft limestone rock that forms the foundation of the lower terraces of the hills.

One day shortly after my arrival in the village, and while the Indian summer was pouring its glories over the land, I wandered up one of these gorges to the foot of a splendid cascade, there known as the Silvermine Falls, and sat down upon a rock under the shadow of an elm, to enjoy the scene before me.

The water came rushing over the jagged limestone ledge in a beautiful shower of spray and foam. It had nothing to do there but to sputter and foam, and laugh and dance along, as wild and free as any mountain stream is wont to be before the hand of man turns it into the channels of labor.

While I sat thus engaged, an old man came walking slowly up the gorge, aiding his uncertain steps with a huge hickory cane. He was tall, with stooping shoulders. His nose and his cheek-bones were prominent; his forehead protruding, his chin somewhat receding; his hair was long and scanty and as white as the driven snow. His garments were tattered and torn, and had been often patched with cloth of different colors.

As he came along he was muttering incoherently to himself, and was so intent upon his thoughts that he did not see me as he passed the spot where I sat. He proceeded a few paces further and sat down upon a log of drift-wood. Removing his hat, which had long before seen better days, he wiped the beaded drops of sweat from his brow, and then gazed at the waterfall.

As the old man sat thus, with his eyes intently fixed upon the foaming waters, he raised his voice above his mutterings into a distinct soliloquy.

"They say it can't be done," said he, "but I say it can.

I say there is water enough running over these falls to turn an overshot wheel of sixty feet in diameter. I say it will run the machinery for the whole village. I will build it some day, too, and it will be my water wheel. They say I never can, but I will. Eunice, too, says I'll never do it, but I shall. She has been a good wife to me. She never complains much, but I do think she ought to have more faith in my water wheel. She says I'm always going to do it, but never get about it. She says she hates people that are always going to do something but never do it. She thinks it is about time, too, that she should have the new silk dress I promised her better than twenty years ago, when she signed the mortgage on the old farm. But I can't get it for her till my water wheel is done. Little Alice—Oh! how I wish she had lived to see my water wheel. There! there! see, see, Alice! It is going now. See how it works! See how the water drips and dashes about it! There is power in it! *I tell you there is power in it!*"

As the old man began to see the vision of the wheel before him, seeming to him so like something real, he arose from his seat, extended his arms convulsively upward, and raised his voice into a shrill tenor. Then as the vision vanished and the blank reality came back, he sank down exhausted to the earth.

I hurried to his side, and dipping some of the cool water of the creek in the hollow of my hand, dashed it into his face. As he partially recovered he began to give utterance to the struggling fancies of his returning consciousness.

"I thought," said he, "I was showing little Alice my water wheel. Poor thing, she died years and years ago, but it seemed to me that I had her in my arms again, and that the wheel was going, and she was looking at it."

Opening his eyes and seeing a stranger thus bending over him, he started at once to his feet with a look of mingled surprise and alarm. While I was endeavoring to make some sort of apology for my involuntary intrusion, he turned upon his heel, and without saying another word, slowly retraced his steps down the gorge. In a few moments he passed around a bend of the stream out of my sight.

After the old man had gone, the laughing waters again entranced me with their pearly splendor. The sun sank slowly down behind the western hills, shedding his blood-red effulgence over the smoky drapery of the landscape, which was now putting on its garb of sadness—its robes of mourning for the dead and dying beauties of the summer.

But sadder than all things else was the heart of that old man, now mourning over his buried hopes.

The next morning I learned upon inquiry that the old man's name was Joseph Dunklee. He was living in a lonely house in the upper part of the village, his aged wife sharing his extreme poverty. They had seen better days. His father had been a thrifty and prosperous miller in a quiet New England village. In due time, being an only child, Joseph inherited his father's property, and was looked upon as one of the most promising young men of the village. His wife was then the comely daughter of a neighboring farmer, who sometimes went with her father to the mill in the bright summer mornings. Joseph, the miller's son was lithe and tall, with ruddy cheeks and dark brown hair, with a merry twinkle in his eye, with a pleasant word and a winning smile that stole her heart. They were soon

29

married and nicely settled in a pleasant home. In a year or two a smiling cherub winged its way into their household—their little Alice. Then the farmer died, and the broad acres of the farm were added to the mill lot. Thus things went on with the young miller Joseph Dnnklee, and his happy wife. This was the golden glow of their life's morning. We shall see how deep were the shadows of its evening.

It is the old story of the unsuccessful. Young Dunklee had inherited his father's property, but not his thrift. His father would go into the mill in the morning, satisfied with the machinery as the millwright had left it, so long as it ran smoothly, and was anxious only to leave it at night with a heavier stock of grain in his toll bin.

The young man had that genius for mechanics which places its possessor in the ranks of the inventors. He could comprehend at a glance all the intricacies of the most complicated machinery, and new combinations of motive power were constantly arising in his mind all unbidden, seeking application to the various wants of human industry. In short, he soon began to spend more time in experimenting with the running gear of his mill than in grinding corn, and the swelling fatness of his father's toll bin dwindled gradually away. Joseph at length conceived the idea of building an immense water wheel that would furnish not only power for his own mill, but sufficient also for all the mills and factories in the village. The idea of such a wheel became indelibly pictured upon his brain. It haunted him day and night. He soon began to see it as distinctly in his waking as in his sleeping dreams, perpetually towering up before him in all its stately proportions. He could no longer resist the temptation to attempt its construction. To raise the necessary funds the mill lot and farm were mortgaged. The services of all the wheelwrights and carpenters for miles and miles around were put in requisition from the opening of spring until the close of an August day, when the different parts were pronounced complete, and were lying scattered along the bank of the mill-stream, awaiting the morrow for the commencement of the raising. A sudden tempest came up before midnight, and the rain fell in sheets till morning. At early dawn the stream was higher than it had ever been known to rise before, and the timbers of the unfinished water wheel were all floating down the wide waste of angry waters into the sea.

Dunklee was ruined.

His neighbors had all laughed at him, had called him an enthusiast—a dreamer, and had sometimes indulged in still harsher epithets. It now seemed as if the hand of Providence even was against him, and had thwarted his endeavors.

The farm and the mill lot were soon to be sold by the sheriff, and Dunklee, his wife, and little Alice were to be sent forth wanderers from their once happy home. But not together. Before the day of sale came little Alice took sick and died. The cherub, it seemed, was but a loan for their life's fair morning. They must return it before the evening shadows came on.

Then Joseph Dunklee and his wife Eunice left behind them the old homestead, his mill and her farm, the peaceful New England village and the grave of little Alice, to bend their steps westward in search of better fortunes. Of all his former possessions he took nothing with him

save the haunting vision of the water wheel. But the
fickle goddess Fortune forever eluded his grasp. By the
labor of his hands he had been able to acquire a scanty
subsistence for himself and wife until old age and failing
strength had brought them to extreme poverty. Such was
their condition when first I saw him.

A short time after the occurrence at the cascade, I was
attracted one afternoon by some unusual noise in the
street. Looking out of the window, I saw the old man
walking along as fast as his feeble legs could carry him.
He was followed by a troop of rude boys, who were all
screaming after him at the top of their voices, "*Water
wheel! water wheel! water wheel!*" Occasionally he would
turn and address the boys a few words of angry expostula-
tion, but they continued to tease him until some kind neighbor took pity upon the poor old man, and drove them away.

A few days after this, a man came into the village from
the country, who had heard of Dunklee's water wheel.
Supposing there was such a thing in existence, the man inquired of some one concerning its locality. The person
inquired of referred him to Dunklee himself, who, it so
happened, was passing near them at the moment. The
stranger accosted the old man. "Mr. Dunklee," said he,
"I have often heard of your water wheel, but never saw it.
Will you tell me where——" "*Heigh!*" yelled the old man,
interrupting him, as soon as he began to comprehend the
subject of the inquiry. "I say," continued the stranger,
somewhat abashed by the old man's warmth of manner, but
raising his voice so that he could be plainly heard by him,
"I say," continued he, "that I never saw your water
wheel——"

But he got no further.   It was too much for the old man.
His cane went down upon the unsuspecting stranger's head
with a crash that sent him reeling to the earth.

The next morning the old man was taken before the village Justice, Esquire Knox, upon a charge of assault and
battery.   He plead the story of his wrongs in extenuation
of his offense.   The kind-hearted Justice imposed a light
fine upon him, and paid it himself, rather than to send the
poor old man to jail.

The stranger from that time forward ceased to indulge
his curiosity in the direction of large water wheels.

During all these years of hopeless poverty, Eunice
Dunklee lived with her husband without upbraiding him.
It seemed to her to be her destined lot in life, so ordered for
some wise purpose, and she accepted it with uncomplaining
resignation.   She had hoped to lean upon him and find
support as the vine does upon the oak.   But he, too, was
but a vine—to her a vine of bitter-sweet.   Kind hands at
last smoothed her dying pillow, and carried her to the
grave.

Then there was but one door left open for the old man—
the door held open by public charity—the Poor House door.
Through this door he entered, his pride humbled by necessity.   At last they laid him in the village burying ground
by her side, and but for this idle tale of mine, Dunklee and
the life-long vision that haunted him would soon have
passed from the memory of men.

II.

THE WORKER.

"Say! Brothers of the dusky brow,
What forge ye now?"

The city of Troy adorns the valley of the Hudson. Its builders have wedged it in between the river and a range of high hills to the eastward. Upon the south the hills crowd down to the river's bank and bar the city's further progress. Toward the north the valley widens and the city breathes more freely as it stretches with rapid strides up the stream. Tall masted vessels and splendid steamers following the swell of the tidal wave until it breaks upon our city's docks a hundred and fifty miles from the sea, fill its warehouses with the riches of the world's commerce. From our city's center radiate toward the north, the south, the east and the west, long lines of railways over which rush a hundred trains of cars each day. Its traffic and trade extend to every country, and the names of its merchants and manufacturers are known in all lands.

In the spring of 18— I left the quiet of the village for the hurry and bustle of the city. The excitement of the city's more intense life intoxicates and bewilders. We forget the pure air and blessed sunshine of the country in the whirl of business and pleasure that is forever surging through the streets of the city. But through it all there will sometimes come unbidden the old love for green fields and babbling brooks—for flowers and trees and growing things.

As the soldier in the fight looks through the smoke of the battle-field upon the green hills far away with longing eyes, and hopes to escape the dreadful dangers which surround him, that he may again roam over them in quietness and peace,—so the dweller in the city looks through the ceaseless toil, the turmoil and strife of his life's battle, into the distant future upon some enchanting spot, some paradise of earth, where he may find peace at last. But oftener than otherwise he finds no rest until his body lies in some Oakwood, Greenwood or Mount Auburn, surrounded at last in death by Nature's charms, the pleasures to be derived from which he denied himself while living.

There is a world of witchery about a city life, but there is nowhere else such terrible unrest.

But what has all this to do with water wheels?

A short time after my arrival, I set out one fine spring morning to view the various iron works in the lower part of the city. Looking through the bell foundries, rolling mills, Bessemer steel works and nail works on the route, I at last arrived at Burden's iron works upon the Wynantskill. Stepping into the office, I registered my humble name among the long list of visitors who had been there before me. The obliging clerk gave me a ticket of admission, and informed me that I would find some one at the gate who would show me around the works.

Before going within I ascended the hill to the southward to view the scene. The Wynantskill has here worn a deep and wide gorge through the slaty rock, and runs down in a series of irregular rapids and cascades into the Hudson. From my point of view the whole valley of the stream was covered with the dusky roofs of the works for acres in extent. From these roofs more than fifty chimneys towered, continually belching forth the flames of as many furnaces,

Upon entering the works the visitor is bewildered at the sight of a mazy labyrinth of ponderous machinery, and deafened by its ceaseless roar. Fiery furnaces, day and night, convert the ore brought from far-off mountain mines into streams of molten metal. This is again changed by another process into lumps of malleable iron, so heated to whiteness that they resemble masses of glittering snow. Heavy rollers soon change these lumps into red-hot iron bars, that seem to wind their way like fiery serpents through the works.

From these red-hot bars, wonderfully constructed machines are forging horseshoes and railróad spikes, day and night, with marvellous facility. Six of these machines make horseshoes. Two strong-armed men at the old-fashioned anvil and forge can fashion some seventy horseshoes only in a day. These machines will each of them turn off sixty every minute, and twelve tons of them every twenty-four hours. These machines at Burden's works, forging horseshoes continually, day and night, with such wonderful rapidity, serve to render the speedy equipment of the vast armies of modern times possible.

These machines thus forging spikes, render it possible to lay the iron rails athwart the continent with the rapidity that accords with our American notions of progress. From this maze of cunningly constructed machinery, which does the work of so many hundred human hands as skillfully as if endowed with human reason, I turned to my guide and desired him to show me the power that put it all in motion. He then led me in among the hissing iron bars, past the fiery furnaces, and up a flight of stairs into the heights of the vast building. Up in those dizzy heights we reached a

platform there constructed.   Standing upon this platform
I saw before me a vast water wheel.   There before me was
an over-shot water wheel sixty-four feet in diameter, over
two hundred feet in circumference, and twenty-four feet in
width.   Through an immense conduit in which a tall man
could walk upright with ease, the waters of the 'Kill were
drawn from a reservoir upon the hill side, and dashed upon
its top with irresistible force.   Its arms reached high above
the platform where we stood, and revolving sank deep into
an excavation in the ground below.   Here then the tireless energy that seemed to pervade the whole works like
some all-controlling spirit of power was explained.   Revolving before me was the largest water wheel in the world.

As I stood gazing at the ponderous wheel, a vague im-
pression arose in my mind that I had seen it before.   When
or where, or whether I had not dreamed it all, I could not
at first conceive.   In another moment, however, scenes
that had lain dormant in the memory for years flashed into
consciousness.   Then the busy scene in which I stood
faded away.   I was again in the gorge of the little stream
that runs through the village of Lowville, and the waters
were dashing and foaming over the Silvermine Falls.   I
saw the old man Dunklee, with white locks streaming in
the wind, with extended arms holding up his little Alice to
see his water wheel.   But the vision of the past vanished
as quickly as it came, and I was again. conscious of the
sharp reality.   "No ! no !" I cried, "this is not Dunklee's
water wheel, it is Burden's."   Dunklee never saw his own
wheel save in dreams.   Here was Burden's wheel, a tangible reality.   Burden had never seen Dunklee—had never
heard of him or his wheel—neither had Dunklee ever seen

30

or heard of Burden. Yet both had conceived the same idea, and both could comprehend alike the magical mysteries of mechanism and of motion. But one was a dreamer and the other was a worker. How vast the difference in the results of their lives.

Dunklee's dreams never found expression in outward works, never lifted an arm in useful labor, never filled a single mouth with bread.

Burden has embodied his conceptions, and they have become tangible shapes, working out wonderful results. His horseshoes ring over the pavements of a thousand cities in the Old World and in the New. At Shiloh, at Antietam, at Gettysburg, at Malvern Hill, in the Wilderness and before Richmond, in Sheridan's ride and Sherman's march, each fiery hoof that pranced along "the perilous edge of battle," was shod with shoes from Burden's works. Each iron rail that forms a link in the almost endless chain of railway that stretches from the Atlantic to the Pacific, helping "to bind the silken chain of commerce round the world," is fastened in its bed with spikes from Burden's mills.

Thus has Burden lightened Labor of her drudgery, and relieved Civilization of her wants. Thus has he given employment to a thousand willing hands, and filled a thousand homes with daily bread.

But can nothing be said for poor Dunklee? Are not the world's inventors, after all, the superiors of the world's workers? Is not invention itself the highest kind of work? Without the inventors, the world's mere workers would be but senseless plodders.

Burden possessed in a high degree the gift of inventive genius, coupled with rare executive ability. But Nature is seldom thus prodigal of her favors, and poor Dunklee was gifted with as high constructive powers as Burden, but like nine-tenths of his class, Dunklee lacked the faculty of getting on in the world.

But constructive power is one of the highest faculties of the human soul. To possess the constructive faculty in a high degree is the distinctive mark of genius. Without it the poet could never weave his undying songs; the sculptor could never fashion his faultless figures, nor the musical composer unfold his immortal symphonies. It is in vain to attempt to belittle constructive power by pointing to the bee, the bird, and the beaver as examples of its existence in a high degree in beings inferior to man. Rather let us stand in awe before their matchless works, for their creations are but the handiwork of the Supreme Architect, who through them and by them manifests His ceaseless care, His changeless love, for his creatures. Call the world in which those persons live who possess high constructive powers, if you please, a world of dreams, yet out of it come all the useful and beautiful things of life. All the wonderful appliances for the aid and comfort of man which mark our era of civilization as the highest the world has ever seen, are the fruits of the world's inventors. All the marvelous works of art which seem to give to life its highest pleasures, come from the glowing ideals of the world's dreamers. The teeming brains of the world's great inventors give them no peace, no rest, until their ideals find outward expression in tangible forms of use and beauty. The world's inventors are the world's great teachers. Yet oftener than otherwise the world shows little favor to such men. "Hunger and nakedness," says Carlyle, "perils and reviling, the prison,

the cross, the poison-chalice, have, in most times and countries, been the market-price it has offered for Wisdom, the
welcome with which it has greeted those who have come to
enlighten and purify it."

But the world's treasures do not satisfy the longings of
such men. And what matters it if they do suffer from
hunger, and thirst, and nakedness? They live in a world
of their own creation, whose sky is blue in eternal beauty,
and in which the nectar of the gods is not sweeter than
their daily food. They have a deeper insight into the hidden
things and beauties of the world around them, in which
we all live, than most men have, and they are, in consequence of it, poets, painters and inventors—in a word, the
world's great teachers.

But the world has been dreaming too much, and working
too little until now. The ages of the past have been ages
of darkness, of superstition, of error, of dreams. The
philosophers and sages of antiquity spent their lives in
dreaming, scorning to do anything useful. The School-men
were dreamers, the Crusaders were dreamers. The age of
Chivalry was an age of romance and of dreams. Yet out
of this chaos of dreams a new order of things has arisen.
This new order is presided over by the genius of Useful
Labor. Henceforth Useful Labor, guided by Science, by
Art, by Inventive Genius, rules the world.

CHAPTER XXIX.

THE STORY OF TOM GARNET'S DREAM.

With a slow and noiseless footstep,
Comes that messenger divine,
Takes the vacant chair beside me,
Lays her gentle hand in mine.
—*Longfellow.*

Take, O boatman, thrice thy fee,
Take,—I give it willingly,
For, invisible to thee,
Spirits twain have crossed with me.
—*John Louis Uhland.*

I.

The Thousand Islands of the St. Lawrence present a scene of the most enchanting beauty. They occur where the river crosses a depression of the Laurentian chain of mountains, that there extend into Northern New York from their Canadian home. There these mountains seem kindly to stoop, as it were, in crossing, to allow the great river to flow on unobstructed to the ocean, their highest points only rising above the surface of the water to form these islands.

From the Thousand Islands the Laurentides extend easterly to the shores of Lake Champlain, southerly to the valley of the Mohawk, westerly to the Black River, and, rising into a vast system of highlands, form the rocky groundwork of the Great Wilderness, with its thousand mountain peaks and its thousand lakes in the intervening valleys.

Here, its current partially obstructed by this mountain chain, the stream spreads into a broad, placid lake, with these thousand islands in fairy-like forms studding its surface. Sometimes they appear only as projecting rocks,

with but room for a single dwarfish tree, or perhaps a sea-
bird's nest—at others as high, rounded forms, forest crowned, and then again as a broad land of miles in extent, covered with cultivated farms. Such a one is Wellesley's
Island, already becoming famous as a camp meeting
ground, and whose Indian name, *Ta-ni-ha-ta*, which it derives from an old village of that name on the Canadian
shore, should now be restored.

In the soft, hazy light of the short Canadian summer,
this "Lake of the Thousand Isles" seems more like the
fabled oceans of the old fairy tales out of which arose the
Islands of the Blessed, than it does like anything that belongs to this work-a-day world of ours.

In the month of June, not many years ago, it was my
good fortune to visit the Thousand Islands upon a short
pleasure excursion. I was accompanied by some friends,
and our little party arrived at the village of Alexandria Bay
on the American shore late in the afternoon of a sultry day.
We were wearied by a long and dusty ride across the flat
country that there skirts the great river, but soon forgot our
troubles in viewing the glorious sunset that we were just in
time for. It was so early that we were greeted at our
hotel as the first guests of the season, and in the morning
had our choice of boats and fishermen.

We had planned a trip of a dozen miles or more up the
river, with the intention of passing the night upon one of
the islands there, and of returning on the morrow. As our
boatmen rowed us slowly along up the broad river, around
and among the islands, with our trolling lines all out, many
a fine pike and pickerel was tempted to take the enticing
bait, and was safely landed in our boats.

In the course of the day one of our fair companions caught two *mas-quin-on-ges*. This was an exploit that she well might be proud of, for the true *mas-quin-on-ge* is quite a rare fish even in these waters, his native home. He is one of the most excellent as well as one of the most gamey fishes in our northern waters, and should not be confounded, as he too often is, with his near relative, although greatly inferior fish, the great northern pickerel. The *mas-quin-on-ge*, I give the old Indian name from Charlevoix, often weighs more than fifty pounds, and is as sprightly and rapid of movement as the brook trout. He affords the most exciting sport to the fishermen, and his firm but delicate, light salmon-colored flesh is prized by the epicure. So our fair friend suddenly found herself quite celebrated among the fishermen, for many an old frequenter of these waters can scarcely boast of having taken a single one of them.

Late in the afternoon we came to the little island upon which we had thought to pass the night. There was a single cottage upon it, built for the accommodation of transient summer guests, containing a half dozen rooms or more, and an ample ice-house in which we secured our store of fish.

The only guest upon the island when we arrived there was a retired officer of the United States navy, who, when in active service, had often cruised in these waters, and had now come to spend a few days in quiet meditation among the familiar scenes of former hardships and dangers.

Strangers meeting in the wilderness, or in lonely places like this, quickly learn to waive all mere formalities; so at our coming the old officer gave us at once a kindly greeting, and we were soon on as familiar a footing as though we had known one another for long intimate years.

After supper we all sat out upon the cottage porch that faced the broad, open stretch of the river, called Kingston Bay, watching the coming on of the evening shadows and listening to the soothing, monotonous cry of the whippor-will upon the Canadian shore. As the sun went down in splendor beneath the western rim of shining waters, the report of the evening gun at the distant British fort at Kingston came booming across the bay. The sound of the gun seemed to awaken tender memories in the mind of the old officer, and we thought, as he turned musingly away, we saw a tear trickle down his weather-beaten cheek.

After we had retired for the night, and the sense of in-tense quiet and repose that seemed to brood over the little island like the spirit of rest had lulled us into slumber, we were suddenly awakened by strange noises and rude voices in the adjoining rooms. We soon learned the nature of our retreat. The position of the little island, in respect to the boundary line, was not well defined, and being under doubtful jurisdiction, it was occasionally resorted to by gamblers, who could there ply their avocation without fear of arrest from either shore. All night long was heard the rattling of cards and dice, making night hideous. It was not until the dawn of the morning that the new comers ceased their horrible din, and we got a little sleep. When we awoke there was no one with us on the island but the old officer, who had been as much disturbed as we. Before the sun rose the gamblers had departed.

Just as the sun was gloriously rising out of the gleaming sea of islands to the eastward, I went out upon the porch.

The old officer was already there to bid me good morning. In another moment the sound of the British morning gun boomed across the bay.

"I never hear," said he, "that single gun at Kingston, but I think of poor Tom Garnet, an old mess-mate of mine, who was killed there in the last war with Great Britain. But sit down," continued he, "and let me tell you his story."

And there in the dewy freshness of that early hour of the summer's morning, we gathered around the old man to hear his story in the very scene of its enactment.

II.

"During the war with Great Britain of 1812," said he, "there were stirring times in these waters. Each nation strove for the mastery of the lakes, and ships and fleets were built and fitted out on both sides with marvelous celerity. It was not an uncommon thing in those days for a sloop of war to be launched all ready for active service from our ship yards, whose timbers forty days before were growing greenly in the forest.

"In November, 1812, I was a young sailor on board the staunch brig Oneida, that was commanded by Lieutenant Woolsey, and was attached to the American fleet then cruising under Commodore Chauncey. For a day or two our fleet had been chasing the British sloop of war the Royal George, among the Thousand Islands, and in the early hours of a bleak morning had driven her into Kingston harbor. Then occurred the daring assault upon the Royal George by our little fleet, under the very guns of the

31

frowning fort, that reflected so much honor upon our gallant seamen.

"Tom Garnet was a sailor on board our brig. He had been for many years in the British service, but had lately enlisted into our navy, and was ordered on board our vessel. Tom had not been long on board before he became the favorite of all the officers and men, and being a most thorough seaman, was made captain of the forecastle. Tom was brave to a fault, unfaltering in the performance of every duty, and always at his post. But he was as gentle as a woman, and at times an irrepressible sadness seemed to weigh down his spirits, and to cast a settled gloom over his life. Some great and abiding sorrow was weighing heavily upon the heart of poor Tom, but none of us knew what it was. What was our surprise then, on the morning of the battle, to see Tom's face beaming with smiles. A great change had suddenly come over his brooding spirits, and Tom was as light-hearted as a child. His comrades quickly noticed the change, and wonderingly inquired the cause.

"Oh! I shall be with them to-day," said Tom, "I shall see them to-day."

"With whom?" said his comrades.

"With Mary, my wife, and our child in heaven," said he, with great earnestness. "Last night I thought, in my dream, I saw her disembodied spirit among the angels, and a little one was by her side whom I had never seen, and they beckoned me to come. I am sure I shall go to-day, and be with them at last. But you cannot understand me," continued Tom, "until I tell you all about how it has been with me. In the first place let me divide between you, my comrades, what few things I have   When I am gone they will remind you of poor Tom. As soon as the morning breaks we shall go into action and I shall be killed. They seemed to tell me so."

The sailors were at first disposed to laugh at what they supposed were Tom's disordered fancies, but his great earnestness of manner indicated his firm belief in the truthfulness of his presentiment, and having a high appreciation of his character, they checked their hilarity, and each in turn received from his hand some little trinket, or a part of his wardrobe as a keepsake.

And after the distribution was made, the sailors of poor Tom's mess gathered round him in the forecastle, in the gloomy dawn of that wild Canadian autumn morning, while the fleet was putting on sail to engage the enemy, and listened to poor Tom's story.

III.

" My father," said Tom, "was a well-to-do English farmer, who lived in the days of our childhood, in the country about forty miles back from Liverpool. I was his first-born and heir, and when I was of age I married the daughter of our nearest neighbor. We were to settle down upon the farm and take care of the old folks, who were already well along in years. A few short, happy weeks flew quickly by, and our honeymoon was over. Then my father loaded his cart with corn, and sent me off to the distant city to exchange it for some things for our housekeeping.

"When I left the old home farm that morning, with my cart and oxen and load of freight, Mary, my wife, kissed me good-bye again and again.

"'You will not be gone long, will you, dear Tom?' said she.

"It was our first and last parting. But twenty years of toil and hardship have not wasted the sweetness of her last kiss from my lips. And her image—how bright and beautiful her image appears to me this morning, as in my memory I see her standing at the old farm gate, bidding me good-bye as I drove the oxen down the lane out of her sight toward the great citw.

"I had never before been in town, and it was to me full of wonders.

" After I had sold my corn, I bought some things for our housekeeping, and had loaded them on my cart, all ready to start on my homeward journey, when I was roughly seized by one of the king's press-gangs, that were the terror of every seaport town in those days, and of which I in my simplicity had never before heard. In spite of my tears and my entreaties, I was rudely bound, hand and foot, and dragged, more dead than alive, on board of one of his majesty's ships that was on the eve of setting sail upon a long East Indian voyage.

" On the morrow the ship sailed. My oxen were left to wander uncared for through the streets of the city, with my precious load of what was to have been our household goods, and before I had the least opportunity to send a single word home to my wife and family to relieve the dreadful anxiety that my long and unaccountable absence must have occasioned them, we were far out upon the broad ocean. In the course of a few months we entered the Indian Ocean, and it was seven long years before our ship again cast anchor, upon her return voyage, in the har-

bor of Liverpool.   During this long time I had never heard
one word from home or friends.

"After our arrival at the home port I was paid my hard-
earned wages and received my discharge.   I soon reached
the welcome shore, and at once hurried out of the now
dreaded city toward my old home in the country.   I was
so changed in appearance by years of exposure under a
burning sun, that I was sure no one would know me.   But
haggard and worn as I was, my heart was light at the
thought of soon meeting my dear wife and friends once
more, and so I pressed eagerly onward until night overtook
me.   I was afraid to call at an inn, lest from my dress and
appearance I should excite suspicion and be arrested as a
deserter from the navy.   Finding a stack of straw in a
lonely nook, I crept under it and slept through the night.
In the morning a dense fog enveloped everything, and I
groped my way on without knowing whither I was going.
It so happened that I wandered into the king's broad high-
way just in time to fall in with another press gang who
were passing by.   They seized me, and utterly regardless
of my entreaties, and in spite of my situation, hurried me
on board another vessel that was soon under weigh for the
distant western coast of South America.

"After we had been cruising about for several years in
the Southern Pacific, I managed to escape from my captivity, and crossing the Andes alone and on foot, arrived,
after many wanderings and hairbreadth escapes, weary and
worn, at an Atlantic port.   There the first opportunity that
offered for sailing was on board of an American man-of-
war that was homeward bound.   Impatient to leave, I enlisted in the American navy as a common sailor for the

term of one year. Our ship arrived in New York harbor a few months ago. I was soon transferred to Commodore Chauncey's fleet, as you now see me.

"I have never heard one word from home since my wife bid me good-bye at the old farm gate, and that is now twenty long years ago. But last evening, as I swung in my hammock, I fell asleep, and I saw her in my dreams, as I have told you already. She and our little one must have died in my absence, and I shall be with them to-day."

IV.

"When Tom had concluded his story," continued the old officer, "there was not a dry eye in that circle of hard-faced men, and in a moment after the command came harsh and loud to clear the decks for action. And then our little ship rode gallantly up under the guns of the fort and poured a broadside into the Royal George. Soon we saw a light puff of smoke curl upward from one of the batteries on the shore, and a nine pound cannon shot went crashing across our deck.

"It struck poor Tom, and he fell dead at our feet. As his body lay upon the deck with face upturned, there was a smile playing upon his stiffening features that will haunt me to my dying day. Death had to him no terrors. He welcomed its coming. It opened to him the door of Heaven, to show him those he loved. The smile upon his face was a smile of recognition."

As the old man concluded his story, he arose from his seat and bade us good-bye.

And now the strangest thing about this story of Tom

Garnet is its truth, for it is not all romance, but veritable history. Dr. Hough, in his "History of Jefferson County, N. Y.," on page 471, places upon record an account of Tom Garnet's singular presentiment and death, which is substantially the same as the one I have woven into the warp of my story. Says the learned historian, in concluding his narrative, and I use his very words :

"Chauncey's fleet sailed and engaged the enemy's batteries in the harbor of Kingston, as above related ; the first shot from which was a nine pound ball, that crossed the deck of the Oneida and passed through the body of Tom Garnet, at his post. He fell instantly dead, with the same smile upon his countenance that habit had impressed. This singular coincidence and verification of presentiment is so well attested by authentic witnesses that it merits the attention of the curious."

I cannot explain these things, dear reader, can you ?

We know not how or why they are so, but this we do know, that the images that fancy paints upon the walls of our memory, of our dear friends long absent or long dead, are beautiful beyond the power of language to describe.

We have hanging on the walls of our habitations the likenesses of our lost or long absent loved ones, that were taken of their frail bodies when they were with us or were with the living : but how different they all are from the magical pictures of them that hang on memory's walls !

Their portraits taken by human hands, once so lovely to us, as time wears on begin to appear is if there was something too gross and earthly about them to be the true images of the absent ones whom they represent, and we at length begin to turn our eyes from them as unsatisfactory, and to

gaze inwardly upon the more enchanting pictures of memo-
·ry. Then it is that the pictures of memory rise up before
us so transcendently beautiful. Then it is that it seems to
our mind's eye that that which was sown in dishonor is already arisen in glory.

Childish innocence, womanly grace and manly power may
be to us attractive beyond measure in the living forms of
those we love, but transfigured in the half-remembered
features of the dead, these blessed attributes of our poor
earthly humanity seem to betray to us mortals some faint
foretaste of the glories of the hereafter.

Again, we know that Sleep, the gentle queen of rest, is
the twin sister of Death, the awful king of terrors. Between their dominions there is but a narrow boundary, and
across it may not their subjects sometimes, in some mysterious way, hold converse? Do not kindred spirits in either
realm sometimes burst through the frail barriers, and half
concealing, half reveal their awful secrets to each other,
that are remembered by the living, when awakened, as but
dreams.

Did the image of his long absent bride haunt the memory of Tom Garnet, until it became to him as it were a
real presence; or did she really whisper to him in his dream
through the prison bars?

As the morning sun rose gloriously in the heavens, we
left the little island, and it soon grew dim and shadowy in
the distance; but the story of poor Tom Garnet was impressed indelibly upon our memories.

The wind arose, and the dancing waves soon entranced
us with their splendor. As our little skiffs rode over their
crested tops among the shining islands on our homeward

way, the story of Tom Garnet's dream as well as the incidents of our night's visit to the little island we had left behind us faded from my thoughts, and in their places the
words of the poet came into my mind, and I fancied I
could hear him singing his song:

" The Thousand Isles, the Thousand Isles,
Dimpled, the wave around them smiles,
Kissed by a thousand red-lipped flowers,
Gemmed by a thousand emerald bowers,
A thousand birds their praises wake,
By rocky glade and plumy brake,
A thousand cedars' fragrant shade,
Fall where the Indians' children played,
And fancy's dream my heart beguiles,
While singing thee, the Thousand Isles.

" No vestal virgin guards their groves,
No Cupid breathes of Cyprian loves,
No Satyr's form at, eve is seen,
No Dryad peeps the trees between,
No Venus rises from their shore,
No loved Adonis red with gore,
No pale Endymion wooed to sleep,
No brave Leander breasts their deep,
No Ganymede, no Pleiades,
Their's are a New World's memories.

" There St. Lawrence gentlest flows,
There the south wind softest blows,
There the lilies whitest bloom,
There the birch has leafiest gloom,
There the red deer feed in spring,
There doth glitter wood duck's wing,
There leaps the *Mas-quin-on-ge* at morn,
There the loon's night song is borne,
There is the fisherman's paradise,
With trolling skiff at red sunrise."

32

CHAPTER XXX.

THE ST. LAWRENCE OF THE OLDEN TIME.

Faintly as tolls the evening chime
Our voices keep tune, and our oars keep time;
Soon as the woods on the shores look dim,
We'll sing at St. Ann's our parting hymn.
Row, brothers, row, the stream runs fast,
The rapids are near and the daylight's past.

Why should we yet our sail unfurl?
There is not a breath the blue wave to curl;
But when the wind blows off the shore,
Oh! sweetly we'll rest on our weary oar.
Blow, breezes, blow, the stream runs fast,
The rapids are near and the daylight's past.
—*Tom Moore.*

I.

THE RIVER OF THE THOUSAND ISLES.

The old Indian *Ho-che-la-ga Ga-hun-da*, the great river of the ancient forest state of that name, now called the River St. Lawrence, still rolls its tide through its mountain barriers and among its wonderful islands as in the days of yore, but in its valley a new race of people have sprung up, who find few traces of the savage warriors and bold explorers who for more than two hundred years after its first discovery by white men, frequented its shores, and sped their bark canoes over its waters.

The first white man who gazed upon the enchanting beauty of the Lake of the Thousand Isles, it is probable, was Samuel de Champlain, the founder of New France. The reader will remember that Champlain, in the autumn of the year 1615, while on a voyage of exploration to Lake Huron, united with a war party of Huron braves in a hostile expedition against the Iroquois of western New York. The trail this expedition took led from the Huron country south-easterly to the River Trent, and down that river to its mouth, at *Catarocoui*, now the city of Kingston, on Lake Ontario, at the head of the great river. From Kingston the Indian trail led down the river around Wolfe Island, and thence up the American channel past Carleton Island, and along the coast of the lake to the mouth of the Oswego river. In pleasant weather they sometimes avoided this circuitous route, and struck boldly across the lake to the westward of Wolfe Island. This last-named route Champlain took on his way to the Iroquois cantons. But this route was a dangerous one for light canoes, and was seldom taken. So Champlain, in following the old trail of the war-path in returning, must have entered the westerly end of the Lake of the Thousand Isles.

After Champlain, the first visitor of note to the upper St. Lawrence and the Thousand Islands was the Jesuit Father, Simon Le Moyne, on his journey to the country of the Onondagas in the summer of 1654. It was while on this visit to the Onondagas that Father Le Moyne became the discoverer of the famous salt springs of Syracuse. The Indians knew of the salt springs, but believed their waters were possessed of a demon or evil spirit, and dare not touch them. Father Le Moyne boiled some of the water, and made a quantity of salt, which he says, in his diary, was equal to that made from the water of the sea.

After Le Moyne came La Salle and Frontenac, De la Barre, La Hontan, Hennepin and Charlevoix, and a long line of names illustrious in Canadian annals.

II.

THE BIRTH-NIGHT OF MONTREAL.

The story of the founding of the city of Montreal is more like a religious romance of the middle ages than veritable history. The reader will not forget that the Island of Montreal was the site of the ancient Iroquois village, *Ho-che-la-ga*, the capital of the old forest state of that name discovered by Jacques Cartier in the year 1535, and that when Champlain first visited the Island in 1603, the old state and its capital had alike disappeared, and its site was occupied only by a few Algonquin fishing huts.

But a newer and more brilliant destiny awaited the site of ancient *Ho-che-la-ga*, the then wild Island of Montreal.

About the year 1636, there dwelt at La Flèche, in Anjou, a religious enthusiast deeply imbued with the mysticism of the times, whose name was Jérôme le Royer de la Dauversière. It is related of Dauversière by the pious historians of the period that one day while at his devotions he heard an inward voice, which he deemed a voice from Heaven, commanding him to become the founder of a new order of hospital nuns, and to establish for such nuns, to be conducted by them, a hospital, or Hôtel-Dieu, on the then wild Island of Montreal.

It is further related that while Dauversière was beholding his ecstatic visions at La Flèche, a young priest of similar mystical tendencies, whose name was Jean Jacques Olier, while praying in the ancient church of St. Germain des Prés at Paris, also heard a voice from Heaven commanding him to form a society of priests, and establish

them on an island called Montreal in Canada for the prop-
agation of the True Faith.

Full of his new idea, Dauversière set out for Paris to
find some means of accomplishing his object.   While at
Paris he visited the château of Meudon near by, and on
entering the gallery of the old castle saw a young priest
approaching him.   It was Olier.   " Neither of these two
men," says the old chronicler, " had ever seen or heard of
the other, yet impelled by a kind of inspiration, they knew
each other at once even to the depths of their hearts ; saluted each other by name as we read of St. Paul, the Hermit, and St. Anthony, of St. Dominic and St. Francis ; and
ran to embrace each other like two friends who had met
after a long separation."

After performing their devotions in the chapel, the two
devotees walked for three hours in the park, discussing and
forming their plans.   Before they parted, they had resolved
to found at Montreal three religious communities—one of
secular priests, one of nuns to nurse the sick, and one of
nuns to teach the white and red children.

By the united efforts of Olier and Dauversière, an association was formed called the Society of Notre Dame de
Montreal, and a colony projected.   The island was purchased of its owners, the successors of the Hundred Associates
of Quebec, and erected into a Seigneurie by the King,
henceforth to be called *Villemarie de Montreal,* and consecrated to the Holy Family.   But it was necessary to have
a soldier-governor to place in charge of the colony, and
for this purpose the Associates of Montreal selected Paul
de Chomedey, Sieur de Maisonneuve, a devout and valiant
gentleman, who had already seen much military service.

It was thought necessary also that some discreet woman should embark with them as their nurse and housekeeper. For this purpose they selected Mademoiselle Jeanne Mance, a religious devotee, who was born of a noble family of Nogent-le-Roi.   She was filled with zeal for the new mission.   In it she thought she had found her destiny.   The ocean, the solitude, the wilderness, the Iroquois, did not deter her from her high purpose, and this delicate and refined woman at once, with enthusiastic devotion, cast her frail life upon the rock of desolation to christianize a strange land, and to soothe with her gentle influence the wildness of barbarous men.

At length in the summer of 1641, the ships set sail with Maisonneuve and his forty men, with Mademoiselle Mance and three other women on board.   But they reached Quebec too late in the autumn to think of ascending to Montreal that season.   While passing the long tedious winter at Quebec, the members of this new company were treated with much coldness by Governor Montmagny, who saw a rival governor in Maisonneuve.   Early in May, 1642, they embarked for their new home, having gained an unexpected recruit in the person of Madame de la Peltrie, another pious lady, who had also cast her fortunes in the wilderness, but it was not until 1653 that the gentle Marguerite of Bourgeoys came to bless the young colony with her presence.   All was seeming peace as they paddled their canoes along near the banks of the stream, decked in the budding beauties of the opening spring-tide; but behind every leafy thicket and rocky island lurked a danger and a terror—the fierce Iroquois on the war-path.

On the eighteenth of May they arrived at the wild island of Montreal, and landed on the very site chosen for a city by Champlain thirty-one years before. Montmagny was with them to deliver the island in behalf of the Company of the Hundred Associates to Maisonneuve, the agent of the Associates of Montreal, and Father Vimont, the Superior of the Jesuit Missions in Canada, was there in spiritual charge of the young colony. Maisonneuve and his followers sprang ashore, and falling on their knees, all devoutly joined their voices in songs of thanksgiving.

Near by, where they landed, was a rivulet bordered by a meadow, beyond which rose the ancient forest like a band of iron. The early flowers of spring were blooming in the young grass of the meadow, and the woods were filled with singing birds. A simple altar was raised on a pleasant spot not far from the shore. The ladies decorated it with flowers. Then the whole band gathered before the shrine. Father Vimont stood before the altar clad in the rich vestments of his office. The Host was raised aloft while they all kneeled in reverent silence. When the solemn rite was over, the priest turned to the little band, and said:

"You are a grain of mustard-seed that shall rise and grow till its branches overshadow the earth : You are few but your work is the work of God. His smile is on you and your children shall fill the land."

As the day waned and twilight came on, the darkened meadow, bereft of its flowers, became radiant with twinkling fire-flies. Mademoiselle Mance, Madame de la Peltrie aided by her servant, Charlotte Barré, caught the fire-flies, and tying them with threads into shining festoons, hung them before the altar where the Host remained exposed.

Then the men lighted their camp-fires, posted their sentries, and pitched their tents, and all lay down to rest. "It was the birth-night of Montreal."*

Old Indian *Ho-che-la-ga* was no more. A new race had come to people the wilderness and unfurl the banner of the Cross on the great river of the Thousand Isles.

III.

CARLETON ISLAND.

" Uttawa's tide ; this trembling moon
Shall see us float over thy surges soon,
Saint of this green isle ! hear our prayers,
Oh ! grant us cool heavens and favoring airs."

In the broad channel of the St. Lawrence, as its waters leave Lake Ontario and run between Kingston on the Canadian and Cape Vincent on the American shore, are several islands. One of the most noted of these is Carleton Island, which is situate in the American channel, four or five miles northerly of Cape Vincent. Carleton Island was known to the old French èxplorers as the *Isle aux Chevreuils*, or Isle of Roe Bucks. It lay in the line of the old Indian trail, which ran from the Canadian shore of Lake Ontario to the Iroquois cantons on its southern border, which trail avoided by its coast line the rough and dangerous waves of the open lake, and it lay also in the line of the great western trail. There being at the head of this island what Father Charlevoix, who, as the reader has already seen, visited it in 1720, calls "a pretty port that can receive large barques," it was a favorite stopping place and camping ground in all the long colonial period.

* Parkman's Jesuits in North America, p. 209, and Charlevoix's History of New France, translated by John G. Shea.

But what render this little island of more historical interest than the many other islands of the group, are the remains of a strong military work, which was constructed
upon it in the latter part of the last century, crowning the
brink of the bluff at the head of the island, overlooking
the " pretty port" and commanding the American channel
of the great river.   This fortification is now known as Fort
Carleton, but in regard to its origin and the date of its construction there has been a great deal of conjecture and not
a little controversy among historical inquirers.   It has been
supposed by some that this fort was begun by the French
during the last years of the French and Indian wars before
the English conquest of Canada, but Pouchot, in his Memoirs, while minutely describing every other fort and
station along the whole northern frontier, says nothing of
this work, and we must believe that had so important a station as this been then fortified, it would not have been
overlooked by so careful and accurate an observer as M.
Pouchot.   Again it has been alleged that these works were
begun by Sir Guy Carleton, Governor General of Canada
during the war of the Revolution, and the island and the
fort at that time named in his honor.   But the histories of
those times are silent on this subject, and the celebrated
French traveler, the Duc de la Rochefoucauld-Liancourt,
in an account of his journey along the St. Lawrence, in the
year 1795, says of this island: " During the American war
the British troops were constantly in motion, and in later
times they were quartered in an island which the French
called *Isle aux Chevreuils*, and which the English have
named Carleton, after Lord Dorchester."

Then again, in a full and complete Canadian Gazetteer,
33

published by David W. Smyth, the able and careful Surveyor General of the upper province, in 1799, no mention is made of any Fort Carleton, but it is said therein of Carleton Island : " Kingston garrison furnishes a detachment to this place." It is therefore more than probable that this fortification was never known to the British as " Fort Carleton," but was merely considered by them as an advance work connected with the defence of Kingston. Kingston was not founded until the year 1784, and this island was not known as Carleton Island until the year 1792, when by the royal proclamation of the 2d of July of that year, the old French and Indian names of several islands of the St. Lawrence, including this, were changed, and called in honor of British generals distinguished in the American wars. Hence we have Howe Island, Gage Island, Wolfe Island, Amherst Island, as well as Carleton Island, all of whose present names date from the proclamation of 1792. Kingston was built upon the site of the old Indian *Catarocoui*, and of the old French Fort Frontenac. Fort Frontenac was begun by Gov. Daniel de Remi, Seiur de Courcelle, in the year 1671, and finished the next year by the chivalrous Louis de Buade, Comte de Frontenac, whose name it bore. It was utterly destroyed by the English under Gen. Bradstreet in 1758, and was never rebuilt.

The work on Carleton Island is a bastioned half-front of a hexagonal fort of some eight hundred feet diameter, open at the rear toward the brink of the bluff overlooking the cove. The ditch, twenty-two feet wide and four feet deep, is excavated in the solid rock. The covered way was twenty-four feet wide, and the parapet four feet high. The front of the fort commands the approach from the island, while a heavy sea-wall, forty feet in height, is built along the bluff that borders the cove. Several chimneys are still standing within the fort and near it, built of stone in a permanent and massive manner, while the remains of guard houses, rifle-pits and wells are still plainly visible. Not far from the fort is an old burying-ground, in which many graves were found, and on the south side of the island was a large clearing of some thirty acres, called the King's garden. Along the western shore of the little cove are still to be seen the remains of a sunken dock. Many relics have from time to time been found near the fort, all bearing marks of British origin.

In 1796 the surveyors of Macomb's purchase found a British corporal and three men in charge of Carleton Island, and four long twelve and two six-pound cannon mounted on the works.

This island was occupied by the British until the war of 1812, when its little garrison was surprised and taken by the Americans, by whom it has ever since been occupied.

After the war the right to Carleton Island became the subject of much diplomatic correspondence between the two governments. This controversy was carried on during the presidency of Mr. Monroe by John Q. Adams, Secretary of State, on our part. It resulted in the boundary line being drawn to the north of the island, leaving it in American waters.

And now this little island, so fraught with historic memories, is the summer resort of the Carleton Island Club, an association of gentlemen who have built their summer cottage and pitch their tents on the meadow that borders the banks of the "pretty port" of the old chronicler, and in sight

of the decaying walls of the old fort. Here in this enchanting spot, among the Thousand Isles, made classic in American story by the presence long ago of a Champlain, a La
Hontan, a La Salle, a Courcelle, a Frontenac, a De la
Barre, a Charlevoix, they take a yearly respite from busy
toil, and while away the fleeting hours of the short Canadian summer in careless repose, dispensing a right royal
hospitality.

IV.

LA PRESENTATION.

The city of Ogdensburgh is in all respects a modern
city. Nothing along her streets, or in her surroundings,
indicates a day's existence earlier than the beginning of the
nineteenth century. Yet she is built upon the site of a city
of the dead, and her modern dwellings rest upon the ruins
of ancient hearth-stones. The mission of *La Presentation*
was founded in the year 1749, on the banks of the St. Lawrence, at the mouth of the Oswegatchie River, by the celebrated Sulspician Missionary Father Picquet, upon the site
of the old Indian village named *Swa-gatch*.

In colonial times, the St. Lawrence was one of the great
highways of the continent. In the olden time an Indian trail
led from the Mohawk Valley to the St. Lawrence. This trail
from the Mohawk ran up the West Canada Creek, and a
branch of it from Fort Stanwix up the valley of the Lan-
sing Kill to the waters of the Black River; thence down
the valley of the Black River to the Great Bend below
Carthage; thence over a short carry to the Indian River ;
thence down the Indian River and through Black Lake into
the River *O-swa-gatch*, and down that stream to the St.

Lawrence.   It was at the northern termination of this old Indian trail at the mouth of the *O-swa-gatch* that the Abbé Picquet founded, in the year 1749, his mission and settlement of La Presentation, so often afterward the terror of the settlers in the Mohawk valley.   As early as the 20th of October of that year Father Picquet 'had completed at his mission a palisaded fort, a house, a barn, a stable, and an oven.   He commenced a clearing, and the first year had but six heads of families, but in 1751 there were three hundred and ninety-six families of Christian Iroquois, comprising in all about three thousand people, in the little colony.   The object of this mission was to attach, if possible, the Iroquois cantons to the French.   In all the battles and massacres of the French and Indian wars in the Mohawk valley, at Lake George and along the Hudson, up to Montcalm's defeat in 1759, the *O-swa-gatch* Indians played a conspicuous part.   But in 1760, at the conquest of Canada, the post of La Presentation fell into the hands of the English, and the fort was for many years afterward occupied by a British garrison.

François Picquet, doctor of the Sorbonne, King's Missionary and Prefect Apostolic to Canada, was born at Bourg in Bresse, on the 6th of December, 1708.   At the early age of seventeen he became a missionary, and at twenty entered the Congregation of Saint Sulspice.   In 1733 he was led to the Missions of North America, where, as we have seen, he labored with such zeal for thirty years that he obtained the title of "The Apostle of the Iroquois." He returned to France, and died at Verjon on the 15th of July, 1781.

To-day two important railroad lines follow the old Indian

trails between the Mohawk and the St. Lawrence, and as the mission of La Presentation took the place of the old Indian village *Swa-gatch* at the northern end of the old war-trail, so, to-day, the modern city of Ogdensburgh, situate at the northern terminus of the railroad lines, takes the place of La Presentation. Of this mission scarce a relic now remains, save the corner-stone of the main building, which is still preserved, bearing the inscription :

In nomine † Dei omnipotentis
Huic habitationi initia dedit
Frans. Picquet, 1749.

CHAPTER XXXI.

THE COUNTY OF CHARLOTTE.

It is finished. What is finished?
Much is finished, known or unknown ;
Lives are finished ; time diminished ;
Was the fallow field left unsown ?
Will these buds be always unblown ?
—*Christina Rossetti.*

I.

Like Tryon county, its twin sister, the county of Charlotte is now almost a mythical name in the annals of New
York. The county of Charlotte, as the reader has already
seen, was set off from the county of Albany and formed on
the 24th day of March, 1772. It was so named in honor of
the Princess Charlotte, daughter of George III, or as some
say, of the Queen Consort, Charlotte of Mecklenburgh-
Strelitz. It included all that part of the state which lay
to the east of the Tryon county line, and to the north of
the present counties of Saratoga and Rensselaer, embracing
the present counties of Washington, Warren, Essex and
Clinton, the eastern part of Franklin county, and the western half of the state of Vermont.

Fort Edward was made the county-seat of Charlotte
county, and the first court was held at the house of Pat-
rick Smith in that village, on the 19th of October, 1773,
by Judges William Duer and Philip Schuyler. The first
clerk of the court was Daniel McCrea, the brother of Jeanie
McCrea, whose tragic death soon after occured near where
the court then sat.

Among the important land grants made in colonial times
was the singular one made by Gov. Fletcher on the 3d of

September, 1696, to his favorite, Godfrey Dellius, the minister of the Dutch church of Albany. This grant was a
large tract of land lying in this county, as will be seen by
the following description, copied literally from the grant,
viz : "A certaine Tract of Land lying upon the East side
of Hudson's River, between the Northermost bounds of
Saraggtoga and the Rock Retsio, Containing about Seventy
Miles in Length, and Goes backwards into the woods from
the said Hudson's River twelve Miles until it comes unto
the wood Creeke, and so far as it goes be it twelve miles
more or lesse from Hudson's River on the East side, and
from said creek by a Line twelve Miles distant from River,
to our Loving Subject the Reverend Godfredius Dellius,
Minister of the Gospell att our city of Albany, He Yielding
Rendering and Paying therefore Yearly and every Year unto
us our Heirs and Successours on the first Day of the An-
nunciation of our blessed Virgin Mary, at our city of New
Yorke the Annuall Rent of one Raccoon Skinn in Lieu and
Steade of all other Rents Services Dues Dutyes and De-
mands whatsoever for the said Tract of Land and Islands
and Premises." But in May, 1699, the Assembly vacated
this grant and suspended Mr. Dellius from the ministry on
account of his complicity in land speculations. It has been
said that Dellius, after his return to Holland, sold his interest in this tract to his successor in the ministry, the Rev.
Johannes Lydius. But John Henry Lydius, son of Johannes, who settled at the Great Carrying Place, now Fort
Edward, on the Hudson, in 1732, claimed the land by virtue of certain grants made directly to himself by the Indians,
and not from Dellius.

When the name of Tryon county was changed to Montgomery, in 1784, the name of the county of Charlotte was changed to Washington.

II.

FORT EDWARD.

Two hundred years ago the site of what is now the villlage of Fort Edward was known in forest annals as " The Great Carrying Place." It was the landing place on the Hudson from which the old Indian trail ran overland for twelve miles through the pine forest to the falls on Wood Creek that runs into Lake Champlain. From these falls the Wood Creek was navigable to the head of the lake. In those days, however, it was called Wood Creek as far down as Crown Point. In the days of the early expeditions planned by the English colonies for the conquest of Canada in the old French and Indian wars, the Great Carrying Place lying in the direct route of the old northern warpath, became the scene of stirring events. The first of those famous expeditions that passed over it was the one fitted out for Gen. Fitz-John Winthrop in July, 1690. But it was not until the year 1709 that a permanent fort was built there. In that year, Col. Peter Schuyler built a stockaded work there, which he named Fort Nicholson, in honor of the commanding general.

On the return of another expedition in the year 1711, Fort Nicholson was burned, and the Great Carrying Place was abandoned to its savage tenants until the year 1721. In that year Gov. Burnet repaired the old fort, built a small block-house there, and stationed in it a detachment of soldiers to protect the interests of the English fur trade in the wilderness.

34

And now one of those prominent characters that so often flit across the dim and shadowy stage of our almost forgotten colonial history, appears upon the scene at the Great Carrying Place. John Henry Lydius was a son of the Rev. Johannes Lydius, a minister of the old Dutch church at Albany. He was six feet and three inches in height, well-formed, and a man of much influence in the colony. For some time he was a successful rival of Sir William Johnson in his influence over the Mohawks, but in the end the Indians became so suspicious of him that they would not allow his presence at their councils. In 1732 he purchased of the Indians a large tract of land, covering the Great Carrying Place. Lydius began a settlement on the ruins of old Fort Nicholson, built a block house known as Fort Lydius, erected a saw-mill, and made various other improvements. For a dozen years he lived there, mostly engaged in the fur trade, and his little colony flourished in its lone forest position until the war of 1745 broke out. Then the French and Indians on their way to the massacre at Saratoga of that year scattered his tenants, burnt his buildings, and sent Lydius a wanderer from his forest possessions never to return. Lydius afterward went to England, where he died in 1791, in the ninety-ninth year of his age. In a biographical notice of him, published in the London *Gentleman's Magazine* of that year, he is styled the "Baron de Quade, Governor of Fort Edward."

In the year 1749, the ruins of his settlement, and of old Fort Nicholson, were visited by the famous Swedish botanist, Peter Kalm, while on his tour through the American wilds in the interest of science. Of these ruins he gives a graphic description in the story of his journeyings.

Again, in the last French war, which began in 1755 and ended with the final conquest of Canada in 1759, and the peace of 1763, the Great Carrying Place became the scene of important military operations. In 1755 Fort Lyman was built on the site of old Fort Nicholson. The next year its name was changed to Fort Edward, in honor of Prince Edward, Duke of York.

Again, in the war of the Revolution, Fort Edward becomes an important military station, but at the close of that war the military prestige of the Great Carrying Place leaves it forever. Yet no event in its long military history possesses half the tragic interest which attaches to the murder of poor Jeanie McCrea there by the Indians under Burgoyne, in the early morning of Sunday, the 27th of July, 1777. But her story has been so often told that I need not repeat it here.

To-day the modern village of Fort Edward stands on this classic ground, made famous by a century of forest warfare, and almost a hundred years of smiling peace have passed over the old Carrying Place of the wilderness. The old fort at the mouth of the creek, the barracks on the island in the mid-river, the Royal Block-house upon the south bank of the river, have crumbled into ruins, and for a hundred summers save one the sweet wild flowers have bloomed over the grave of Jeanie McCrea, the one maiden martyr of the American cause, whose innocent blood, crying from the ground, aroused her almost despairing countrymen to renewed effort, to vengeance, and to final victory over the invader at whose hands her young life was ended.

III.

SKENESBOROUGH.

Major Philip Skene, the founder of Skenesborough, now Whitehall, at the head of Lake Champlain, was of noble lineage, and some of the best blood of Scotland coursed through his veins. His fraternal grandmother was the Lady Elizabeth, daughter of Sir Thomas Wallace, a descendant of the unfortunate William Wallace, of patriot and soldier memory.

Philip Skene entered the British army in 1739, and remained in the service until the year 1782. During these forty-three years of soldier life, he was a participator in many a scene of carnage, both in the Old World and in the New. His regiment accompanied the British expedition against the Spanish-American province of New Granada, and he was at the taking of Puerto Bello in 1739, and engaged in the unsuccessful seige of Carthagena in 1741. Returning to the battle-fields of Europe, he was one of the fourteen thousand who made the daring but disastrous charge led by the Duke of Cumberland through the bloody ravine of Fontenoy in Belgium, on the 11th of May, 1745, and the following year, with his regiment, met successfully the terrible onslaught of the infuriated Highlanders upon the bloody field of Drummossie Moor, near Culloden House, on the 16th of April, in the rebellion of 1746. In 1747 he was at the battle of Lafeldt, where the Duke of Cumberland was again beaten by Marshal Saxe. In the year 1756 he came to America, and on the 2d of February in that year was promoted, by Lord Loudon, to the command of a company in the 27th, or Inniskillen, regiment of

foot.   He was engaged in the bloody assault by Gen. Abercrombie upon Fort Carrillon, at Ticonderoga, in July, 1758,
where he was wounded, and on the 31st of July, 1759, was
raised to the rank of brigade major by Gen. Amherst.   In
October following he was left in command of the British
garrison at Crown Point and Ticonderoga, and was induced
by Gen. Amherst, in 1761, to project a settlement in the
wilderness at what is now Whitehall.   But his soldier life
was not yet ended, for in 1762 he was ordered on the expedition, under Lord Albemarle, against Martinique and
Havana, and at the storming of Moro Castle was the first
man to enter the breach made in its walls by the British
guns.

Returning once more to northern New York, Philip
Skene found his infant settlement of Skenesborough reduced to fifteen souls, and, retiring from the army under half-
pay, at once began its re-establishment.   He first went to
England, and obtained from the Crown, in 1765, the grant
of a large tract of land, containing some twenty-five thousand acres, lying on both sides of Wood Creek.   Upon this
tract he began his improvements.   He built for himself, in
1770, a stone mansion house and a large stone building one
hundred and thirty feet long, which was used for military
purposes.   He also erected a stone forge, and began the
manufacture of iron.   He owned a sloop on the lake, with
which in summer he kept up a regular communication with
Montreal.   He cut a road through the forest at his own
expense, a distance of thirty miles, to Salem, for use in the
winter.   In 1773 there were seventy families in the settlement of Skenesborough, and a population of 379 persons,
including forty or more negro slaves brought by Skene from

Havana. But Skene had a still more ambitious project in view. This was no less than the founding of a new royal province out of the then disputed territory of Vermont and of northern New York, of which he was to be the Governor. But the war of the Revolution soon coming on put an end both to his flourishing settlement and to his ambitious scheme of founding a new royal province in the old wilderness.

Skenesborough was in the line of the old war-path that ran through the great northern valley. Skene espoused the royal cause, and, in May, 1775, the Americans took possession of his house, and he became a fugitive from his settlement, never to return. In 1776 an American garrison was stationed there, and upon the retreat of the Americans in 1777 before Burgoyne, its fort was blown up, its buildings all burned, and the place was left in utter ruins. Major Skene rejoined the British service, served under Lord Howe in New York, joined the expedition of Burgoyne, took part in all the battles of the campaign, and became a prisoner of war at the surrender of Saratoga. After the war his estates in America were all confiscated, and returning to Scotland, his native country, he died there in the year 1810, at an advanced age.

Such are the main incidents in the eventful career of Philip Skene, who was styled in an obituary notice "Lieut.-Governor of Crown Point and Ticonderoga, and Surveyor of his Majesty's Woods and Forests bordering on Lake Champlain," and who was one of the most famous pioneers of the Champlain valley, and the founder of another of the frustrated settlements of the old wilderness. To-day, the modern village of Whitehall, disputing with her rival sisters the supremacy of the beautiful valley of the "Lake of the Iroquois," occupies the site of the ruined colony of Skene.

IV.

THE NEW ARGYLESHIRE.

The Isle of Islay was in ancient times famous as the home of the Lords of the Isles. It is the most southerly of the Hebrides, and is situate fifteen miles off the coast of Argyleshire, Scotland. To the clan Campbell, to which the Duke of Argyle belongs, also belonged, about the year 1737, a Highland chieftain whose name was Laughlin Campbell. Like the Duke, he was a descendant of the Lords of the Isles, and was the owner of large landed possessions in the Isle of Islay.

About this time, a proclamation was issued by the governor of the Province of New York, and circulated in Scotland, offering liberal inducements to and inviting "loyal protestant Highlanders" to come and settle on the wild lands bordering the easterly side of the upper Hudson, between Saratoga and Lake Champlain. Attracted by this proclamation, Capt. Laughlin Campbell, in the year 1737, visited this country. He traversed the lands, and was pleased with the soil and situation. The Indians whom he met, admiring his athletic form, and delighted with the gay colors of his tartan costume, invited him to settle in their country. Lieut.-Governor Clarke, the acting governor of the province, also urged him to come, and, as an inducement, offered him a grant of thirty thousand acres free from all charges save those of the survey and the King's quit-rents. Thus allured, Capt. Campbell returned to Scotland,

sold his lands in the Isle of Islay, and gathering a company
of eighty-three families of protestant Highlanders, comprising in all, of adults and children, more than five hundred souls, set sail for America to settle the howling wilderness.

On the eve of their departure, Capt. Campbell and the
principal heads of families were met by the Duke of Argyle
in council, and a plan of settlement was agreed upon in
conformity to the advice of the Duke.

But these adventurers from the Hebrides were destined
to long delays, bitter disappointments, and many sad calam-
ities before they reached the goal for which they aimed.
Upon the arrival of Capt. Campbell and his band of immi-
grants in New York, the governor and surveyor-general,
incited by the love of gain, refused to make out to him the
promised conveyance of the thirty thousand acres, except
upon payment of their usual exorbitant fees therefor, and
then only on condition that Campbell would allow them a
share in the grant.   Laughlin Campbell was a man of too
much spirit to be thus dishonestly imposed upon, and utterly refused to accept the grant upon such unexpected conditions.   The governor then pathetically appealed to the
assembly to grant "these poor strangers," as he styled them,
the gift of seven pounds to each family to enable them to
settle their lands.   But the assembly, justly suspicious that
this money would all find its way into the pockets of the
avaricious governor for his fees, refused the grant.   Thus
all hopes of building up a new Argyleshire on the banks
of the Hudson by these people, were cruelly dispelled,
and they hardly knew where their wives and little ones
could find daily bread, unless the ravens fed them.   Some

of them enlisted in the expedition then fitting out in the
harbor of New York against the Spanish West Indies, and
died of the pestilence in the harbor of Carthagena. The
others separated themselves, and wandering from the city
found homes among the Dutch settlers of the river counties
above New York. In a few years, Capt. Campbell, failing
to obtain his grant upon any reasonable terms, died broken-
hearted, leaving a widow and six children almost penniless.

At length, in 1763, after twenty-five years of tedious
waiting, the heirs of Capt. Campbell received a grant of ten
thousand acres, which embraced nearly a third of the present town of Greenwich, Washington county. The next
year, 1764, a grant was also made of 47,450 acres to the colonists who came over with Campbell, and had been so cruelly
disappointed as to their possessions in the New World.
By the instrument of conveyance the tract was also erected
into the township of Argyle. Thus were the long-deferred
hopes of these settlers about to be realized, and dazzling
visions of the future importance of their township and of
their own wealth as land-owners arose at once before them.
They at once proceeded to devise on paper a plan of their
township like the one projected for them by the Duke of
Argyle on the eve of their departure from old Argyleshire.
An avenue seven miles long and twenty-four rods wide was
laid out, passing through the center of the town, entirely
across it, from east to west. This magnificent avenue was
called "The Street," a name by which it is still well known.
Along this avenue a village lot was laid out for each inhabitant, twenty-two rods front, and reaching back one hundred
and seventy-five rods, while in the rear the remainder of
the town was divided into large "farm lots" of several

35

hundred acres each for every inhabitant.   In strict accord-
ance with this plan, which appeared so well on paper, the
survey was made, and the "darling Street" was laid out.
Yet in the actual survey it crossed many a craggy bluff and
steep hillside, that never could be worked, or used for
travelling purposes.   In a short time many of them moved
upon their lands, and commenced their little clearings in
the grim old forest.   Such is the origin of the modern town
of Argyle.

Like the children of Israel wandering with Moses in the
desert, seeking Palestine for forty years, these children of
the Hebrides, after wandering for twenty-five years in the
wilderness, also found their promised land, and their leader,
Laughlin Campbell, like Moses, never reached it, but only
saw its sunny slopes from some far-off mountain peak.

CHAPTER XXXII.

OSWEGO AND THE WESTERN WAR-PATH.

It is over. What is over?
Nay how much is over truly?
Harvest days we toiled to sow for;
Now the sheaves are gathered newly—
Now the wheat is garnered duly.
—*Christina Rossetti.*

I.

SWA-GEH.

The city of Oswego sits at the mouth of the river of the same name on the south-eastern shore of Lake Ontario, the "Beautiful Lake" of the Iroquois, the long silent guns of her protecting fort overlooking its peaceful waters. Her harbor is filled with the teeming commerce of the great lakes, which seeks through her ports an outlet overland to the Atlantic seaboard, and her shipping and railroad interests are among the most important in the land. This is the Oswego of to-day. But her authentic history runs back for more than two hundred years, into the legendary lore of the Oswego, the Indian *Swa-geh*, of the olden time, the famous lake-port of the populous Iroquois cantons of western New York. The Indians, in all their journeyings through the wilderness, made their trails along the water courses. They threaded the winding streams with their frail bark canoes for hundreds of miles, carrying them on their backs around the numerous falls and rapids. To each end of these carrying places, and to all the points where they reached some large stream or some lake, they gave significant names. Many of these ancient names are still retained, and among them is *Os-we-go*, the lake port of the Iroquois.

II.

THE WESTERN WAR-TRAIL.

In colonial times, between Albany on the Hudson and the Canadian cities in the valley of the St. Lawrence, there were two great routes of travel over which the old war-trails ran. One of these was the great northern route, running up the Hudson and down the Champlain valley, and the other was the western trail, which ran up the Mohawk valley, through Oneida Lake, and down the Oswego River to Lake Ontario.

The first carrying place on the great western route was from the Hudson at Albany through the pine woods to the Mohawk at Schenectady. This carrying place avoided the *Ga-ha-oose* Falls. At the terminus of the old Indian carrying place on the Hudson, now called Albany, the Dutch, under Hendrick Christiensen, in 1614, built Fort Nassau on Castle Island. This island was situate on the east side of the river, a little below the city, and after 1630 was known as Patroon's Island. It has long since been joined with the mainland, and lost in the improvements made on that side of the river. In 1617 they built another fort at the mouth of the Normanskill, at the old Indian *Ta-wa-sent-ha* —"the place of the many dead." In 1623 Fort Orange was built by Adriaen Joris, and eighteen families built their bark huts and spent there the coming winter. In 1630 Kilian van Rensselaer, a rich diamond merchant of Holland, the original patroon, sent over his colonists, the Manor of Rensselaerwyck was founded, and a little fur trading station grew up under the guns of Fort Orange, which has since developed into the modern city of Albany. The Mohawk name for Albany was *Ska-neh-ta-de*, meaning "the place beyond the pine openings."

In the year 1662, Arendt van Curler, and other inhabitants of Fort Orange, "went west" across the old carry through the pines to the rich Mohawk flats and founded a settlement.   To this settlement they applied the old Indian name of Albany, calling it Schenectady.   From Albany it was the new settlement on the Mohawk beyond the pines. The true Indian name for Schenectady was *O-no-a-la-gone-na*, meaning "pained in the head."

From Schenectady the western trail ran up the Mohawk to what is now the city of Rome, where there was another carry of a mile in length, to the Wood Creek which flows into Oneida Lake.   This carrying place, afterward the site of Fort Stanwix, was called by the Indians *Da-ya-hoo-wa-quat*.   From it the old trail ran through the Oneida Lake, and down the Oswego River to Lake Ontario.   At the mouth of the Oswego River, on Lake Ontario, was the old Indian village called *Swa-geh*, the lake-port of the Iroquois.

From *Swa-geh* westward the navigation was unobstructed for almost a thousand miles through the great lakes to the old Indian *Chik-ah-go*, (Chicago) which was situate at the eastern end of the trail which led from the great lakes westward to the Indian *Me-che-se-pa* "the mysterious river, the Father of Waters toward the setting sun."

III.

OSWEGO.

For a period of one hundred and eighty years, from its earliest settlement in 1614 up to the end of the last French war, the chief business of Albany was dealing in furs and peltries with the Indians of the North and West. But the French at Montreal and Quebec at length began to divert the western fur trade, and it became necessary for the merchants of Albany to adopt measures to retain it. So, in 1720, the citizens of Albany pushed boldly out on the old western trail to *Swa-geh*, on Lake Ontario, and established a fur trading station there upon what the French claimed was their territory. The importance of this measure will be readily seen, for *Swa-geh* commanded the fur trade of the great West. *Swa-geh* thus became the lake-port for Albany as well as for the cantons of the Iroquois.

As early as the year 1700 Col. Romer, after making a careful exploration of the country of the Five Nations, mentioned *Swa-geh* as an important station on Lake Ontario for the prosecution of the fur trade with the Indians of the great West. But it was not until 1721 that *Swa-geh* was occupied by the English, and not till 1727 that Gov. Burnet built a fort there and it was called Oswego. In a letter to the Board of Trade by Gov. Burnet, dated May 9th, 1727, he says: "I have this spring sent up workmen to build a stone house of strength at a place called Oswego, at the mouth of the Onnondaga River, where our principal trade with the Five Nations is carried on." This building was eighty feet square, and of great strength. In 1744, at the beginning of the French and Indian war of that date, it was mounted with cannon transported with much toil from Albany up the wild valley of the Mohawk.

In 1756 Oswego was the northern rendezvous of Gen. Shirley, with fifteen hundred men, on his expedition against the French forts Frontenac and Niagara. From this period Oswego became an important military post on the northern frontier, and an object of jealousy to the French. At length it was attacked in 1757 by five thousand men under Gen. Montcalm, and captured after a gallant resistance on the part of its garrison. On retiring from Oswego, Montcalm left it a heap of ruins, but in 1758 Gen. Bradstreet appeared upon the scene with his army of three thousand three hundred and forty men, on his march against Fort Frontenac, and soon rebuilt the decaying fort. After the close of the last French and Indian war, Oswego was occupied by an English garrison until the year 1798, when it was abandoned to the Americans.

IV.

OLD FORTS ON THE WESTERN WAR-PATH.

Up to the end of the last French and Indian war, Albany and Schenectady were strongly fortified and surrounded by palisades. They were as much walled cities as those of mediæval times in Europe. In Albany a huge frowning fort called Fort Frederick, bristling with cannon, filled up State street a little below where the Capitol now stands, its northeast bastion resting on the ground now occupied by St. Peter's church. At Schenectady was a wooden fort in the line of palisades which surrounded the village, with four block-houses as flankers. Between Schenectady and *Swa-*

geh was a line of forts built for the protection of the traveling fur-traders, and as barriers to French and Indian in-
vasion from the valley of the St. Lawrence. The first of
these was at the mouth of the Schohariekill, and was called
Fort Hunter. It was built on the site of old Indian *Te-
hon-de-lo-ga*, the lower castle of the Mohawks. Above Fort
Hunter, near the Indian *Ga-no-jo-hi-e*—"washing the basin"
—the middle Mohawk castle, was Fort Plain. The Indian
name of Fonda was *Ga-na-wa-da*—meaning "over the
rapids." Of Little Falls, it was *Ta-la-que-ga*—"small
bushes," and of Herkimer the Indian name was *Te-uge-ga*,
the same as the river. At Herkimer was Hendrick's castle
and Fort Herkimer, near *Ga-ne-ga-ha-ga*, the upper Mohawk castle.

The Indian name for Utica was *Nun-da-da-sis*—meaning
"around the hill." At Utica, the Indian trail from the west
crossed the river. To defend this ford of the Mohawk at
Utica, a small earth-work was built in 1756, and named Fort
Schuyler. From the little settlement began at this old fort
Utica has become the queen city of the Mohawk valley.
The territory upon which the city of Utica has been built
was granted in 1734 to Gov. Cosby, and was long known in
colonial annals as "Cosby's Manor."

A little above Utica was a small Indian station called
Ole-hisk—"the place of nettles." This is now Oriskany,
one of the famous battle-grounds of the Revolution. At
the carrying place between the Mohawk River and Wood
Creek was the Indian *Da-ya-hoo-wa-quat*, meaning "the
carrying place." Here Fort Williams was built in 1732, and
on its site, in 1758, was built Fort Stanwix. During the
Revolutionary war the name Fort Stanwix was changed to

Fort Schuyler, and should not be mistaken for the little fort at Utica of that name. At Wood Creek, a mile from Fort Stanwix, Fort Bull was built in 1737.

At the mouth of Wood Creek, on the Oneida Lake, a Royal Block-house was built, and at the west end of Oneida Lake, in 1758, Fort Brewerton was built. The Indian name for Wood Creek was *Ka-ne-go-dick;* for Oneida Lake was *Ga-no-a-lo-hole*—"head on a pole." For Syracuse the Indian name was *Na-ta-dunk*, meaning "pine-tree broken with top hanging down," and the Indian name of Fort Brewerton was *Ga-do-quat*. Fort Brewerton, the remains of which may still be seen from the railroad track, was an octagonal palisaded fort of about three hundred and fifty feet in diameter. After the close of the French war, and during Pontiac's war, Fort Brewerton was commanded by Capt. Mungo Campbell, of the 55th Highlanders. Mrs. Grant, of Laggan, in her *Memoirs of an American Lady*, gives an interesting description of this fort, which she visited while on her way to Oswego about the year 1763.

At the falls on the Oswego River, (now Fulton) Gen. Bradstreet built a small stockaded fort in 1758, and garrisoned it with one hundred men. In 1755, a new fort was built at Oswego by Col. Mercer. This fort is now known as Fort Ontario.

Such was the line of defences bristling along the old western war-path between Albany and Oswego at the close of the last French and Indian war. For a hundred years this old western trail was the pathway of contending armies, its streams were often crimsoned with blood, and its wild meadows filled with nameless graves.

36

CHAPTER XXXIII.

SARATOGA AND THE NORTHERN WAR-PATH.

She stood beside the well her God had given
To gush in that deep wilderness, and bathed
The forehead of her child until he laughed
In his reviving happiness.   *   *   *
                                —*Willis.*

I.

INDIAN SARATOGA.

Among the earliest dates in which the name Saratoga appears in history is the year 1684. It was then not the name of a town, nor of a county, nor of a great watering place, but it was the name of an old Indian hunting ground situated along both sides of the Hudson River. The Hudson, after it breaks through its last mountain barrier above Glens Falls, for many miles of its course runs through a wider valley. After winding for a while through this wider valley, it reaches the first series of its bordering hills, and this old hunting ground was situate where the outlying hills begin to crowd down to the river banks. In the Indian tongue it was significantly called *Se-rach-ta-gue*, meaning "the hillside country of the great river.*

It also has been said Saratoga, in the Indian language, means the "place of the swift water," in allusion to the rapids and falls that break the stillness of the stream where this hillside country begins on the river.†

An Indian whose name was *O-ron-hia-tek-ha* of Caugh-

*Steele's Analysis, p. 13.

† Vide Judge Scott's historical address at Ballston Spa, July 4th, 1876, also, Reminiscences of Saratoga, by Wm. L. Stone, p. 5.

na-wa-ga on the St. Lawrence, who was well acquainted
with the Mohawk dialect, informed Dr. Hough, the historian, that Saratoga was from *Sa-ra-ta-ke*, meaning "a
place where the track of the heel may be seen," in allusion
to a spot near by, where depressions like foot-prints may be
seen in the rocks. Yet Morgan, in his *League of the Iroquois*, says the signification of Saratoga is lost.

But whether its meaning be this, that, or the other, I am
sure that it is gratifying to us all that this famous summer
resort, situate as it is on American soil, bears an American
name.

As early as 1684, this hillside country of the Hudson,
the ancient Indian *Se-rach-ta-gue*, was sold by the Mohawk
sachems to Peter Philip Schuyler and six other eminent
citizens of Albany, and the Indian grant confirmed by the
English government. This old hunting ground then became known in history as the Saratoga patent. As set forth
in the Indian deed and described in the letters patent, it
was a territory of fifteen miles in length along the river
and six miles in width on both sides. It reached from the
Di-on-on-da-ho-wa, now the Battenkill, near Fort Miller, on
the north, to the *Ta-nen-da-ho-wa*, now the Anthony's kill,
near Mechanicville, on the south. The towns of old Saratoga and Stillwater on the west side of the river, and the
town of Easton (the east town) on the east side of the
river, are within the bounds of this ancient patent. This
was Saratoga of the olden time, called on some old maps
So-roe-to-gos land.

In the year 1687, three years after the Mohawks had sold
this hunting ground, and the patent had been granted, Gov.
Dongan of New York attempted to induce a band of

Christian Iroquois that the French missionaries had led to *Cach-na-oua-ga* on the St. Lawrence, to return and settle in ancient *Se-rach-ta-gue*. This was done to form a barrier between the then frontier town of Albany and the hostile French and Indians on the north. Some of the descendants of these Indians still make an annual pilgrimage to the springs, and encamping in the groves near by, form an interesting part of the great concourse of summer visitors.

It will be seen, however, that the ground on which the village of Saratoga Springs is built, and the region in which the famous mineral springs were found, formed no part of the old hunting ground and patent of Saratoga. The *So-roe-to-gos* land of the olden time lay along both sides of the Hudson, and extended no further west than Saratoga lake.

II.

KAY-AD-ROS-SE-RA.

The Indian name for the territory in which the famous mineral springs were found was *Kay-ad-ros-se-ra*.*

Like Saratoga, it was one of the favorite hunting grounds of the Iroquois. It lay in the angle between the two great rivers, to the south of a line drawn from Glens Falls on the Hudson westerly to near Amsterdam on the Mohawk. *Kay-ad-ros-se-ra* means in the Indian tongue, the "lake country." Its principal lake, now Lake Saratoga, was the Lake *Kay-ad-ros-se-ra* of the Mohawks, and its largest stream the *Kay-ad-ros-se-ra* river. On the old French maps Saratoga Lake is called *Cap-i-a-qui*. The Indian name for Round Lake, now famous as a camp-meeting ground, was *Ta-nen-da-ho-wa*.

* So written in Claude Joseph Sauthier's map of 1779.

The forests of ancient *Kay-ad-ros-se-ra* were full of game, and its lakes and streams swarmed with fish. The herring ran up the west side of the Hudson, and through Fish Creek, giving rise to its name, into Lake Saratoga in immense numbers. The shad ran up the east side of the river, and lay in vast schools in the falls and rapids above and below Fort Edward. The sturgeon frequented the "sprouts" of the Mohawk, and sunned themselves in the basin below Cohoes falls.

The wild animals of *Kay-ad-ros-se-ra* were attracted in immense numbers by the saline properties of the mineral springs that bubbled up in its deepest shades, all unknown save to them and its Indian owners. In this "paradise of sportsmen" the Mohawks and their nearer sister tribes of the Iroquois, the Oneidas and Onondagas, and sometimes the further off Cayugas and Senecas, every summer built their hunting lodges around its springs, and on the banks of its lakes and rivers. It will be seen that ancient wild *Kay-ad-ros-se-ra* was as famous in the old time to the red man as modern Saratoga is to-day to the white man.

The first grant made by the Mohawks of any part of *Kay-ad-ros-se-ra* bears date the 26th of August, 1702. In this deed the Indians sold to David Schuyler and Robert Livingston, Jr., a tract of land lying on the west bank of the Hudson, above the Saratoga patent, running up as far as the Great Carrying Place, (Fort Edward) "and westward into the woods as far as their property belongs." In the spring following, Samson Shelton Broughton, attorney general of the province, obtained a license from the governor in behalf of himself and company to purchase from the Indians a tract of land known by the Indian name of

Kay-ad-ros-se-ra. This license is dated April 22, 1703. In pursuance of this license, a purchase was effected of *Kay-ad-ros-se-ra*, and an Indian deed given the 6th of October, 1704, signed by the sachems of the tribe. At length a release was obtained from David Schuyler and Robert Livingston, Jr., of their title acquired by the deed of the 26th of August, 1702, and on the 2d day of November, 1708, a patent was granted by Queen Anne to "her loving subjects Nanning Hermance, Johannes Beekman, Rip van Dam," and ten others, of the whole of *Kay-ad-ros-se-ra.* Yet it was not until the year 1768 that the deed given by the Indian sachems in 1704 was confirmed by the tribe, and then only through the powerful influence of Sir William Johnson.

The sachems said they were told by the agents of the purchasers that the description in the deed covered only " land enough for a good sized farm," and that they never intended by it to convey to the whites " for a few baubles," their great hunting ground containing half a million acres. After more than sixty years of fruitless quarrels over this old title, the Indians had grown weak and the whites had grown strong, and it is the old story, the weaker gave up to the stronger.

On the 24th day of March, 1772, three years before the war of the Revolution broke out, and about the time the first white settler was building his rude cabin at the Springs, these two patents of *Kay-ad-ros-se-ra* and Saratoga were united by the colonial government into a district. The name *Kay-ad-ros-se-ra* was dropped, and the district was named after the smaller patent, and called the District of Saratoga. The old hunting ground, the beautiful lake and the famous springs of *Kay-ad-ros-se-ra* have, since the Act of the 24th of March, 1772, all borne the name of Saratoga. Since then the grand old Indian name *Kay-ad-ros-se-ra,* so far as territory is concerned, has fallen out of human speech, and is only heard in connection with the principal stream and mountain chain of the great hunting ground so famous in Indian story.

III.

THE NORTHERN WARPATH.

The territory which now comprises the county of Saratoga lay in the angle between two great pathways, one from the north, the other from the west. And lying as it did in the angle of the war trails, it became the battle ground of nations. Whoever possessed it was master of the situation and held the door of the country. For the hundred and seventy years in which its authentic history runs back, before the close of the war of the Revolution, there was scarcely an hour of peaceful rest unbroken by the fear of the savage invader in this battle ground of Saratoga, in this angle between the great northern and western war trails.

In previous chapters the reader has already been apprised of some of the main incidents in this long warfare down to the return of the Marquis de Tracy's expedition to the Mohawk country in the war of 1666, after which there was a comparative peace for twenty years.

Again in 1686, after these twenty years of peace were ended, the French and Indian war broke out afresh, and lasted through nine weary years to the peace of 1695. During this period of nine years, numerous war parties passed through *Kay-ad-ros-se-ra* and Saratoga on their way to and from the hostile settlements on the St. Lawrence and the Mohawk and lower Hudson. In the month of August, 1689, nine hundred Mohawk warriors passed over the old trail that led across the Greenfield hills, which twenty-three years before had been trodden by the victorious Tracy with his veteran soldiers and train of French noblemen. During the twenty years' peace these wild savages had been nursing their wrath, and now their hour of sweet revenge had come. Launching their bark canoes, they swept down though Lakes George and Champlain, and landing on the island of Montreal, like so many ravening wolves, carried the war to the very gates of the French forts on the St. Lawrence.

Six months later, in February, 1690, Lieut. Le Moyne de St. Helene passed up Lake Champlain and down the Hudson on snow shoes, and traversing Lake Saratoga upon the ice, and winding up the *Kay-ad-ros-se-ra* river and the Mourningkill to the little hamlet, now below Ballston, called East Line, passed over Ballston Lake, and in the dead of the night of the 9th of February, swept down upon the sleeping inhabitants of Schenectady with indiscriminate slaughter.

On his hasty return, Lieut. de St. Helene was followed by Major Peter Schuyler, at the head of a company of two hundred whites and a band of Mohawks, as far as Lake Champlain, and fifteen French prisoners were taken and brought back to the Mohawk castles.

And now we come during these nine years of war to the first of those military expeditions that were undertaken upon a large scale by the English colonies for the conquest of Canada, which passing through Old Saratoga, made it a place of note in the annals of savage warfare.

On the 1st day of May, 1690, the first American Congress met at the old fort in the city of New York. In pursuance of its recommendations, a joint expedition of the colonies was planned and fitted out for the conquest of Canada, the command of which was given to General Fitz John Winthrop of Connecticut.

On the 14th day of July, 1690, Gen. Winthrop, with the New England troops, left Hartford, and passing through a virgin wilderness, whose interminable shades were broken only by the little settlements at and near Albany, arrived at Stillwater on the first of August.

Stillwater was " so named," says the old chronicler, " because the water passes so slowly as not to be discovered, while above and below it is disturbed, and rageth as in a great sea occasioned by rocks and falls therein."

On the day after, he arrived at *Sar-agh-to-ga*, near where Schuylerville now is. Here at Saratoga he found a block-house and some Dutch troops under Major Peter Schuyler, mayor of Albany, who had preceded him with the New York forces. From this date, the second day of August, 1690, six years after the old patent was granted, and almost two centuries ago, Saratoga takes its place among the long list of our country's geographical names.

Major Schuyler had already pushed up to the second carrying place, now Fort Miller Falls, where he had stopped to.build some bark canoes. The next and third carrying place above was from the Hudson at Fort Edward to what is now Fort Ann, on Wood Creek. This portage ran through a magnificent grove of pines for twelve miles, and was known in old forest annals as the " Great Carrying Place."

37

This expedition proved an utter failure. Before its return, however, Capt. John Schuyler, brother of the mayor, and grandfather of Gen. Philip Schuyler of revolutionary memory, pressed on down Lake Champlain, and made his famous raid upon the Canadian settlement of La Prairie.

In the next year, 1691, Major Peter Schuyler, at the head of two hundred and sixty whites and eighty Mohawks from their camp at Saratoga Lake, following in the track of his brother, made another descent upon the doomed settlement of La Prairie.

To retaliate these injuries, Comt de Frontenac, Governor General of Canada resolved to strike a blow upon the Mohawk settlements. Accordingly, in January, 1693, he sent a force of six hundred and twenty-five men, including Indians, who passed down over the old trail that led from Lake George to the bend of the Hudson above Glens Falls, and from thence through Wilton, Greenfield, and along the brow of the *Kay-ad-ros-se-ra* range to the Mohawk castles. On its return march over this old trail, this war party was followed by Major Peter Schuyler and his forces, who overtook it in the town of Greenfield or Wilton, Saratoga county.

Near the old Indian Pass over the Palmerstown range on the border of Wilton, almost if not quite in sight of Saratoga Springs, in the month of February, 1693, a battle was fought, or rather a series of engagements took place, in which the French loss amounted in all to thirty-three killed and twenty-six wounded. At the conclusion of the fight the French retreated towards the Hudson. It had been thawing, and the ice was floating in the river. When the French arrived on its banks a large cake of ice had lodged in the bend of the stream. The French crossed over on this cake of ice in safety, but before their pursuers came up it had floated away, leaving them no means of crossing, and the chase was relinquished. This closes the record of the nine years' war from 1686 to 1695. From the year 1695 until the year 1709, a period of fourteen years, peace again spread her white wings over the grim old wilderness along the great northern war-path.

IV.

THE WAR OF 1709.

In the year 1709 the war known as Queen Anne's war broke out between England and France, and the warfare of the wilderness again began its savage butchery. In this war we come to the founding and construction of the military works in old Saratoga and along the great northern valley, which lasted unto comparatively modern times, and with whose names we have been so long familiar.

In 1709 a joint expedition like that led by Gen. Winthrop in 1690, was planned for the conquest of Canada. In that year, Major Richard Ingoldesby, who had come over in command of the Queen's four companies of regulars, was lieutenant-governor of the province. Peter Philip Schuyler was now a colonel in the service, as well as one of the governor's council and a commissioner of Indian affairs, while his brother John had been advanced to the rank of lieutenant-colonel. The command of the expedition was given by Ingoldesby in May to Gen. Nicholson.

About the 1st of June, Col. Schuyler, in command of the vanguard of the English forces, comprising three hundred men, including pioneers and artificers, moved out of Albany upon his northward march. At Stillwater, Colonel Schuyler halted his command, and built a small stockaded fort for provisions, which he named Fort Ingoldesby, in honor of the lieutenant-governor. Halting again at old Saratoga, where he had built a block house in 1690, and which in the meantime had become a little hamlet in the wilderness, Col. Schuyler built another stockaded fort. This fort was built on the east side of the Hudson, below the mouth of the Battenkill, on the hill nearly opposite the mouth of Fish Creek, and was known as Fort Saratoga.

Proceeding up the river, Col. Schuyler built another fort at the second carrying place of Fort Miller Falls. From Fort Miller Falls Col. Schuyler built a military road along the east bank of the Hudson up to the Great Carrying Place. At the beginning of the Great Carrying Place on the Hudson, now Fort Edward, Col. Schuyler built another stockaded fort, which he named Fort Nicholson, in honor of the commanding general. Proceeding across the Great Carrying Place to the forks of Wood Creek, which runs into Lake Champlain, he built another stockaded fort, which was first called Fort Schuyler, but which two years later was named Fort Anne, in honor of the Queen. I need not follow the fortunes of this expedition to its failure and return.

Two years later, in the year 1711, another expedition in command of Gen. Nicholson left Albany on the 24th of August, and proceeding up the northern valley of the Hudson, crossed the Great Carrying Place to Fort Anne. While there, Gen. Nicholson learned that her Majesty's fleet in the St. Lawrence, which was to co-operate with him in the conquest of Quebec, had been shattered by storms with the loss of a thousand men. So he returned to Albany with all his forces, and the third expedition fitted out for the conquest of Canada proved, like the other two, a most mortifying failure. In 1713, peace was again declared between England and France, which lasted until 1744, and for a period of thirty-one years there was peace along the great northern war-path.

During this period of thirty-one years of quiet in the old wilderness, the French were not idle on Lake Champlain, neither were the Schuylers idle at their little settlement of Old Saratoga. In 1731, during this period of profound peace, the French built Fort St. Frederick, at Crown Point, on Lake Champlain. This fort soon became a menace and a terror to the people of the valley of the Upper Hudson. There grew up under its protecting guns a little French village of near fifteen hundred inhabitants, and the valley of Lake Champlain became as much a province of New France as was the valley of the St. Lawrence. During this period of thirty-one years of peace, the landing place of Old Saratoga grew into a little forest hamlet containing some thirty houses and over one hundred inhabitants.

V.

THE WAR OF 1744.

The war of 1744 found Saratoga, with its little tumble-down stockaded fort on the hill near by, the extreme northern outpost of the English settlements. There was but a single step, as it were, between it and the frowning walls of the French fort St. Frederick at Crown Point, from which a deadly blow might be expected at any moment. In November, 1745, the blow came. At midnight on the 15th of November the sleeping inhabitants of Old Saratoga were awakened by the terrible war-whoop. The place was attacked by a force of three hundred French and Indians under the command of M. Marin. The fort and houses of the village were all burned to the ground. Of the inhabitants, thirty were killed and scalped, and sixty made prisoners.

The celebrated French missionary, Father Picquet, the founder, in 1749, of the mission and settlement La Presentation, at the mouth of the Oswegatchie, now Ogdensburgh, on the St. Lawrence, accompanied this expedition.

During this short war no less than twenty-seven marauding parties swept down from Fort St. Frederick at Crown Point upon the settlers of what are now Saratoga and Rensselaer counties. It was the midnight war-whoop, the uplifted tomahawk, the scalping knife, the burning dwelling, the ruined home, that made the whole country a scene of desolation and blood.

In the spring of 1746 the English rebuilt and enlarged the Fort at Saratoga, and named it Fort Clinton, in honor of the governor of the Province. During the night of the 17th of June, 1747, Fort Clinton at old Saratoga, was approached by a band of French and Indians under the command of La Corne St. Luc. While the main body of the French were lying in concealment near by, La Corne sent forward six scouts with orders to lie in ambush within eight paces of the fort, to fire upon those who should first come out of the fort the next morning, and if attacked, to retreat pretending to be wounded. At daybreak in the morning two Englishmen came out of the fort, and they were at once fired upon by the French scouts, who thereupon fled. Soon after the firing began, a hundred and twenty Englishmen came out of the fort, headed by their officers, and started in hot pursuit of the French scouts. The English soon fell in with the main body of the French, who, rising from their ambuscade, poured a galling fire into the English ranks. The English at first bravely stood their ground and sharply returned the fire. The guns of the fort also opened upon the French with grape and cannon shot. But the Indians soon rushed upon the English with terrible yells, and with tomahawk in hand drove them into the fort, giving them scarcely time to shut the gates behind them. Many of the English soldiers, being unable to reach the fort, ran down the hill into the river, and were drowned or killed with the tomahawk. The Indians killed and scalped twenty-eight of the English, and took forty-five prisoners, besides those drowned in the river.

In the autumn following this disaster, Fort Clinton of Saratoga was dismantled and burnt by the English, and Albany once more became the extreme northern outpost of the English colonies, with nothing but her palisaded walls between her and the uplifted tomahawks of the ever-frowning north. In May, 1748, peace was again proclaimed, which lasted for the brief period of seven years, until the beginning of the last French and Indian war of 1755, which ended in the conquest of Canada.

During this short peace of seven years, the settler's axe was again heard upon many a hillside, as he widened his little clearing, and the smoke went curling gracefully upward from his lonely cabin in many a valley along the upper Hudson.

It was in the summer of 1749, during this short peace, that Peter Kalm,* the Swedish botanist, traveled, in the interests of science, through this great northern war-path. He gives, in his account of the journey, a graphic description of the ruins of the old forts at Saratoga, at Fort Nicholson and Fort Ann, which were then still remaining in the centres of small deserted clearings in the great wilderness through which he passed. He made many discoveries of rare and beautiful plants before unknown to Europeans, and in our swamps and lowlands a modest flower, the *Kalmia glauca*, swamp-laurel, blooms in perpetual remembrance of his visit. But there were no mineral springs in the Saratoga visited by Peter Kalm.

VI.

THE WAR OF 1755.

We now come to the stirring events of the last French and Indian war. This short war lasted only four years, from 1755 to 1759, but during its continuance great armies marched through the old northern war-path, dyeing its streams with blood, and filling its wild meadows with thousands of nameless new-made graves, and at its close the sceptre of the French kings over the valleys of Lake Champlain and the St. Lawrence dropped from their hands forever. In this war the tide of battle moved northward, and settling around Lakes George and Champlain, passed beyond the limits of Saratoga.

* Vide Kalm's Travels, in Pinkerton, vol. 13.

Space will hardly permit me to give more than the names of the vast armies—vast armies for those times and for those northern wilds—whose movements then made that fair scene the classic ground of our country's history.

The first expedition was that under Sir William Johnson, who in the summer of 1755 took his position at the head of Lake St. Sacrament, changed its name to Lake George,* in honor of the English King and in token of his empire over it, and successfully defended it in the three bloody battles of the 8th of September with the French and Indians, in command of the veteran French general, the Baron Dieskau.

It was while on his way to Lake George, in the month of August, 1755, that Gen. Lyman halted his troops and built a fort in old Saratoga, at the mouth of Fish Creek, now Schuylerville, on the Hudson, and named it Fort Hardy, in honor of Sir Charles Hardy, the governor of New York. After the battle of the 8th of September, 1755, Sir William Johnson built Fort William Henry, at the head of Lake George, naming it in honor of the Duke of Cumberland.

Of Gen. Winslow's fruitless expedition of 1756, during which he built Port Winslow, at Stillwater, in the place of Fort Ingoldesby, built by Col. Schuyler in 1709; of the campaign of 1757, in which Gen. Montcalm invested and destroyed Fort William Henry, at Lake George, whose surrender was followed by the dreadful massacre of a part of its garrison by the Indians; of the magnificent army led

---

* Doc. His. of New York, Vol. I, p. 429 : "I am building a fort at this lake, which the French call Lake St. Sacrament, but I have given it the name of Lake George, not only in honor of his Majesty, but to ascertain his undoubted dominion here."—Sir William Johnson to Board of Trade, September 3d, 1775.

38

by Gen. Abercrombie, in 1758, against Fort Carillon, at
Ticonderoga, into the jaws of slaughter and defeat, and of
the final triumph of the English forces, under Gen. Amherst, on Lake Champlain, and under Gen. Wolfe, at Quebec, in 1759, I shall make but this passing mention.*

The peace of 1763, between England and France, brought
joy to the war worn inhabitants of the great northern valley. The hardy settlers, now that all fear of the northern
invader was gone, left the banks of the rivers and the protection of the forts, and began to push their way into the
heart of the old wilderness, and with them came Dirk
Schouten, the first white settler among the Indian wigwams
near the High Rock spring, in the summer of 1773.

Before we briefly trace the history of Schouten's little
clearing, with its rude cabin, through its slow development
into our modern village of Saratoga Springs, we must glance
at some of the important events that occurred during the
war of the American Revolution, and also notice the important battles of that war, which, taking place on the soil
of old Saratoga, have shed such lustre on her name.

VII.

CAMPAIGN OF 1777.

In the campaign of 1777, Saratoga again became the battle ground of the great northern valley.

In the early summer of that year, Gen. Burgoyne, with
the British army under his command, swept down from the
north through the old war-path, driving everything before

* See Silliman's Tour, Pouchot's Memoirs, Butler's Lake George and
Lake Champlain, History of Queensbury, by Dr. A. W. Holden, and
Narrative of Father Roubaud in Kip's Early Jesuit Missions.

him. On the 30th of June, at Crown Point, Burgoyne uses this striking language in his general orders to his army: "The army embarks to-morrow to approach the enemy. The services required of this particular expedition are critical and conspicuous. During our progress occasions may occur in which nor difficulty, nor labor, nor life, are to be regarded. This army must not retreat." On the 29th of July the British army arrived on the banks of the Hudson at Fort Edward. About the same time the American forces under General Schuyler retreated down the Hudson, and made a stand on the islands at the mouth of the Mohawk, where the rude earthworks then thrown up by them can still be seen by the curious traveler as he rides near them and even over them in the cars of the Delaware and Hudson Canal Company's railroad.

Before the middle of August, Burgoyne passed down the east side of the river to the Fort Miller Falls and the mouth of the Battenkill, where he remained for over a month, until he crossed the Hudson on the 13th and 14th of September, and encamped on the heights of Saratoga, on his way to Bemis' Heights.

On the 19th of August, Gen. Gates superseded Gen. Schuyler in the command of the northern army, and on the 23d, Col. Morgan's regiment of riflemen arrived in the American camp from Virginia.

It has always seemed to me that the removal of General Philip Schuyler from the command of our northern army, although at the time so loudly called for by the disaffected, and perhaps necessary to appease their clamor, was really an act of injustice to that distinguished son of New York, and that much of the brilliant success of that army in the end was due to the prudent plans and wise forethought of Gen. Schuyler.

On the 8th of September, Gen. Gates marched his army up to Stillwater, and a day or two after went two miles further up the river and took up his position at Bemis' Heights. At Bemis' Heights the hills crowd down to the river bank, and leave only a narrow defile through which the great northern road runs up and down the valley. At the foot of the hill by the roadside near the bank of the river, stood a little tavern kept by one J. Bemis. His farm ran up over the hills back into the woods to the west of his tavern stand, and the hills were called after him Bemis' Heights.

Gen. Gates took possession of this narrow defile on the river bank, and extending his left wing back from the river over the heights to the westward, threw up intrenchments, and awaited the approach of Burgoyne. He did not wait long.

On the 13th, Burgoyne moved down on the west side of the river to Coveville. On the 17th he encamped near Sword's house, within four miles of the American army. Between him and the American camp, along the hills back from the river, there were several deep ravines to cross, and Burgoyne spent the 18th in making roads and bridges over these ravines.

At ten o'clock on the morning of the 19th of September, Burgoyne broke up the camp at Sword's house, and dividing his army into three divisions, took up his march to attack the Americans in their intrenchments. General Burgoyne, in command of the center column, followed the road which he had cut the day before through the woods and across the ravines about a mile back from the river. Gen. Fraser, in command of the right wing, took a circuitous route about a mile further back from the river than Burgoyne, while Gen. Phillips and Gen. Riedesel, with the left wing proceeded down the road along the river's bank.

The country was then all covered with its primeval forests, in which was here and there a small clearing with its lonely, deserted log cabin. On the road which Burgoyne took with his center column, there was one of those little clearings, which lay about a mile north of the American camp, and a mile back from the river. This clearing contained some twelve acres of ground. It was about the size of two city blocks, and was called Freeman's farm.

In that little clearing in the old wilderness, on that 19th day of September, 1777, was fought one of the few decisive battles of the world.*

I will not weary the reader with its details. The battle began about noon, at the log house, where a company of Morgan's Riflemen was stationed when the pickets of the center division of the British army reached the clearing. The British pickets, who were commanded by Major Forbes, were soon driven back to the main column, and the pursuing American riflemen routed in turn.

Reinforcements soon coming up from the American camp,

---

* Henry Hallam, author of the celebrated work, the "View of the State of Europe during the Middle Ages," defines decisive battles as "those battles of which a contrary event would have essentially varied the drama of the world in all its subsequent scenes." E. S. Creasy, professor of history in the University Col. of London, has selected fifteen battles, beginning with Marathon, which took place 2366 years ago, and ending with Waterloo, in 1815, as the only ones coming within this definition. Among the fifteen he names Saratoga.—Vide Gen. Bullard's Historical Address at Schuylerville, July 4th, 1876.

and the main central British column under Burgoyne advancing into the clearing, at three o'clock the battle became general. Like the waves of a stormy sea the combatants drove each other back and forth across that little clearing all the afternoon for four weary, bloody hours, until night closed the scene.

When the shadows of that night passed over that bloody field, *the cause of American Independence was won !*

At the conclusion of the fight, the Americans returned to their camp on the heights. They had scarcely a single round of ammunition left in their magazines. Had the British renewed the attack on the morrow, they would have achieved a bloodless victory, but they were too much crippled by the fight to renew it again so soon. Upon how slender a thread does the fate of nations sometimes hang. Gen. Gates alone knew the terrible secret, and a large supply coming up from Albany the next day, the danger was averted.*

The British encamped on the field of battle, and occupying the plain to the east of it, down to the river's bank at what is now called Wilbur's Basin, threw up a line of intrenchments from the river to the Freeman farm, corresponding with the American works at Bemis' Heights. The two armies remained in this position for eighteen days.

Again on the afternoon of the 7th of October, the British marched out of their encampment to make another attempt to turn the left wing of the American army. The Americans marched out of their intrenchments to meet them, bearing down upon them with such fury that in less than

* Neilson's Burgoyne's Campaign.

an hour the British were driven into their camp with great slaughter.

Then around the British camp at Freeman's Farm the battle raged furiously till nightfall, the Americans carrying the British out-posts at the point of the bayonet as the darkness set in. Once more on Freeman's Farm, and on the hill to the west of it where the first attack was that day made, the dead bodies of the slain lay upon the ground "as thick as sheaves in a fruitful harvest field."

On the morning of the eighth the British were all huddled down around the Smith house at Wilbur's Basin, and the victorious Americans had advanced to the plain just below them.

At sunset on the evening of the eighth the British buried Gen. Fraser in the great redoubt on the bluff overlooking the river near the Smith house, and soon after took up their midnight retreat toward the plains and heights of Saratoga.

Then on the morning of the 17th of October, amid the crimson and golden glories of our American autumn forests, the like of which they had never seen before, the British marched out of their perilous camp " to the verge of the river where the old fort stood "—Fort Hardy—and laid down their arms as prisoners of war to the victorious Gates.*

The Americans were now masters of the great northern valley. These old hunting grounds in the angle of the war

* The Duc de la Rochefoucauld-Liancourt, who in the year 1795, while on his tour through this country, visited this old battle-ground, and had all the points of interest pointed out to him by eye-witnesses of the scenes, says that the spot where Burgoyne surrendered his sword to Gates was in one corner of the grounds in front of the Schuyler mansion.

trails were theirs. The country itself was from that day theirs.

It is proposed to build a monument on the heights of old Saratoga in honor of the surrender. It is well to do something worthy of a grateful people to keep in remembrance so important an event in their history as the surrender of Burgoyne and his army. If the ground on which the final surrender of the already beaten and conquered British army took place is worthy of such honor, should there not also be something done to mark the spot where the *terrible wrench of the battle came* and was so bravely met in the field of that little clearing in the old wilderness, on the 19th of September, and the 7th of October, 1777? It has been objected that what was then called Freeman's Farm, where those battles occurred, is an out of the way place, where few would ever see a monument. Every man, woman and child in our country should make a pilgrimage to that old battle ground, and a monument be built upon it so high that all the people in the land can see the spot where their country was saved.

VIII.

THE SMALL BEGINNINGS OF MODERN SARATOGA.

The village of Saratoga Springs lies on the south-eastern corner of the great highland region of the wilderness, and on the very edge of the system of old Laurentian rocks. Along in the valley which runs through the village, the hard Laurentian rocks terminate, and the softer rocks of the Trenton limestone and Hudson river slates begin. In the geologic fault or fissure which here occurs between these two systems of rocks, the mineral springs burst forth. The most easterly of the five great mountain chains of the wilderness, the Palmertown range, ends in the northern part of the village, while the next chain westerly, the *Kay-ad-ros-se-ra* range, fills up its western horizon. Thus this village of Saratoga Springs sits at the foot of the Adirondacks, and while it sips its mineral waters, it breathes the pure invigorating air of the mountains.

The first white man who visited Saratoga Springs, says Sir William Johnson, was a sick French officer whom an Indian chief brought from Fort Carillon for the benefit of the waters.*

The next, it is believed, was Sir William Johnson himself, who came here in August, 1767. His faithful Mohawks brought him through the woods from Schenectady by the way of Ballston Lake to the High Rock spring.

The High Rock of Saratoga, with its wonderful spring, is too familiar to need a description here. It was doubtless formed by slow accretions from the mineral substances deposited by the flowing waters, until it assumed its present shape, with the water flowing over the top and down the sides. For a long time, however, before Sir William's visit,

---

* " An Indian, it is said (of those no doubt
    Whom French intrigues had from this country drawn)
    In earlier wars a sick French captain led
    To these rare fountains to regain his health."
                 —Mineral Waters, by Reuben Sears, 1819

Sir William Johnson made this observation when he sold this tract of land to private individuals: " In tracing the history of these mineral springs, I could only learn that an Indian chief discovered them to a sick French officer in the early part of their wars with the English, but whether they were these very springs in this basin, or those at ten miles distance properly called Saratoga Springs, I know not."—Vide Morse's Gazetteer, article Ballston.

39

it had ceased to flow over the top, and had found some other outlet.

According to an old Indian legend, while it was still flowing over the top, some squaws once bathed in it their sooty faces against the will of the water's spirit, and the offended waters, shrinking from their polluting touch, sank down in shame into the bosom of the rock, and never afterward were seen to flow over its surface.*

In the partition and division of the patent of *Kay-ad-ros-se-ra* among its owners, which occurred on the 22d of February, 1771, lot 12 of the 16th allotment fell to the share of Rip Van Dam. This lot 12 was about three miles long and one and three-fourths wide. It contained over three thousand acres, and in it were all the mineral springs of Saratoga. Rip Van Dam having died many years before the division, his executors sold lot 12 to Jacob Walton, Anthony Van Dam and Isaac Low. After the war the state took possession of Low's interest in lot 12, and sold it to Henry Livingston and his brothers. In 1793 Walton purchased Anthony Van Dam's interest, and from that time the original title to most of the lands in the village can be traced to the Waltons and the Livingstons.

In the year 1773, Dirk Schouten, the pioneer settler of Saratoga Springs, came up to chop his small clearing, to plant a few potatoes, and build his humble cabin on the bluff a little west of the High Rock spring. Schouten's route to the springs was from the Hudson to the east side of Saratoga Lake, thence across the lake in a bark canoe to the mouth of the *Kay-ad-ros-se-ra* river, thence up the river two miles to an Indian trail that led to the springs.

* Chancellor Walworth's speech at Saratoga Springs, August 23, 1866.

The way to the springs is much plainer now-a-days than it was a hundred years ago. Before Schouten's cabin was completed, he quarrelled with the Indians, and they drove him away.

In the next summer, that of 1774, John Arnold, from Rhode Island, with his young family, tried his fortunes at Saratoga Springs. He took possession of Schouten's deserted cabin, and, making some improvements, opened a kind of rude tavern for the visitors of the springs. This pioneer hotel had but a room or two on the ground floor, with a chamber overhead. In sight of it were sixteen Indian cabins, filled with their savage occupants. In the rocky ledges near by were numerous dens of rattlesnakes. There were so many of these reptiles then at the Springs, that the early visitors often had to hang their beds from the limbs of the trees to avoid them. Nightly, the wolves howled and the panthers screamed; daily, the black bears picked berries in the little clearings, and the wild deer and the moose drank from the brook, while the eagles yearly built their nests on the tops of the towering pines. Such was the style, and such were the surroundings of the first rough hotels of the wilderness springs of a hundred years ago, that led the way in the long line of magnificent structures that have since adorned the modern village.

Arnold kept his little forest tavern for two summers, and was succeeded by Samuel Norton, who was driven away by the war of the Revolution, and for six years the springs were again left to their savage occupants.

In the spring of 1783, a son of Norton returned to his father's deserted cabin, and remained until 1787, when Alexander Bryant became the owner of the Schouten house.

Bryant built a blacksmith shop, and another log tavern near by. It was in 1783, also, that Gen. Schuyler cut a road from old Saratoga, now Schuylerville, on the Hudson, into the Springs, and in the following year built his rude frame summer-house near the High Rock spring.

In 1789 Gideon Putnam and Dr. Clement Blakesley settled at the Springs. Dr. Blakesley occupied the Schouten house, and Putnam located on his farm a mile west of the village. It is to the enterprise of Gideon Putnam that the village is indebted for much of its early prosperity.

In 1790, Benjamin Risley, from Vermont, bought the Schouten house, and opened a hotel which was for ten years the rival of Bryant's house on the opposite corner of the little clearing near the High Rock spring.

It was in the month of August, 1792, that Governor John Taylor Gilman, of New Hampshire, who had been a delegate in the Continental Congress, was staying at the Schouten house. Upon a sunny afternoon he took his gun and wandered up the creek into the deep woods in search of game. Coming to a little waterfall he found at the foot of it a small jet of sparkling water issuing from the rocky bank of the stream. Stooping down to taste it, he found the little sparkling jet, no bigger than a pipe-stem, to be mineral water. Hastening back to his boarding place, Gilman made known his discovery.*

Every person in the settlement was soon at the foot of

---

* In May, 1875, I published an article entitled "Saratoga" in the Troy *Times*. In the summer following, the Messrs. Taintor, of New York, published their guide book entitled "Saratoga, and how to See it." In their guide book the Messrs. Taintor inserted large portions of my article on Saratoga without giving me credit for it. Some of the matter so taken I have reclaimed.

that cascade in the deep, wild woods, wondering at the curious spectacle. You could almost count them all upon your fingers' ends. There were Risley and his family of the Schouten house. There was Alexander Bryant, the patriot scout of the Revolution, who kept the only rival tavern. There were Gen. Schuyler, and Dr. Blakesley, and Gideon Putnam, and Gilman's brother, and a few more guests who were at the little log tavern were all doubtless there. There too, were Indian Joe from his clearing on the hill, near where the Clarendon now is, and some of his swarthy brethren from their huts near the High Rock, wondering at the strange commotion among the pale faces at the little waterfall in the brook. All, gathering around it, each in turn tasted the water of the newly-found fountain, and pronouncing it of superior quality, they named it then and there the Congress Spring, out of compliment to its distinguished discoverer, and in honor of the old Continental Congress of which he had been a member.

For many years afterward the water was caught in glasses as it ran from the rock. In attempting to increase its capacity by removing a part of the rock the spring was lost. But bubbles of gas were noticed in the bed of the creek near by, and turning the creek one side, excavations were made in its bed. The spring was found and tubed, and has long since been world renowned.

In the year 1794 John and Ziba Taylor opened a small store in one of the rooms of the Schouten house, and became the pioneer merchants of the Springs.

In the year 1800 a new era dawned upon Saratoga Springs. In that year Gideon Putnam bought of Henry Walton an acre of land on what is now the site of the Grand Union, then in the depths of the old forest, and clearing off the heavy growth of pines, built the first of the large, commodious and elegant hotels for which Saratoga has since become so famous. Of the large hotels the Congress Hall was first opened in 1815, and the United States in 1824. Such were the small beginnings of the first quarter of a century of this great watering place up to a period within the memory of living men.

During these, the centennial years of the first rude openings of the Springs in the northern wilds, this whole village is crowded with hotels, the largest, grandest, best appointed in the world, within a stone's throw of each other, and glittering with more than oriental splendor. When all lighted up of a summer evening, the streets filled with gay promenaders—the wit, the wealth, the fashion and the beauty of half the world all there, the scene presented is like that of some fairy land. Surely has some enchanter touched with magic wand those rude hotels of a century ago, and transformed them into palaces like those famous in eastern story.

In reviewing these historical memories we have seen how the old Indian trails that surrounded Northern New York; how the valleys of the St. Lawrence, the Hudson, and the Mohawk, how the shores of Lake Ontario, Lakes George and Champlain, as well as the old hunting-grounds of *Kay-ad-ros-se-ra* and *Sa-ragh-to-ga* were for a hundred and seventy years the scenes of sanguinary warfare. To-day we look around us upon a brighter scene, and see how ninety years of smiling peace have made the fair borders of the grim old wilderness to "bud and blossom even as doth the rose." We have seen how a hundred years ago no one came to these old springs of the forest *Kay-ad-ros-se-ra*, now modern Saratoga, but serpents and wild beasts, and still wilder men. To-day we see how many steps from all the nations of the earth, in the pomp of modern travel, still following the routes of the old war-paths,* are turned toward this great watering place—this Mecca of our country's highest civilization; we see how all eyes are gazing at its sparkling, bubbling fountains, and how all lips are tasting of their healing waters.†

* In the first chapter I give the names of ten populous cities that now lie along the great modern thoroughfares which have taken the places of the old Indian and colonial war-paths that surrounded Northern New York. Below I give their Indian names, with the signification of each :

ALBANY,........*Ska-neh-ta-de*—Beyond the open pines.
TROY,.........*Pa-an-pa-ak*—The field of standing corn.
COHOES,........*Ga-ha-oose*—The shipwrecked canoe.
SCHENECTADY,..*O-no-a-la-gone-na*—Pained in the head.
UTICA,.........*Nun-da-da-sis*—Going around the hill.
ROME,..........*Da-ya-hoo-wa-quat*—Place for carrying boats.
SYRACUSE,......*Na-ta-dunk*—Pine tree broken with top hanging down.
OSWEGO,........*Swa-geh*—Flowing out.
WATERTOWN,...*Ka-hu-ah-go*—Big river.
OGDENSBURGH,. *O-swa-gatch*—Flowing around the hills.

† See Saratoga and Kay-ad-ros-se-ra, an Historical Address, delivered by the author at Saratoga Springs, July 4th, 1876.

INDEX.

Also available:

A History of the Adirondacks.
By Alfred L. Donaldson. Reprint of the 1921 ed. With a new introduction by John J. Duquette, Saranac Lake Village Historian. 2 volumes, 856 pp., 34 illus. and maps.   cloth **$39.50**

The Birch Bark Books of Henry Abbott.
Sporting Adventures and Nature Observations in the Adirondacks in the Early 1900s.
By Henry Abbott. Reprint in one volume of 19 books publ. privately 1914-1932. With an introduction by Vincent Engels. 288 pp. illus., maps.   cloth **$19.95**

Wild Northern Scenes,
or, Sporting Adventures in the Adirondacks with Rifle and Rod. By S. H. Hammond. Repr. of the 1857 ed. 341 pp., illus.   cloth **$12.50**

Trappers of New York,
or, A Biography of Nicholas Stoner and Nathaniel Foster; together with Anecdotes of Other Celebrated Hunters, and some Account of Sir William Johnson and his Style of Living. By Jeptha R. Simms. Repr. of the 1871 ed., with new preface and an index. 320 pp., illus.   cloth **$15.00**

Why the Wilderness is called Adirondack.
The Earliest Account of the Founding of the MacIntyre Mine. By Henry Dornburgh. Repr. of the 1885 ed., with new preface and added illus. 32 pp.   paper **$3.95**

Woods and Waters, or the Saranacs and Racket.
By Alfred Billings Street. 386 pp., illus. map. Reprint of the first ed. 1861.   cloth **$14.50**

The French Occupation of the Champlain Valley, 1609-1759.
By Guy Omeron Coolidge. Repr. of the 1938 ed. 175 pp., maps.   cloth **$9.75**

History of the Lumber Industry in the State of New York.
By William F. Fox. With 22 full-page illustrations from 19th-century photos and a large foldout map of New York State in full color showing first settlements. Reprint of the 1901 ed.   cloth **$13.95**

A Brief History of the Printing Press in Washington, Saratoga and Warren Counties.
Together with a Check List of their Publications prior to 1825, and Selection of Books relating particularly to this Vicinity. By William H. Hill. 118 pp., Reprint of the Fort Edward 1930 edition (privately printed)   cloth **$8.50**

Harbor Hill Books, P.O. Box 407, Harrison, N. Y. 10528